CONSPIRACIES UNCOVERED

COVER-UPS, HOAXES, AND SECRET SOCIETIES

CONSPIRACIES UNCOVERED

COVER-UPS, HOAXES, AND SECRET SOCIETIES

Written by

Dr. Lee Mellor

DK | Penguin Random House

Senior Editor Alastair Dougall
Copy Editor Megan Douglass
Designer David McDonald
Jacket Design Lisa Lanzarini
Senior Picture Researcher Sumedha Chopra
Senior Production Controller Louise Minihane
Senior Production Editor Jennifer Murray
Managing Editor Sarah Harland
Managing Art Editor Vicky Short
Art Director Lisa Lanzarini
Publisher Julie Ferris
Publishing Director Mark Searle

Cover image: NASA

First American Edition, 2021
Published in the United States by DK Publishing
1450 Broadway, Suite 801, New York, NY 10018

ISBN: 978-0-7440-2723-5

DK books are available at special discounts when purchased in bulk for sales
promotions, premiums, fund-raising, or educational use. For details, contact:
DK Publishing Special Markets, 1450 Broadway, Suite 801, New York, NY 10018
SpecialSales@dk.com

Set in 10.5/13.5pt Bembo MT Pro
Typeset by Jouve (UK), Milton Keynes
Printed and bound in Great Britain by Clays Ltd, Elcograf S.p.A.

For the Curious

www.dk.com

Contents

"Them"

Who is really running things? What are they keeping from us? What do they want? Questions such as these, crucial to every conspiracy theory, all imply the secret existence of a "them," lurking in the shadows, pulling strings behind the scenes . . .

"Just because you're paranoid doesn't

mean they aren't after you."

Joseph Heller, *Catch-22*

The Oxford English Dictionary describes a "conspiracy" as: "A combination of persons for an evil or unlawful purpose; an agreement between two or more persons to do something criminal, illegal, or reprehensible (especially in relation to treason, sedition, or murder); a plot."[1]

Implicit in this definition is the notion of a plurality of people. We often use the term "them" or "they" in casual speech, as if knowledge of whomever we are referring to is a given—eg, "Well, *they* just want to keep us lazy and stupid, so we'll sit at home and consume while *they* slowly take over the world." Given that hidden hierarchies have governed mankind since the first agrarian civilizations, there is no reason to think that the average person voicing suspicions about an ill-defined hidden hierarchy operating clandestinely—a "them"—is a novel phenomenon. Marketing companies have even picked up on this predilection, bombarding us with slogans such as "the weight loss secret *they* don't want you to know about," implying there is a group who are concealing information from the general public because it would hurt their bottom line.

Thus, the existence of a "them" is, by necessity, indispensable to any conspiracy theory. And, throughout the ages, there have been no shortage of "thems" to whom secret actions and sinister motives have been ascribed.

—

In the Western world, perhaps the oldest "them" has been Jews, or, "*the* Jews" (in "them"-speak). The tragic irony is that this belief has repeatedly led to systematic persecution and murderous pogroms perpetrated against the Jewish people—a cycle one would think an

2

allegedly powerful tribe could and would have prevented. Instead, European Jews were brought to the brink of extermination by Nazi Germany and its collaborators during the 1941–45 Holocaust, in which approximately six million—or two thirds of the Jewish population—were annihilated. Though this should lead any reasonable person to conclude that their near-extermination constitutes startling evidence to the contrary, conspiracies involving a hidden Jewish cabal manipulating events persist to this day.

The roots of anti-Semitism in the West date back at least to the crucifixion of Jesus Christ as depicted in the New Testament. According to the gospels of Matthew, Mark, and Luke, Jesus ran afoul of Jewish elders in the Temple who questioned his authority and divinity. The elders presented him to the Roman governor of Judea Pontius Pilate as a man claiming to be the King of the Jews. This act of treason resulted in Jesus' crucifixion.

Roughly one hundred years later, when the Jewish people were banned from Jerusalem by their Roman conquerors, the Jewish Diaspora began. Dreaming of a return to their ancestral homeland, exiled Jews migrated to kingdoms all over the Middle East, Europe, North Africa, and Eurasia. As Christians were forbidden from lending money and pawn-broking by the Catholic Church, Jews were encouraged to fulfill these roles, and prospered accordingly. They were also renowned for their acumen in the field of medicine.

Both this diaspora and monopoly on usury were double-edged swords. On the positive side, they allowed Jews to capitalize on far-flung connections that existed along tribal lines. Jewish merchants, already extremely competent, leveraged these connections along-side pawn-broking and money-lending to thrive financially. Tragically, this helped lay the groundwork for the "Jewish world domination" conspiracy theories that emerged during the 18th and 19th centuries with terrifying results.

Though Jews and Christians always viewed one another with suspicion, in the Early Middle Ages, they worked side by side in an array of professions with relatively little animosity. During the 6th century CE, Pope Gregory I issued a Papal Bull instructing Christians to protect the Jewish people. Moreover, he also opposed the forced conversion of Jews to Christianity.

With the onset of the Crusades, European attitudes toward Jews took a turn for the worse. Wild rumors that Jews were ritually sacrificing Christians, especially infants, proliferated across the continent. Jewish knowledge of medicine became linked to magic and alchemy, and Jewish spells were blamed for everything from plagues to birth defects. Widespread outbursts of anti-Semitic slaughter followed. Jews were prohibited from joining numerous guilds, which allowed members to practice trades and crafts. This left few options outside pawnbroking and money lending (which was now increasingly incorporated into banking): professions many Jews had mastered. By the Renaissance era, Jews found themselves largely segregated in specific areas of major cities called "ghettos"—originating from the Venetian word "gheta" for the slag biproduct of iron foundries.

By the Industrial Revolution, animosity toward Jews reached an unprecedented level thanks to a confluence of events. During the late-1700s and early-1800s, a Jewish family consistently implicated by conspiracists rose to prominence: the Rothschilds. Ironically, their success was largely modeled on the gentile Habsburg monarchs who dominated Europe at the time. Realizing that it was advantageous to keep money and secrets in the family, patriarch Mayer Bauer Rothschild encouraged each of his five sons to marry within their own bloodline, sending them to open de Rothschild Frères banks in several major European cities. Upon Mayer's death, his first son, Anselm Rothschild, took over as head of the Frankfurt bank; second son Salomon had already established a bank in Vienna; third son Nathan in London; fourth son Calmann in Naples; and youngest son Jacob in Paris. Profiting from wise investments they had made during the Napoleonic Wars, the Rothschild dynasty accumulated the largest private family fortune in the world, and to this day, remains a financial powerhouse. The family's success, more than any other Jewish banker or money lender, fueled the vile and pernicious conspiracy theory that "the Jews"—originally the five Rothschilds, but more recently updated to eight who supposedly run the US Federal Reserve—have complete or near-complete control of banking all over the world.

In 1905, a fraudulent document began circulating in Tsarist Russia purporting to outline an international Jewish conspiracy to conquer the world: *The Protocols of the Elders of Zion*. Also included in the text as unwitting pawns of "the Jews" was another favorite "them": the Freemasons. *The Protocols* claimed that this menacing alliance was using liberalism—with its accompanying pornography, alcohol, narcotics, and false notions of individual freedom—along with Masonic control of the printing press and court systems, to weaken the Russian state and subvert Christianity. It proposed that Jewish influence over international banking had brought economies to ruin, and that Jews and Freemasons were employing blackmail to control politicians and governments. Apparently, according to the Protocols, Jews and Freemasons also frequently use war as a pretext to remove civil liberties that are never restored, even after the fighting has ended. In reality, the culprits for subversive tactics such as these are neither Jews nor Freemasons, but corrupt administrations working alongside military or intelligence agencies. Of course, many conspiracists will counter that the Jews and/or Freemasons are actually running these institutions from the shadows, but offer little proof to support their claims.

—

Despite attempts by both Freemasons and outsiders to convince the world otherwise, the origins of Freemasonry can be traced to the stonemasons' guild of York in 926 CE. The stonemasons were artisans in medieval England, revered for constructing castles and cathedrals. The guild—like many others—trained apprentices, fixed prices, and offered quality assurance. Its members met at a wooden structure called a "lodge," where they received education, dined together, initiated apprentices, and slept. The earliest record of masonic guilds, the Regius manuscript, dates back to 1390 CE.

In the 1640s, stonemasons began allowing "speculative" non-stonemasons—who did not actually practice the craft—into their lodges, thus establishing the basis of modern Freemasonry. By the latter half of the 1600s, such lodges could be found all over England and Scotland. Throughout the 18th century, an increasing number of non-laborers from the monied classes were admitted into Free-mason lodges in London. In 1717, the members of four local lodges congregated at the Goose and Gridiron pub in Castle Baynard, central London, to officially found the Premiere Grand Lodge of England. Each of the First Grand Officers elected was a non-operative gentleman. At this point, Freemasonry became the entirely speculative philosophical fraternity it is today. Why these radical changes occurred is unknown, but henceforth, for the first time, the ruling classes began to view Freemasonry as a nefarious organization bent on world domination.

A significant contributor to this suspicion is a fabricated mythology linking the Freemasons to ancient Middle Eastern secret societies. This connection seems to have been drawn in 1730 with the writings of Scottish expatriate Chevalier Andrew Michael Ramsay, a Jacobite in France. Ramsay declared that the first masons had actually existed before ancient Egypt, and unlocked esoteric secrets, only to later lose them. However, during the Crusades, European knights had recovered this knowledge and returned it to the masonic order. Unfortunately, Ramsay did not specify which knights he was referring to—although, apparently, it was the Knights of St. John, later wrongly interpreted as being the Knights Templar. This narrative expanded, seemingly of its own accord, with claims that the Templars had unearthed these forgotten secrets from Solomon's Temple, where the Order was headquartered in the early 11th century. Having fallen into debt to the Order, King Phillip IV of France pressured Pope Clement V to disband the

Knights Templar. Phillip pursued them relentlessly, torturing and immolating those who fell into his clutches. However, some of the remaining Templars fled to Scotland, where they were said to have been key players in many of the kingdom's historical triumphs. It was here, safe in the hills and mountains of Caledonia, that they allegedly developed the rituals of Freemasonry.

The proliferation of this Templar myth has been attributed to attempts by Scottish lodges to establish an older historical pedigree than their English counterparts. Yet, they also captured the imaginations of Freemasons in Europe, who incorporated the Knights Templar fable into their foundational narratives. In the years since, the myth has mutated in some lodges to hold that the masons were descended from the Old Testament engineers who erected the Tower of Babel and Solomon's Temple, from Egyptian pyramid builders, or that they had once been disciples of the Ancient Greek philosopher, religious teacher, and mathematical genius Pythagoras.

The author and Freemason Christopher L. Hodapp proposes that while many of his brothers likely knew the difference between masonic mythology and its true origins, non-members have largely accepted it, or at least, its possibility. This general supposition has opened the door to the widespread misconception that Freemasons dabble in the occult. In actuality, like many of the demonized secret societies in this chapter, Freemasonry was established by Enlightenment thinkers who extolled reason and science above all else. However, as Freemasonry arose during a historical period in which witch-hunting was prevalent, its members were forced to exchange and explore Enlightenment ideas in the safety and secrecy of their lodges. Tellingly, discussion of religion or politics was strictly prohibited.

A second reason why Freemasons fell under suspicion was the considerable number of politicians, clergymen, bankers, and wealthy businessmen who came to occupy their ranks. While Freemasonry speaks of universal brotherhood, in reality, during much of its history it was an exclusive club for the powerful. In an age of turmoil, where monarchies and religious institutions were threatened by revolutionaries and secular thinking, it is no surprise that the nobility and the Catholic church viewed Freemasons unfavorably. This view was particularly prevalent among the monarchs of France and the various German kingdoms, but much less so in Britain, owing to the fact that members of the Royal Family held prominent positions in the Order.

While Hodapp rightfully calls Freemasons "the world's best-known and least hidden secret society"[2]—conspiracists maintain that most members are blissfully unaware of the megalomaniacal machinations of the hidden upper tier. Yet, according to Hodapp, there is no international governing body of Freemasonry. A separate Grand Lodge with its own sovereignty and rules of conduct presides over smaller lodges in every American state. Outside the US, a Grand Lodge exercises the same authority in each country.

Nevertheless, Freemasons have been persecuted by totalitarian regimes of differing stripes. The Order was outlawed in the Soviet Union, Fascist Italy, and Nazi Germany, where many were sent to Nazi death camps alongside Jews, gypsies, homosexuals, and political dissenters. This persecution continues in [21st]-century Islamist regimes practicing Shariah law, where Freemasons have been executed. Even in the UK, Freemasons are viewed with suspicion, owing to the influence of tabloid media. In the last decade of the 20th century, allegations of masonic influence over the British criminal justice system led to official hearings, though no evidence was ever found to support these assertions. Nevertheless, judges, police officers, and other British government employees are legally required to disclose membership of a mason's lodge.

Masons have largely been viewed favorably in the US, and heralded as benefactors of the community. Perhaps this is because the one successful plot to overthrow a government concocted by Freemasons—George Washington, Benjamin Franklin, John Hancock, Paul Revere, and the Marquis de Lafayette—was the American Revolution!

Currently, there are less than two million Freemasons in the US and about five million members internationally. In the US and Canada, freemasonry is hardly a secret at all. Besides the famous rings bearing a square and compass with a "G" denoting "God" and "geometry" at its center—the symbol of the Great Architect (belief in a supreme creator is a requirement of Freemasonry)— American masons often sport t-shirts, belt buckles, and other apparel advertising their lodge. Their community activities are covered in local newspapers with a total lack of controversy.

The hierarchy of masonic membership and many of the rituals involved are an open secret. For instance, the proceedings that take place when a newcomer is initiated into a lodge have long been publicly available. During this first step, they become an Initiate. The next degree of Freemasonry—the details of this ritual are also easily accessible—is that of Fellow Craft. Only the ritual elevating a mason to the third and final degree, Master Mason, remains closely guarded. Aside from this, the secrets of Freemasonry largely revolve around handshakes, passwords, symbols, and private matters disclosed in confidence from one masonic brother to another— with murder and treason being notable exceptions.

—

The Rosicrucians, also known as The Order of the Rose Cross, are a secret society, whose existence was supposedly "revealed" in three pamphlets published by Lutheran minister Johann Valentin Andrae in the early-17th-century—*Fama Fraternitatis Rosae Crucis* (1614), *Confessio Fraternitatis* (1615), and *Chymical Wedding of Christian Rosenkreutz* (1616). According to Andrae, the Rosicrucians formed in the early-15th century under Christian Rosenkreutz, a German monk who wandered east to study under occultists and mystics. Upon returning to Germany in 1407, Rosenkreutz founded the Rosicrucians—whose insignia is a cross with a rose at its center—along with three other monks. Headquartered in Dominus Sancti Spiritus (House of the Divine Spirit), their aim was to collect and fuse all mystical and scientific knowledge. This would allow them to arrive at a universal message that would prepare them for the Final Judgment of God. As their numbers grew, more and more Rosicrucians traveled the world, bringing esoterica back to Dominus Sancti Spiritus. According to Andrae, Rosenkreutz died in 1484 at the age of 106, and was interred somewhere in the building. The whereabout of his remains were forgotten until 1604, when a renovator stumbled upon them inside a plaster wall. Not only did Christian Rosenkreutz appear no different than when he had first died but he had also been buried with voluminous texts of Rosicrucian knowledge. In the years since, Andrae claimed Rosicrucian societies had sprung up clandestinely around the globe to study these lost teachings.

Andrae's whole pitch was a well-meaning hoax. He simply wanted to attract people to his own Rosicrucian group to seek truth for the betterment of mankind. Yet, by 1620, unaffiliated Rosicrucian societies had arisen in Germany and Holland. Even when Andrae admitted his deception, passing it off as a bit of fun, few believed him. The world quickly polarized into wannabe Rosicrucians who wished to join the order and unlock its ancient secrets and those who were suspicious of this hidden organization with its strange interest in magic.

As science and reason flourished in the 18th century, the interest in Rosicrucianism waned. It made a comeback with the Romantic movement in the 19th century, only to be subsumed by outlying masonic groups or appropriated by former Freemasons disappointed with the secrets revealed to them. One particularly notorious organization, The Hermetic Order of the Golden Dawn, which boasted members such as the poet William Butler Yeats and "The Wickedest Man in the World" Aleister Crowley, would itself become a "them" for conspiracists, along with Crowley's off-shoot group Ordo Templi Orientis. Today there are five masonic Rosicrucian chapters in the world: England's Socitas Rosicruciana in Anglia (SRIA), Scotland's Socitas Rosicruciana in Scotia (SRIS), the

American Societas Rosicruciana in Civitatibus Foederatis (SRICF), Societas Rosicruciana in Canada (SRIC), and Portugal's Societas Rosicruciana in Lusitania (SRIL). Rosicrucians practice a fusion of alchemy, Christianity, Egyptian mysticism, Kabbalah, and magic, with much of their attention devoted to reincarnation.

While Freemasons and Rosicrucians were progeny of the Enlightenment, more than any other secret society, the Illuminati embodied its values. Rather than squandering their energies on mysticism or the occult, Illuminati members were devoted to political and epistemological philosophy. Though this should be to their credit, the organization arose at a time when the divine rights of monarchs and religion were threatened by the emergence of reason, the scientific method, and individual rights. These institutions were justified in their fear of the Illuminati, who sought nothing less than to infiltrate the establishment and bring it down.

First called the Perfectabilists, and then the Bees, the Illuminati—whose name represented the light of knowledge flaring up after a long, dark historical period of ignorance—was founded in 1776 by Adam Weishaupt, a young professor and chair of canon law at the University of Ingolstadt in Bavaria. Weishaupt had been unexpectedly promoted to this position when the Pope at the time, Pius VI, had a falling out with the Jesuits, expelling them from the school. Little did he know that Weishaupt was secretly (and virulently) anti-Catholic.

At first, the Illuminati consisted only of Weishaupt, who used the codename "Spartacus," and four others. These five founders labeled themselves the Areopagites. The title of their organization was encrypted, symbolized by a circle with a dot in its center that represented the sun illuminating the other planets in the solar system. Illuminati intellectuals aimed to gain access to influential Freemason lodges—this Weishaupt managed to accomplish the following year, joining Lodge Theodore of Good Council in Munich. Weishaupt then began scouting for potential Illuminati recruits. By 1779, he had secured total control of the lodge.

One of the keys to winning over Freemasons was to establish rituals, which largely mirrored those of the Freemasons, and create a membership hierarchy. Weishaupt's friend and fellow mason, Baron Adolf Franz Friedrich Knigge, aided him in this regard. The German poet Johann Goethe became a member and soon membership ballooned to a minimum of 2,000 men, distributed across Europe. The Illuminati now had a presence in universities, militaries, and religious institutions all over the continent.

However, within six years of its establishment, the Illuminati began to crumble. In 1782, groups of Freemasons from Austria, France, Holland, Italy, and Russia convened at the Congress of Masonry in Wilhelmsbad to air their grievances about this strange new order. Emboldened by his success, Professor Weishaupt had started launching into anti-Catholic tirades in front of his largely Catholic students. Paradoxically, Baron Knigge began to suspect him of being a Jesuit spy. In 1784, Knigge left the Illuminati. His departure was followed by a number of others. Inevitably, some of these individuals talked. Duke Carl Theodore, the ruler of Bavaria, was made aware of the Illuminati and handed a list of its members. He responded by banning all groups not officially authorized by the Bavarian government. A year later, he issued arrest warrants for the Areopagites, prompting Weishaupt to flee to the German duchy of Saxe-Gotha-Altenburg. However, in his haste, the absent-minded professor left a trove of incriminating documents, including the Illuminati's strategy to take over the world. Duke Theodore saw to it that their plans were disseminated all over Europe, which resulted in Illuminati members being purged from institutions across the continent, typically followed by imprisonment or exile. Weishaupt was more fortunate, taking up a teaching post at the University of Gottingen, Lower Saxony.

Though the Bavarian Illuminati were no more, their name and sinister agenda were not forgotten. In the years since, numerous unrelated groups have co-opted the Illuminati brand without bearing any resemblance to Weishaupt's, while others have found

themselves tarnished with the label. During the 18th century, baseless rumors spread that 14 Illuminati lodges had sprouted up in 13
American states, and even the revered figure of Thomas Jefferson
was falsely accused of belonging to an alleged Virginia chapter. In
the 19th and 20th centuries, the concept of the Illuminati broad-
ened to include any subversive or powerful group. from Communists
to bankers, to leaders of multinational corporations. Similarly,
establishment politicians in rival political parties were accused of
secretly sharing the same views and agenda, and saddled with the
label. Naturally, they could be tied to business interests, bureaucra-
cies, and transnational organizations such as the United Nations and
European Union, which led to accusations of being "globalists"
seeking to dominate the human race by establishing a tyrannical,
one-world government. At one point, President Franklin Roosevelt was suspected of being an Illuminati member, owing to his
implementation of social programs to lift the United States out of
the Great Depression. Even if the Illuminati were not presidents,
prime ministers, or monarchs themselves, they were seen as being
the hidden hand directing key government institutions.

—

When the French Revolution resulted in the deposing of King
Louis XVI and establishment of a Republic in 1792, anti-
Republican writers began looking for somebody to blame. In
1792, Cadet de Gassicourt's *The Tomb of Jacques Molay*, described
how the Knights Templar had survived by rebranding themselves
as Freemasons, and spent the last 450-plus years plotting revenge
against the Catholic church and French monarchy. Five years later,
following The Reign of Terror, in which the Jacobin revolutionary
faction guillotined more than 16,500 people and allowed another
10,000 to perish in prison, the Scottish scientist James Robison
penned *Proofs of a Conspiracy Against All Religions and Governments of
Europe Carried On In The Secret Meetings of Freemasons, Illuminati,*

and Reading Societies. Disenchanted with the Enlightenment, Robison claimed that the Illuminati had taken over the continental Freemasons and turned them into Jacobins. These conspiracy theories were synthesized by Abbé Augustin Barruel, a French Jesuit, who authored and published a voluminous, four-part series entitled *Memoirs Illustrating the History of Jacobinism* from 1797-98. Barruel accused French Enlightenment philosophers such as Voltaire, Denis Diderot, Jean-Jacques Rousseau, and Baron de Montesquieu of opening the door for a sect of Freemasons and Illuminati to influence the Jacobins to seize power. In 1806, Barruel received a letter from a Captain Giovanni Battista Simonini in Piedmont, praising his work but insisting that Jewish conspirators were pulling the strings behind the Freemasons and Illuminati in order to destroy Christianity, enslave all gentiles, and rule over a one-world government. Simonini's letter was printed and circulated, linking these groups in the public consciousness. As the Knights Templar became the Freemasons and took their rituals from Solomon's Temple, and the Illuminati were also Freemasons, then all these groups must be in league with the Jews. The fact that most French Freemasons were noblemen who had been executed during the French Revolution was ignored by these conspiracists. Unsurprisingly, many historians believe Simonini's letter served as a prototype for the aforementioned, anti-Semitic *Protocols of the Elders of Zions.*

With supposed links between caricatures of "international Jewry," Freemasonry, the Knights Templar, Rosicrucians, and Illuminati, along with their mutual agenda of world domination, now established in the minds of conspiracists, these groups could be folded into a single overarching conspiracy: the New World Order. Essentially, whether it was President Woodrow Wilson's League of Nations, its successor the United Nations, or Marxism, any [20th]-century effort to gather nation states or citizens around the world together under a single governing body has been viewed by conspiracists as an attempt to establish the New World Order.

Often this alleged conspiracy is simply referred to as "The Elite" or "The Globalists." Depending on where a conspiracist lives, the emphasis on which version of "Them" is behind the New World Order plot changes. In the US, "the Jews" and Illuminati tend to be the central antagonists, with the Knights Templar and Rosicrucians minimized or omitted. It is not uncommon for far-right conspiracy theorists to use the acronym ZOG—Zionist Occupied Government—to refer to the American Federal Government, which they claim is merely a puppet for their so-called Jewish masters.

Variations on New World Order conspiracy theories number in the thousands, but the history outlined here serves as a useful template to understand and interpret them in the 21st century. Paraphrasing the historian Daniel Pipes, Christopher Hodapp argues that "almost all conspiracy theories have as their origin the same two boogeymen—Jews and secret societies, most notably Freemasons. They have simply been recycled and renamed, again and again, as events have transpired over the last 250 years. For example, if you take almost any conspiracy about the Jews from the 19th century and erase 'Jews' and substitute 'military-industrial complex' or 'neocons,' you find that very same theory in dozens of books and on hundreds of Websites about the sinister forces behind the 9/11 'conspiracy.'"[3]

—

For some conspiracists, the idea that human forces are vying to control the world is only a part of what is *really* going on. They maintain that human organizations are simply covering up or working with much more powerful, extraterrestrial entities. And if these conspiracy theorists' certainty that aliens have visited Earth is not outlandish enough, they have actually developed a taxonomy of extraterrestrials that includes their origins, morphology, and motives.

To students of history, the Anunnaki are deities worshipped by the ancient Sumerians, Babylonians, Akkadians, and Assyrians. Depicted wearing horned crowns, they are descended from An, god of the sky, and the goddess of Earth, Ki. However, the controversial archeologist and author Zecharia Sitchin claims the Anunnaki are, in fact, inhabitants of the undiscovered planet Nibiru (aka Marduk) which supposedly passes Earth every 3,600 years. Apparently, the Anunnaki first arrived on Earth approximately 500,000 years ago, only to discover the planet contained vast deposits of gold. Nibiru was facing ecological devastation owing to a depleted atmosphere, and the Anunnaki learned that they could counteract this by sending particles of gold into the heavens to shield the planet. Needing laborers to mine gold on Earth, the Anunnaki's Chief Scientist, Enki, augmented *homo erectus*, our primitive ancestor, with their own DNA through *in vitro* fertilization, creating a hybrid: *homo sapiens*—us. Conspiracists and fringe historians believe the Anunnaki were responsible for teaching humans agriculture, along with erecting the pyramids, Stonehenge, and other ancient wonders.

While the Anunnaki are usually viewed as a benevolent species, British conspiracist David Icke begs to differ. The former BBC sportscaster refers to the Anunnaki as the Archons: lizard-like beings who arrived on Earth with malevolent intentions.

Having originally proclaimed himself the son of the Godhead in 1991 and made various erroneous apocalyptic predictions, Icke has spent the years since regurgitating conspiracy theories about a shadowy elite who manipulate global events and opinions to establish the New World Order and enslave humanity. They allegedly intend to do so by creating a monolithic global government, banning free speech, disarming the population, and fitting mankind with microchips.

Given what we have learned, it should come as no surprise that Icke repeatedly and controversially cites *The Protocols of the Elders of Zion*, but claims the document was actually an Illuminati agenda, and that only "Zionist" Jews were involved. Furthermore, he claims that the Illuminati are actually shapeshifting Reptilians. Created by the mysterious, interdimensional Archons some 7,000 years ago, the Reptilians of "The Babylon Brotherhood" are a blend of Archon and human DNA. In their lizard form they are 12 ft (3.7 m) tall and scaled, with lizard eyes. Yet, they can access their mammalian DNA to transform into beings who look human. In order to do this, they participate in Satanic child molestation and sacrifice, "drinking human blood, particularly the blood of blond-haired, blue-eyed people, [which] seems to be beneficial to holding mammal codes open."[4]

According to Icke, members of the Reptilian Elite include the Merovingian Dynasty, Rothschilds, British Royal Family, Rocke-fellers, every American president since JFK up to at least Barack Obama, Henry Kissinger, Jed Bush, Hillary Clinton, former British Prime Minister Ted Heath, Al Gore, Kris Kristofferson, Bob Hope, and even the country singer Boxcar Willie. Together, the Reptilians control the Freemasons, United Nations, International Monetary Fund, World Bank, Round Table, Council on Foreign Relations, Chatham House, Club of Rome, Royal Insti-tute of International Affairs, Trilateral Commission, Bilderberg Group, CIA, MI6, Mossad, and the Internet; as well as almost every institution, whether media, military, religious, or scientific.

Another alien conspiracist species are the so-called "Grays." The first mention of these allegedly small, gray-skinned extrater-restrials with huge, opaque, oval eyes seems to have appeared in the writings of author HG Wells, and echoed by subsequent science-fiction writers. The Grays first entered the American popular imagination as "real" beings in 1965, when the alleged abduction of Betty and Barney Hill four years earlier became public knowledge. While driving home a mile south of Indian Head, New Hampshire, at 10:30 pm on September 19, 1961, the Hills were reportedly hypnotized by alien beings and taken aboard a flying saucer. Betty described their captors as standing 5 ft to 5 ft

4 in (1.5 to 1.6 m) tall with gray skin and dark eyes. In the following years, representations of gray aliens with large black eyes appeared with increasing frequency in media from the films *Close Encounters of the Third Kind* and *Communion* to episodes of the *X-Files*. Those who believe extraterrestrial bodies were recovered during the 1947 Roswell UFO incident largely accept that these beings were Grays. Though nearly 75 per cent of reported extraterrestrial encounters in the United States are with Grays, there is no consensus regarding their natures and motives among conspiracists and UFOlogists.

—

When conspiracists talk about secret societies, extraterrestrials, or ethnic groups as "thems", they are almost always well wide of the mark. Government bureaus, agencies, and departments, on the other hand, have been repeatedly exposed conspiring to commit truly shocking acts. Britain's Special Operations Executive (SOE)—formed in 1940 and a forerunner of the OSS—was referred to in hushed tones as "The Ministry of Ungentlemanly Warfare." This group of spies, saboteurs, and assassins was a secret subsection of the national intelligence agency MI6, and operated behind enemy lines to undermine Nazi Germany. In perhaps its greatest achievement, Operation Anthropoid, two Czech nationals trained by the SOE, Jan Kubiš and Josef Gabčík, assassinated the infamous "Blonde Butcher" Reinhard Heydrich outside Holešovice on May 27, 1942. Though the majority of British generals opposed the SOE for circumventing the laws of war, a thoroughly dishonorable endeavor, Prime Minister Winston Churchill thought the organization both necessary and desirable.

When President Franklin Roosevelt asked Churchill if the British had played a role in Heydrich's death, the Prime Minister apparently winked. Two weeks later, Roosevelt authorized retired American General William Donovan to create the Office of Strategic Services (OSS), modeled on Britain's SOE. For the remainder of World War II, both organizations worked together under the Joint Chiefs of Staff. Six weeks after the end of the war, President Harry S. Truman, who disliked Donovan and the OSS cutthroats, gave orders for it to be disbanded. However, Truman's idealism soon received a much-needed wake-up call following an unsettling meeting between American representative Walter Bedell Smith and Soviet leader Josef Stalin. On July 26, 1947, he signed the National Security Act, giving birth to the OSS's successor: the Central Intelligence Agency (CIA). More than any other "Them", the CIA will pop up with stunning regularity throughout this book, and with good reason.

Besides the CIA and MI6, nearly every intelligence agency around the globe has been implicated in conspiracies, whether accurately or not. From 1918 through the Cold War years, Russia's intelligence service was the *Glavnoye razvedyvatel'noye upravleniye* (GRU) or Main Intelligence Directorate, which transformed simply into the GU in 1992.

Under the leadership of Nikita Khrushchev, in 1954, a second Soviet intelligence agency emerged: the infamous *Komitet Gosudarstvennoy Bezopasnosti* (KGB). After the fall of the USSR, this became the *Federalnaya Sluzhba Kontrrazvedki* (FSK) from 1991-95, before shapeshifting once more into the *Federal'naya sluzhba bezopasnosti Rossiyskoy Federatsii* (FSB). It was from the FSB, or Federal Security Service of the Russian Federation, that Vladimir Putin ascended to become Russian prime minister, and, since 2012 Russian president. Nefarious Russian intelligence activity has reared its head on a number of occasions, notably in the poisonings of Russian dissidents of various stripes, including Aleksander Litvinenko, Sergei and Yulia Skripal, and Alexei Navalny.

Though generally portrayed in a more benevolent light than the CIA, the Federal Bureau of Investigation (FBI) has also been implicated in a number of conspiracy theories, largely owing to the authoritarian bent and meddling of its first director, J. Edgar Hoover. Founded on July 26, 1908, this federal law enforcement agency has jurisdiction over Indian Reservations, National Parks, and crimes occurring across state lines.

—

Two pervading "thems" that have not been detailed in this chapter are Nazi Germany and the Catholic Church. Their absence is partially owing to space, but also because public knowledge of their origins and nature is already relatively well-established and widespread. It is fitting, then, that the next two chapters will focus on these organizations: one an indisputably ruthless and evil 20th century regime, and the other a near-two-millennia-old religious institution.

Operation Grey Wolf

The end of World War II was finally in sight. The Soviet army was closing in on Berlin. Adolf Hitler had committed suicide. However, as time went by, rumors grew that somehow Hitler's private secretary, ruthless, resourceful Martin Bormann, had plotted an elaborate escape route for the loathed *führer* of Nazi Germany. This alleged plan even had a name: Operation Grey Wolf.

The official narrative holds that on his 56th birthday—April 20, 1945—Hitler emerged from his Berlin *Führerbunker* for the final time to present Iron Crosses to Hitler Youth in the ruins of the Reich Chancellery garden. He then returned to his subterranean lair. With Soviet General Georgy Zhukov's army due to reach the outskirts of Berlin the following day, Hitler began issuing nonsensical military instructions. On April 22, upon learning his orders had been ignored, Hitler admonished his commanders as traitors and imbeciles. Declaring all was lost, he announced his intentions to remain in the bunker and shoot himself, depriving the Soviets of the pleasure of capturing him.

As the days passed, allegiances between key members of the Third Reich fractured. In the west, SS head Heinrich Himmler began secretly negotiating peace with the encroaching Allied forces, while *Luftwaffe* commander-in-chief Hermann Göring vied to replace Hitler as Führer. Resigned to his fate, Hitler married his long-term mistress Eva Braun just after midnight on April 29. Later that day he would learn his ally Benito Mussolini, the father of fascism, had been executed by gunshot in northern Italy. On April 30, with Joseph Stalin's soldiers two blocks away from the

Reich Chancellery, bid farewell to Martin Bormann, propaganda minister Joseph Goebbels and his family, and the bunker staff, and retired to his private study. Hitler and Eva Braun both took cyanide pills; Hitler also fired a failsafe bullet from a Walther PPK 7.65 into his own skull. He had chosen this method on the advice of Dr. Werner Haase. Hitler had insisted Haase first prove the poison's potency by administering it to his beloved dog, Blondi. The Alsatian died quickly.

Loyal soldiers acting on Hitler's last requests carried the bodies upstairs to the garden and doused them with gasoline. Bormann, whom Hitler had appointed the new Minister of the National Socialist Party, set them ablaze.

In the bunker beneath, Joseph Goebbels and his wife Magda tricked their six children into swallowing cyanide capsules before following them into death.

On May 1, a radio broadcast by Admiral Karl Dönitz over *Reichssender Hamburg* informed the German people that the Führer had been killed while valiantly defending the capital. In accordance with Hitler's wishes, Dönitz announced he was now President of the German Reich.

That night, Martin Bormann fled the *Führerbunker*, accompanied by three men, including Hitler Youth leader Artur Axmann, and hurried down a deserted U-Bahn tunnel. They emerged at Friedrichstraße station and made their way to the Weidendammer Bridge, taking cover behind a tank as they crossed the Spree River, Soviet artillery exploding all around them. Eventually reaching the other side, Axmann parted ways with Bormann. Encountering Soviet troops, he made his way back, only to find the corpses of Bormann and another SS member lying dead on a bridge.[1] Axmann hurried on, and Bormann's body was lost in the chaos. As his death could not be confirmed, Bormann was tried for conspiring to launch a conflict of aggression, war crimes, and crimes against humanity *in absentia* at Nuremberg. Convicted on the latter two counts, he was sentenced to die by hanging on October 15, 1946, although his whereabouts remained a mystery.

—

With the mysterious deaths of Hitler and Bormann, conspiracy theories sprouted up like weeds. One of the most popular hypotheses, known as the **Operation Grey Wolf** account, holds that Bormann and General Heinrich Müller, chief of the Gestapo, had long since prepared a contingency plan—Operation Grey Wolf— to facilitate the Führer's escape if Germany fell. This was simply one piece of a larger plot dubbed *Aktion Feuerland* (Project Land of Fire) to establish a Fourth Reich in South America. Hitler would make his way to Spain by air and then continue on to Argentina by submarine. By April 28, Bormann had sent an encrypted message to his secret network of operatives both on land and in U–Boats, reading, "Agree proposed transfer overseas."[2] All parties knew what that meant: Adolf Hitler was on the move.

Just after midnight on April 28, Hitler, Eva Braun, Blondi, Bormann, Braun's brother-in-law Hermann Fegelein, and a party of SS guards left the *Führerbunker* and made their way to Hitler's private headquarters in the Old Reich Chancellery. Opening a secret panel, they entered an escape tunnel and headed toward a bunker. There, Adolf Hitler and Eva Braun came face-to-face with their lookalikes—most likely Hitler's regular "stand-in" Gustav Weber and a young actress selected by Goebbels. Eva Braun scrawled a letter instructing her mother and father not to be concerned if she did not contact them for a while, and passed it to Bormann for safekeeping.

At this point, so the theory goes, Bormann led the two stand-ins back into the *Führerbunker* to fulfill their gruesome roles in the operation, while Hitler, Braun, and Fegelein changed into steel helmets and camouflage. Then, accompanied by their SS guards and Blondi, they descended into the U–Bahn near Kaiserhoff

Station (now renamed Mohrenstrasse) and embarked on a 4-mile (6.5-km) journey through the subway tunnels of war-torn Berlin. After traveling more than three hours on foot, they finally emerged at Fehrbelliner Platz station. There they were joined by Eva's sister, Ilse, and SS General Joachim Rumohr and his wife. Exiting through the main entrance, they boarded two armored personnel carriers and three tanks which drove them to a Junkers Ju 52/3m transport plane on a temporary airstrip on the Hohenzollerndamm. It was now 3 am. Veteran *Luftwaffe* pilot Captain Peter Erich Baumgart welcomed his six still-disguised passengers and their dog aboard and took off. Only once the passengers were in the air and had removed their helmets did Baumgart realize their identities and status.

Captain Baumgart landed his plane in the city of Magdeburg on the Elbe. Dawn was breaking, and it was a necessary measure to avoid Allied fighters. Once he was reasonably sure the path was safe, he flew northwest to a former German zeppelin base in the inconspicuous town of Tønder in south Denmark. It was April 29 when Baumgart and his passengers finally alighted onto the runway. Baumgart claims the Führer shook his hand, slipping a check for 20,000 Reichsmarks in the name of "Adolf Hitler" into his palm.[3] Another SS officer, 24-year-old Friedrich von Angelotty-Mackensen, later claimed to have seen Hitler deliver a 40-minute speech on the airfield.[4]

According to Baumgart, he was instructed to fly back to Berlin in another airplane to pick up more evacuees. A second pilot took control of the Ju 52, flying Hitler and company to nearby Travemünde in the port city of Lübeck in northern Germany. It was there, having ultimately decided to remain in Germany, that Ilse Braun and the Rumohrs bid the others farewell. By this time, Martin Bormann had learned from German military intelligence in Spain that an airfield in the southern Catalonian city of Reus had been prepared to receive the Führer on the next leg of his escape.

Hitler, Eva Braun, Hermann Fegelein, and Blondi boarded a Ju 252, and approximately six hours later touched down in Spain. They were then whisked away to a second Ju 52—without Spanish air force markings—while the plane they had arrived in was destroyed to dispose of any evidence. They were subsequently flown to Fuerteventura—one of Spain's Canary Islands—where they stayed at the Villa Winter on the Jandía peninsula. The SS-staffed Villa Winter was a luxurious stopover specifically constructed by German military intelligence in 1943 for *Aktion Feuerland*.

Meanwhile, Martin Bormann and Heinrich Müller were tying up loose ends in the bunkers of Berlin. On the afternoon of April 30, Eva Braun's stand-in was poisoned with cyanide while Hitler's double was shot in the head. Their bodies were covered in blankets and taken upstairs to the Chancellery Garden where they were burned beyond recognition. Bormann also ensured an Alsatian resembling Blondi was given a cyanide capsule. Before abandoning the bunkers once and for all, on May 1, Bormann sent a message to Admiral Karl Dönitz stating that Hitler was dead and had appointed Dönitz as his successor. Soon after midnight on May 2, Bormann fled to the Hotel Atlas where he had stowed civilian clothing, identification, and Reichsmarks. Joined by SS Major Joachim Tiburtius, he headed for the Schiffbauerdamm road, which ran alongside the Spree River. He and Tiburtius became separated, but Bormann, though wounded in the foot by shrapnel from Soviet artillery bombardment, managed to hobble 12 miles (19 km) to the town of Königs Wusterhausen the next day. Eventually, he was able to sneak past British lines and reach a safehouse near Flensburg on the Danish border where he reconvened with Müller. Learning that Dönitz had surrendered unconditionally, Bormann decided to travel south to the Bavarian Alps to plan his next move.

By this time, Hitler, Eva, and Blondi were being transported across the Atlantic in the belly of a Type IXC U-boat. The vessel is believed to have been the U-518, commanded by 25-year-old Hans-Werner Offermann, although, according to the official narrative, that vessel had been sunk northwest of the Azores a week earlier by the USS *Carter* and USS *Neal A. Scott*. Stopping to anchor for only a few hours at the Cape Verde Islands on May 4, the U–518 continued south, reaching south, reaching the Argentine beach of Necochea around 1 am on July 28, 1945.

Lieutenant General Fegelein, who had parted ways with them at Villa Winter, had raced toward Argentina in U–880, arriving five days before U–518 to prepare for the Führer's arrival. While the crew unloaded, he escorted them to their automobile. They spent their first night at the main house on Estancia Moromar; the loot they had brought with them was transported to Nazi banks in Buenos Aires. On the morning of April 30, Hitler, Eva Braun, and Blondi accompanied Fegelein onto a Curtiss biplane, courtesy of the Argentine air force, and flew to Estancia San Ramón in Patagonia, roughly 12 miles (19 km) from San Carlos de Bariloche. This isolated ranch was owned by Prince Stephane zu Schamburg-Lippe, a Nazi consul in Buenos Aires who had been thoroughly briefed on *Aktion Feuerland*. Hitler and Eva Braun remained at Estancia San Ramón for nine months while their permanent residence, Inalco, was prepared.

Modeled after the Führer's beloved Alpine home, the Berghof, Inalco was located in the province of Neuquén about 21 miles (34 km) from the Chilean border in northwest Patagonia and 56 miles (90 km) from Estancia San Ramón. It would serve as their main Patagonian abode from 1947 to 1955. The surrounding area even became known as Adolf Hitler's Valley. It hosted a Nazi colony called the Center which was governed by escaped war criminal General Ludolf von Alvensleben: a man who had personally overseen countless mass murders in Crimea and Western Poland. Originally captured by British troops in April 1945, Alvensleben had managed to escape his internment camp during the Christmas festivities and was smuggled to Argentina using Red Cross travel documents obtained in Genoa.[5] In these early days, President Juan Perón would often stop by the valley to mountaineer with his new Nazi *amigos*.

Back in Europe, Bormann was alive and plotting. After five months hiding out in the Bavarian highlands, he had ventured into Munich in October 1945 to obtain a visa to enter Spain. He was still working on this a year later, when he was tried *in absentia* at the Nuremberg International Military Tribunal and sentenced to hang. By mid-1947, Bormann was ready to move on. Secure in the knowledge that Hitler had been living undetected in Argentina for two years, he conspired with Juan and Eva Perón to resettle in Argentina accompanied by his friend and coconspirator Heinrich Müller. Narrowly escaping the British Army in December while leaving Udine, Italy, Bormann boarded a ship bound for Argentina in the Adriatic port of Bari. At some point, he must have changed vessels, for when he arrived in the Argentine capital in Jesuit attire on May 17, 1948, it was aboard the *Giovanna C* out of Genoa. According to his Vatican passport, he was Reverend Juan Gómez. Bormann obtained the proper paperwork, rendezvoused with the Peróns who gave him a meager quarter of the considerable Nazi wealth he had smuggled into Argentina (which he had little option but to grudgingly accept), and traveled to Inalco to meet with the Führer. Though Bormann allegedly had a home in San Carlos de Bariloche, he reportedly spent most of his time in Buenos Aires, where he continued to administer the funds to keep Adolf Hitler's Valley and its denizens thriving.

Among the Nazis said to have been living in Patagonia were "Architect of the Holocaust" Adolf Eichmann, "Butcher of Mauthausen" Aribet Heim, "Angel of Death" Josef Mengele, "Butcher of the Ardeatine Caves" Erich Priebke, "Executioner of Riga" Eduard Roschmann, and the infamous SS sadist Josef Schwammberger. Though Bormann's plan to launch a Fourth Reich in the South seemed plausible in the late-1940s, by the 1950s, Hitler's visible deterioration, along with the gradual realization that militant National Socialism was not due for a comeback, led most former Nazis to tone down their rhetoric, drift apart, and go on to lead mostly normal lives.

In 1954, Eva Braun reportedly left the ailing Hitler and Inalco, and moved 230 miles (370 km) from San Carlos de Bariloche to the town of Neuquén where she was well cared for by Bormann. When the Perón government was toppled in a Catholic military coup in mid-September 1955, Bormann saw the writing on the wall, and ordered that Hitler be relocated from Inalco to a smaller, more remote property called La Clara. Only Bormann knew its true whereabouts. Now aged 66, the shock of the upheaval caused the already frail Hitler to deteriorate even further. He allegedly spent his final years in suicidal melancholy, alone, save for his physician Dr. Otto Lehmann, and a sailor named Heinrich Bethe. After suffering partial facial paralysis in January 1962, the now 72-year-old Führer began experiencing terrifying hallucinations before falling into a coma after a stroke on February 12. At 3 pm the following day, Dr. Lehmann declared Adolf Hitler dead.

The last reported sighting of Martin Bormann and Heinrich Müller was in 1980 in Argentina. Both would have been roughly 80 years of age.

———

While Hitler's demise was initially subject to far less scrutiny, during the Cold War, the West German Government and CIA spearheaded an unsuccessful effort to locate Martin Bormann. Then, on December 7, 1972, construction workers unearthed human skeletons near where a German civilian had reportedly buried bodies on Soviet orders. These remains were forensically identified as Bormann's, a claim that was further supported by facial reconstruction. Still, the authorities could not be absolutely certain.

The Operation Grey Wolf account of Martin Bormann's relocation to South America is but one of many conspiracy theories. In 1996, John Ainsworth Davis—writing under the pen name Christopher Creighton—claimed to have participated in a top-secret British intelligence operation led by future James Bond author Ian

Fleming in which they rescued Bormann from certain death in his bunker. According to his book *OPJB: The Last Great Secret of the Second World War*, the aim of the mission was to recover the substantial Nazi funds that Bormann had squirreled away in Swiss bank accounts. Ainsworth Davis claimed Bormann was temporarily removed to the United Kingdom, ultimately dying in Paraguay in 1959. Though never printed in the US, *OPJB* was a bestseller in France and Germany. In fact, the book caused such consternation among members of the German government that it spurred DNA analysis of the 1972 remains. The results confirmed that one of skeletons was that of Martin Bormann.[6] *OPJB* was not reprinted.

In light of the additional evidence of Bormann's May 2, 1945, demise, all conspiracy theories in which he escaped Berlin must be considered thoroughly debunked.

However, there is less certainty surrounding the fates of Adolf Hitler and Eva Braun. On hearing news of the Führer's death, Joseph Stalin had demanded proof. Commander Ivan Klimenko had found the burned bodies of what he believed to be Hitler, Braun, and Blondi on May 4 in a shell crater near the Reich Chancellery. They were transported to Soviet counterespionage in Buch where, on May 11, Käthe Heusermann, a former assistant to Hitler's dentist, and dental technician Fritz Echtmann identified a segment of the Führer's lower jaw. However, owing to the Cold War's prevailing culture of secrecy, the USSR did not publicize details of the autopsy until 1968. Four years later, American forensic odontologists at UCLA confirmed the dentists' findings. By this time, the Soviets had reduced the charred remains to ash and dumped them in a tributary of the Elbe River. This short-sighted decision rendered any future attempt at DNA analysis impossible.

The chronology of events in the official narrative and the Operation Grey Wolf conspiracy theory both hold that Martin Bormann did not escape the bunker until May 2, 1945. By then, Adolf Hitler and Eva Braun would have been safely ensconced in U-518 *en route* to the Cape Verde Islands. Given this timeline, a third possibility emerges: Martin Bormann was indeed killed trying to flee Berlin *and* Operation Grey Wolf was a complete success. However, if we are to discount the dozens of witnesses in both Europe and South America who claimed to have seen or even conversed with Bormann after May 2, then how reliable is similar testimony about Adolf Hitler and Eva Braun? At the end of the day, scientific evidence must take precedence.

—

Though Martin Bormann and likely Adolf Hitler did not survive to make it to the Americas, the sickening truth is that hundreds of Nazi war criminals did. Worse, they were aided and abetted by individuals and institutions who were widely seen as virtuous, by way of aptly-named "ratlines . . ."

Nazi Ratlines

By the spring of 1945, with the Red Army closing in on Berlin, the Third Reich's days were clearly numbered. High-ranking Nazis began fleeing Germany like vermin from a fire. Many were assisted by rogue Catholic priests operating so-called "ratlines." But were those priests *truly* rogue, or acting on orders from the Vatican?

The conduit for Nazi and fascist escapees in the final days of World War II in Europe necessarily entailed collaboration between certain members of the Catholic Church and sympathetic regimes, such as that of General Francisco Franco in Spain, and Juan and Eva Perón in Argentina. The role of rogue priests acting on their own accord versus a top-down policy orchestrated by the Vatican—including Pope Pius XII himself—remains hotly contested. For the most part, the church denies any knowledge on behalf of the late pontiff and high-ranking members of his clergy; however, opponents assert that such a large-scale evacuation of Nazi officials simply could not have happened otherwise.

The first and most important player in the ratlines was the rabidly anti-Communist Austrian Bishop Alois Hudal. After working as a Professor of Old Testament Studies at the University of Gratz, Hudal was named Rector of the Pontificio Collegio Teutonico di Santa Maria dell'Anima in Rome by Pope Pius XI. Located on Via della Pace, this 14th-century church and hospice was transformed into a theological seminary for Germanophones in the mid-1800s. Hudal's appointment came within four months of Fascist dictator Benito Mussolini's ascent to power. Having obtained his position on the recommendation of Austrian diplomat

Ludwig von Pastor, Hudal advocated strongly for his countrymen and homeland within the Catholic church.

By 1933, Hudal had been consecrated Titular Bishop by Eugenio Cardinal Pacelli—who would succeed Pius XI as pope in 1939—and began openly espousing pan-Germanic nationalism and railing against the Jews. The Austrian bishop traveled extensively through Italy and Germany, orating to large audiences of German-speaking Catholics in order to promote unity between the church and Nazi regime. Hudal's 1937 publication *The Foundations of National Socialism* sang Hitler's praises, and in April of the following year he organized a vote concerning Germany's March 12 annexation of Austria for clerics from both nations.

When the tide of war began turning against the Axis powers in 1944, Hudal made a complete about face, publicly positioning himself as an oppressed Austrian patriot and long-time champion of democracy. Yet, all the while, the Austrian bishop was plotting to rescue rousted Nazis from what he considered immoral "Allied Vengeance."[1] Over the next two years, he dedicated his energies to hiding and transporting Nazis to safety. His task was made easier by the sheer number of displaced persons from all over Europe—many of whom were Catholic—stranded in Italy, Germany, and Austria in the wake of the war. While the overwhelming majority were genuine victims of authoritarian regimes, their sheer numbers enabled fascists to conceal their identities with comparative ease. Furthermore, the Holy See had successfully lobbied the Allies to allow specific priests to enter civilian and POW camps to attend to refugees' physical and spiritual needs.

In December 1944, the Vatican selected a bishop to minister to German-speaking civil internees in Italy—none other than the once unabashedly pro-Nazi Alois Hudal. He was thus in a prime position to infiltrate civilian camps teeming with displaced Germans and Austrians and identify and assist potential Nazi war criminals. Through his relationship with Giovanni Montini, an undersecretary to Pope Pius XII (Pacelli), Hudal had access to Vatican passports and other documents used for identity and travel, along with a mandate to dispense them. Allegedly, Montini also allowed Hudal to access funds from the Caritas, a charitable organization that covered travel and living expenses for refugees. As of this writing, the Vatican refuses to release bank records concerning the allocation of moneys to displaced persons in the late and post-World War II era. Montini would himself later become pontiff in 1963.

While much noise has been made about the role of Vatican passports in helping fascist war criminals flee Europe, in truth, passports issued by the Red Cross were far easier to obtain and played a much greater factor. Nevertheless, pro-Nazi clergymen were instrumental in getting these Red Cross passports into the hands of fascist fugitives holed up in their churches, religious colleges, and monasteries.

Enabled by the highest echelons of the Catholic Church, whether knowingly or unknowingly, Hudal still needed allies on the ground to man hubs along his ratline. While there are countless theories as to how the virulently anti-Communist Archbishop Siri of Genoa and Walter Rauff, former Chief SS Security Officer of Northwest Italy, became key players in Hudal's network, their involvement has been established beyond a reasonable doubt. From 1945–1951, this triad smuggled hundreds of Nazis—including some of the most heinous characters in history—to South America and Spain. Typically, once a Nazi fugitive entered Italy, he contacted Rauff in Milan. Rauff then arranged his transfer to the Pontificio Collegio Teutonico di Santa Maria dell'Anima in Rome. There, sheltered by Alois Hudal, the fugitive received the necessary documentation before being transported to Siri in Genoa. Once there, he boarded a ship, usually for Spain or South America. Among the most despicable Nazi war criminals to escape via Hudal's ratlines were Alois Brunner, Adolf Eichmann, Dr. Josef Mengele, Franz Stangl, and Gustav Wagner. These five men alone were responsible for the deaths of millions.

The first of the five to flee Europe using Hudal's ratlines was the infamous "Angel of Death," Dr. Josef Mengele. Born in Bavaria, Mengele was an intelligent child who moved to Munich to study philosophy. In the early 1930s, he joined the paramilitary wing of the Nazi party, the Sturmabteilung ("Assault Division) or SA, and in 1935, earned a PhD in anthropology. Mengele worked as research assistant on the genetics of facial deformities under Dr. Otmar Frei-herr von Verschuer—and was awarded a Doctor of Medicine in 1938 from the University of Frankfurt. That same year, Mengele joined the SS. When war broke out he served in medical reserve battalions of the *Waffen-SS* and 5th SS Panzer Division Wiking. After suffering a serious combat-related injury, he relocated to Berlin to work in the SS Race and Settlement Main Office head-quarters with Dr. von Verschuer.

On the advice of his old mentor, Mengele transferred to Auschwitz-Birkenau where he accepted a position as chief physician of Birkenau's Romani camp. Tasked with assuring the proper administration of Zyklon B, he presided over the gas chambers of crematoriums IV and V, inspecting the hospital barracks each week to add sick patients to the kill list.

Mengele's reputation for unfathomable cruelty was cemented by his human experiments. The countless atrocities he is known to have perpetrated include deliberately infecting his subjects with diseases, needlessly amputating their limbs, injecting chemicals into their irises to alter the color, and sewing twins back-to-back, causing them to slowly die from gangrene.[2]

In June 1945, Mengele and his unit fled west from the advancing Soviets, only to fall into American hands. At the time, he was not listed as a war criminal, and was released the following month thanks to forged documents that identified him as Fritz Hollman. After heading back east to recover some documents from Auschwitz that he had entrusted into the care of a nurse, Mengele worked on a farm in Bavaria, before traveling to Genoa along Hudal's ratline. There, he was given a Red Cross passport identifying him as Helmut Gregor, which he used to sail to Argentina in July 1949.

Under the leadership of Nazi-hunter Simon Wiesenthal, Israeli intelligence agency Mossad ascertained that Mengele was alive and living in Buenos Aires. But by the time they had obtained a warrant for his arrest, formally petitioning the government of Argentina for his extradition in June 1959, the "Angel of Death" had already escaped to Paraguay. Within a year he relocated to Brazil, though Mossad continued to stay on his trail, coming within a hair of capturing him in 1962.

On February 7, 1979, Josef Mengele had a stroke while swimming in the ocean at Bertioga and drowned. He was buried under the name Wolfgang Gerhard, and in 1985 the West German authorities finally learned of Mengele's fate and the whereabouts of his final resting place. His body was exhumed on June 6 of that same year, and in 1992, his identity was finally confirmed through DNA analysis.

The Mossad team who had come to Argentina in search of "The Angel of Death" were also pursuing a bigger quarry: "The Architect of the Holocaust. "

Lieutenant-Colonel Adolf Eichmann ran the department of the SS which dealt with the "Jewish Question" under "Blond Butcher" Reinhard Heidrich. Their "answer" to this so-called question quickly escalated from ghettoization in preparation for mass deportation to systematic genocide following the Wannsee Conference of January 20, 1942. Eichmann harnessed the notoriously efficient Nazi bureaucracy to arrange the transfer of millions of Jews to extermination camps, particularly Auschwitz II-Birkenau, Belzec, Sobibór, and Treblinka.

When World War II ended, Eichmann was living in Austria with his wife and children. He was captured by American troops but used forged documents to pass as Otto Eckmann. Routinely transferred from one SS officer camp to another, he learned that his true identity had been uncovered in Cham and escaped while on work detail. Taking on yet another identity, Otto Heninger, Eichmann fled to bucolic Lower Saxony. Through Bishop Hudal, in

1948 Eichmann gained a permit to enter Argentina along with false identification papers stating he was a Croatian refugee named Rikardo Klement. In 1950, Eichmann used these documents to obtain a Red Cross passport, and scurried along Hudal's ratline to a Genoese monastery controlled by Archbishop Siri. Like so many other Nazi butchers, he eventually made his way to Argentina.

Eichmann was apprehended outside his Buenos Aires home by Mossad agents on May 11, 1960. His eldest son, Klaus, had bragged about his father's past to his Argentine girlfriend, Sylvia Hermann. Sylvia's father, Lothar Hermann, was a half-Jewish German who had presciently moved to Argentina in 1938. Lothar contacted the West German government, who passed the information on to Mossad. On April 11, 1961, Eichmann stood trial in Jerusalem, Israel, for crimes against humanity, war crimes, and 13 other charges. On December 12, he was convicted of crimes against Jews, Poles, Slovenes, and Romani and sentenced to death. Adolf Eichmann was executed by hanging at a Ramla prison on June 1, 1962.

Despite widespread knowledge of his role in the Nazi ratlines, Bishop Alois Hudal continued his operation with impunity until an August 6, 1947, article in the newspaper *Milano Sera* accused Pius XII of fraternizing with SS war criminals and propagating the myth of the persecuted "poor German."[3] Now that the Vatican itself was under attack, Hudal came under immense pressure from its diplomats and clergymen. Dubbed "Nazi, fascist Bishop"[4] by colleagues, he nevertheless continued running the ratline until December 1951, when he announced that he would be stepping down from his position at Pontificio Collegio Teutonico di Santa Maria dell'Anima within seven months. Though effectively disavowed by the church, Hudal was open and unapologetic about his actions, later writing: "I thank God that He [allowed me] to visit and comfort many victims in their prisons and concentration camps and [to help] them to escape with false identity papers . . . I felt duty bound after 1945 to devote my whole charitable work mainly to former National Socialists and Fascists, especially to so-called 'war criminals.'"[5] Hudal was disowned by Pius XII and banned from Rome. He died in May 1963. When the Hudal-Rauff-Siri ratline fell, it was replaced by a second even more efficient one run primarily by Croatian nationalist clergymen. Headed by Father Krunoslav Dragonović and headquartered in Rome at the Confraternity of San Girolamo, it focused primarily on securing safe haven for fugitive Ustaše from Ante Pavlić's fascist Croatia—men fleeing reprisal at the hands of the Yugoslavian Communist dictator Tito. As with Hudal's ratline, the usual point of departure was Genoa. Incredibly, Dragonović's operation transported the genocidal Pavlić himself to Argentina: a leader so callous and brutal he was known to have kept a bowl containing 40 lbs (18 kg) of Serbian eyeballs in his office. Pavlić once even admonished Hitler for going too easy on the Jews.

—

Perhaps the greatest controversy surrounding the Catholic Church during the rise of Nazi Germany, World War II, and the operation of its ratlines has been the degree to which Pope Pius XII, and to a lesser extent, his successor's successor, Paul VI (Giovanni Montini), enabled these processes. At either extreme of the debate are two Brits: the author and academic John Cornwell who (in)famously dubbed Montini "Hitler's Pope"[6] and the late Sir Martin Gilbert, a chronicler of Jewish history and the Holocaust. On the basis of Pius XII's letters before he became pope, which repeatedly link the Jews to Bolshevism, Cornwell argues that the pontiff was an anti-Semite. In addition, just before he became pope, Pacelli was involved in drawing up an encyclical titled *Humani Generis Unitas* (The Unity of the Human Race) that purported to reject anti-Semitism, but did nothing of the kind. Instead it claimed that "the Jews were responsible for their own fate." This, combined with Pacelli's pursuit of Papal absolutism—the notion that the office of pontiff should be highly centralized and dictatorial—led him to form concordats and collude with Mussolini, Hitler, and other right-wing authoritarians.[7] Gilbert counters with claims that Pacelli used monasteries and convents, some of which were in the Vatican itself, to hide 4,000 Roman Jews when the Gestapo unexpectedly stormed into the Italian capital to round up its Jewish population.[8] The pontiff also sheltered hundreds in his personal summer Palace of Castel Gandolfo.[9]

Australian journalist Mark Aarons and former American federal prosecutor and army intelligence officer John Loftus propose that "the evidence clears the Vatican of actively assisting Hitler, but convicts it of aiding war criminals, knowingly laundering stolen property in order to protect its own investments in Nazi Germany, and violating the norms of international diplomacy."[10] Pointing to Pius XII's clandestine support of the Black Orchestra—a secret society of German aristocrats and high-ranking soldiers who privately despised National Socialism and sought to usurp Hitler— Aarons and Loftus disagree with Cornwell's conclusion that Pius XII was pro-Nazi. At the same time, they accuse the Holy See of knowingly facilitating Hudal's ratlines, only replacing the Austrian with Dragonović when he became a liability. Aarons and Loftus cite British and American intelligence reports to support this claim. Having followed a trail of smuggled gold and laundered money to the Vatican bank, they propose that "on balance of probabilities"[11] the Holy See's motivation for running the ratlines was profit, with anti-Communist concerns coming in a distant second (if at all).

Fortunately, we may soon have an answer as to whether Pius XII was a Nazi collaborator, unsung hero, or someone altogether different. When Pope Benedict XVI, himself a former member of the Hitler Youth, venerated Pius XII in 2009, the United States Holocaust Memorial Museum and a number of Jewish organizations lobbied the Vatican to release over one million classified documents concerning Pacelli from their archives.[12] Benedict XVI began the process, and in March 2020, Pope Francis completed it. A thorough evaluation of this voluminous material is expected to take years as the Vatican offices can only accommodate a maximum of 60 scholars at any given time.[13]

—

While Argentina and the Catholic Church have borne the brunt of global condemnation for their role in trafficking prominent fascists to safety, the United States and Soviet Union also took Nazi scientists under their respective wings. In the US, this intelligence project entailed secreting war criminals in the deserts of the American southwest to develop advanced weaponry in exchange for turning a blind eye to their pasts.[14]

Unlike Argentina, Spain, or the Catholic Church, neither the US or USSR were motivated to provide sanctuary for Nazis out of misplaced sympathy or ideological solidarity. Rather, it was a matter of practical necessity.

In 1943, the Germans had begun mass production of *Vergeltungswaffe*[i] missiles at Mittelwerk, a subterranean complex and concentration camp at Nordhausen in the Harz Mountains. The miners and munitions workers at Mittelwerk consisted of enslaved laborers from occupied Europe. Approximately half of the 60,000 workers brought to Nordhausen perished due to Nazi brutality[15], with a minimum of 20,000 dying during the construction of *Vergeltungswaffe-2* (V-2) missiles.[16] The V-2 was the first long-range guided ballistic rocket. Measuring 46 ft (14 m) in length, it could hold up to 2,000 lbs (907 kg) of explosive material.[17] Where its predecessor, the V-1, was vulnerable to British antiaircraft guns, the V-2's ability to travel faster than the speed of sound at an altitude of 50 miles (80 km) made it virtually invincible.

By September of 1944, London, Antwerp, and several other Western European cities were bombarded by V-2s, resulting in approximately 7,000 fatalities.[18] General Dwight D. Eisenhower,

i *Vergeltungswaffe* roughly translates from German to English as "vengeance."

Supreme Commander of the Allied Expeditionary Force in Europe, once remarked that "it seemed likely that, if the German had succeeded in perfecting and using these new [V–2] weapons six months earlier than he did, our invasion of Europe would have proved exceedingly difficult, perhaps impossible."[19]

With the fall of the Third Reich and its allies in the late summer of 1945, history's most catastrophic war opened the door to a seemingly imminent conflict between the western capitalist democracies and Communist USSR. Only now, the threat of nuclear weapons—having been successfully deployed by the US on the Japanese cities of Hiroshima and Nagasaki—was a terrifying reality. In light of this impending war of apocalyptic proportions, both superpowers were more than willing to scoop up key Nazi scientists, especially those involved in the V–2 program, in order to benefit from their destructive brilliance before their competitor beat them to it. These Nazi-grabbing operations were dubbed Paperclip and Osoaviakhim in the US and Soviet Union, respectively.

Among the more than 1,600 German scientists and engineers granted safe haven in the US were V–2 program boss Major General Walter Dornberger, physicist Dr. Wernher Von Braun, Mittelwerk operations director Arthur Rudolph, and Mittelwerk general manager and engineer Georg Rickhey, along with doctors Ernst Steinhoff, Walter Ziegler, and Walther Riedel.

Many of these refugees could have easily stood trial beside Hermann Goering and Karl Dönitz at Nuremberg. For instance, Rickhey, von Braun, Dornberger, and Rudolph had all met on May 6, 1944, to discuss where to acquire additional enslaved people to replace the prisoners they had worked to death at Nordhausen. They ultimately decided on 1,800 skilled French laborers.

These "Paperclips" would spend a significant portion of their new American lives at the Los Alamos National Laboratory in New Mexico: birthplace of the atomic bomb. Los Alamos was also the future residence of a bespectacled young man named Robert Lazar, whose revelations would shock the world 45 years later . . .

Area 51

For years, a certain United States Air Force facility in the Nevada desert became the focus of feverish rumor and speculation. Was top-secret military research going on there? And if so, what kind? Did it house recovered UFOs and even their real, live, extraterrestrial pilots?

Today, Area 51 is a household name, but it only became so in May 1989, when Las Vegas TV station KLAS aired an interview with "Dennis"—who claimed to have worked as a physicist at the S-4 facility in the Area 51 compound at Nellis Air Force Base. Filmed in silhouette, the alleged whistleblower informed the nation that he had witnessed "nine flying saucers . . . of extraterrestrial origin . . . [at S-4] being test-flown and basically just analyzed."[1] Dennis said that he knew very little of the overall scope and vision of the project because his superiors only provided staff with information on a "need to know" basis. The particular Rubik's Cube Dennis had been handed was to understand and reverse-engineer the alien craft's propulsion and power source. When investigative reporter George Knapp proposed that the technology might have been created by the US government itself, Dennis replied that this was impossible as the vehicle used an anti-matter power source and gravity to propel itself—both which defy known physical laws.

"One of the reasons I'm coming forward with this information," he proclaimed, "[is] it's not only a crime against the American people, it's a crime against the scientific community."[2] Dennis concluded by acknowledging that he had been threatened with charges of espionage and even death.

This local media story soon featured on news programs around the globe. People had reported seeing UFOs in the vicinity for over 40 years, and at long last somebody was coming forward with the truth *they* had been hiding from the public.

—

Area 51 is a military facility in the northeast corner of the greater Nevada Test and Training Range (NTTR) located 75 miles (120 km) from Las Vegas in the Mojave Desert and covering a vast area—4,687 square miles (7,543 sq km). The US only officially acknowledged its existence in 2013. As it turns out, there was plenty to conceal.

Throughout the 1930s, the Department of the Interior used this stretch of the Mojave as a sanctuary for wild horses, cougars, antelope, and bighorn sheep. However, with the US's entry into World War II in December 1941, the area was transferred from public to government-only access and repurposed into a bombing range. After Operation Crossroads—the 1946 test detonations of two nuclear bombs, *Gilda* and *Baker*, at the South Pacific coral reef of Bikini Atoll—leading atomic physicist Dr. Edward Teller, "the father of the hydrogen bomb," advocated for a domestic location to carry out future tests, mainly due to logistics. President Harry S. Truman supported the idea, and in 1950, Project Nutmeg determined that the most feasible place to carry out these tests was the desert in south Nevada encompassing the World War II bombing range. The convenient proximity of the government-owned airfield, Indian Springs, less than 7 miles (11 km) away sealed the decision.

A section of land comprising just over a quarter of the total area was designated the Nevada Test Site. At 5:45 am on January 27, 1951, the USAF dropped an atomic bomb on Frenchman Flat, a dry lake bed near the site's southern boundary. This was the first time an aerial nuclear bomb had been detonated on American soil, and the first of 928 nuclear explosions at the NTTR, the last occurring in 1992.

Although the military went to great lengths to deny or cover up the unintended consequences and mishaps—bovine fatalities, birds gobbling up radioactive worms, and birth defects in Utah—there was simply no hiding the detonations. In the 1950s, the exciting promise of distant mushroom clouds drew crowds of tourists to Las Vegas, and the "City of Lights" shook with the ensuing tremors. CIA special assistant Richard Bissell used these mushroom clouds to the agency's advantage, correctly surmising that no sane American civilian would go anywhere near the base. This made it the perfect spot for the CIA, USAF, and Lockheed corporation to perfect their highly classified new Cold War project—the U-2 spy plane.

The U-2 began with Colonel Richard Sully Leghorn: a seasoned USAF pilot who had flown over Axis-controlled Europe nearly 100 times between 1943-1945. Leghorn had been summoned to Bikini Atoll in 1946 to photograph the underwater atomic blast from the skies. The shocking power he witnessed that day convinced him the world could not survive a full-scale nuclear conflict. He reasoned the best strategy to prevent this was to collect intelligence on the USSR's weapons capabilities. Moreover, this had to be done sooner rather than later. Leghorn proposed that there should be regular flights over the Soviet Union to observe and document what the Russians were up to. His ideas were dismissed by Truman and the Joint Chiefs of Staff in the 1940s, but, in the following decade, the Korean War changed minds as American F-86 Sabres and Soviet MiG-15s, developed by Nazi scientists on either side of the Iron Curtain, engaged in dogfights over the peninsula.

Following the cessation of the war in 1953, the USAF reviewed the enemy's capacities and noted that Soviet MiGs flew at a maximum altitude of 45,000 ft (13,700 m). If the US could develop a plane that reached 60,000 ft (18,300 m), the Soviets would be unable to reach them. This would allow Leghorn's proposed spy plane to photograph the USSR with impunity.

President Dwight D. Eisenhower was enthusiastic about Leghorn's plan. He assigned the CIA's Richard Bissell to oversee the development of the U-2, codenamed Project Aquatone. Eisenhower's decision to entrust Aquatone to the CIA rather than the USAF was because the program needed to be a "black op," with Congress, foreign governments, and even the military itself kept in the dark. Any US Air Force pilot flying in Soviet airspace was required by international law to wear a uniform, which would be viewed as an act of military aggression. However, if the CIA recruited a pilot from the USAF, this would circumvent the mandate to wear a uniform, and allow Eisenhower plausible deniability of military involvement in the event of a crash. Bissell even convinced the President to excise the Development Project Staff tasked with running Aquatone from the CIA's organizational chart, making the program virtually autonomous. Aquatone was essentially an intelligence program hidden from its own agency, with Bissell in total control.

In early 1955, Bissell and Lockheed aerodynamicist Kelly Johnson flew out to Groom Lake, another dried up bed on the NTTR, just northeast of the Nevada Test Site by Area 51. Soon after landing, they realized it was completely shielded from public view by mountains. The location was optimal.

By September, Area 51 had 200 residents: 33 percent were CIA; 33 percent USAF; and 33 percent from the Lockheed Aircraft corporation. Operating on a budget of $22 million (the equivalent of $210 million in 2020), the men behind Project Aquatone were tasked with designing and building the U-2, conducting covert test flights, and accustoming pilots to the unparalleled intensity of flying at such extreme altitudes. Even before they set foot in a U-2, chosen pilots were subjected to torturous physical and psychological exercises. These included electric shocks, orifices flooded with liquids, confinement in boxes, lengthy stints in boiling hot rooms, and arms plunged into ice water for as long as they could bear. If these tests sound suspiciously like the cruel experiments conducted by Dr. Josef Mengele and his ilk, it is because they were administered by medical doctors brought in under Operation Paperclip, some of whom had actually worked at Nazi concentration camps.

Each U–2 was transported unassembled in a C–124 from Lockheed's plant in Burbank, California, with every individual piece concealed in a white sheet. Project Aquatone operated under a policy of sensitive compartmentalized information (SCI), so that only a select few had a complete picture of what they were building. Once the U–2s were pieced together, test flights began within a maximum radius of 200 miles (322 km) from Groom Lake as Bissell and his colleagues anticipated multiple crashes which would need to be recovered with the utmost speed and discretion. Eventually, the U–2 was able to fly at an altitude of 70,000 ft (21,336 m).

At 6 am on July 4, 1956, Hervey Stockman piloted the U–2's first aerial reconnaissance mission over the Soviet Union. While the operation was highly successful—photographing naval bases, airfields, and antiaircraft batteries across 400,000 square miles (643,737 sq km) and purportedly revealing the "real intentions and objectives of the Soviet Union . . . behind this 'Iron Curtain' . . . "[3]—the resulting diplomatic fallout far outweighed the benefits. Despite Bissell's assurances, the U–2 had been tracked by Soviet radar and Secretary Nikita Khrushchev, the Soviet Union premier, was incensed. Eisenhower informed Bissell that he had become disenchanted with the U–2 program. Not only did radar-absorbing paint used to coat the spy planes after the Stockman incident not work, it was learned that Soviet surface-to-air missiles would be capable of striking U–2s within a year-and-a-half. It seemed the U–2 program was doomed.

Fortunately for Bissell and those employed at Area 51, on October 4, 1957, the USSR shocked the world by launching the world's first operational satellite, *Sputnik*, into orbit. Overnight, the development of military and espionage sciences became a priority for both the frightened American public, still unaware of the U-2 program, and President Eisenhower alike.

Lockheed aerodynamicist Kelly Johnson now recruited radar expert Edward Lovick into the company's classified "Skunk Works" program to develop a spy plane that would vastly exceed the U-2: the Archangel-12 (A-12). Flying at an altitude of 90,000 ft (27,430 m) with Mach 3 speed, it would be nearly impossible for Soviet missiles to shoot down. Lovick suggested adding chines to the sides of the aircraft, reducing its cross section by 90 percent. This adjustment, combined with ionizing the engine's exhaust, would make the plane virtually undetectable by radar. All Skunk Works needed was a full-scale laboratory to test their design. Unfortunately, Area 51 had fallen prey to Operation Plumbbob, a series of 30 nuclear detonations at the NTTR. On July 5, 1957, the explosion of the 74-kiloton (74,000-metric ton) Hood bomb at Area 9 had gone awry, severely damaging Area 51 buildings and covering the vicinity with radioactive debris. Though deserted for two-and-a-half years, Johnson knew it was nonetheless the best location to test the A-12 in secrecy and he convinced Bissell to let Lockheed return to Area 51 in January 1960.

Five months later, on May 1, 1960, a Soviet surface-to-air missile shot down a U-2 flying near Sverdlovsk and the pilot, Gary Powers, was captured. This triggered a major international incident during which Khrushchev finally revealed the US's regular U-2 incursions to the world. He demanded an apology from Eisenhower. The president's refusal led Khrushchev to clandestinely transport nuclear warheads to a Soviet military base in Cuba, eventually culminating in the Cuban Missile Crisis of October 1962, during which the US and USSR seemed on the brink of nuclear war for 13 days. Ironically, the U-2 would also reveal the presence of Russian nukes while conducting aerial reconnaissance mission over the island. This soon-to-be-legendary stand-off spurred the Pentagon to inform the CIA that they needed the A-12 urgently. The aircraft's development thus became a national priority. April

25, 1962, marked the first A-12 test flight around Area 51, and by May the following year, there were five A-12s soaring through Nevada's skies on a regular basis.

—

Beginning in the summer of 1947 when pilot Kenneth Arnold described seeing nine "saucerlike" objects in the skies near Mount Rainier, Washington, and ranch foreman Mac Brazel discovered mysterious wreckage and the dead bodies of "little creatures" in New Mexico—famously dubbed the Roswell Incident—men and women across the United States began reporting Unidentified Flying Objects (UFOs) with stunning regularity. Several witnesses were commercial pilots or members of the USAF, accustomed to seeing aircraft, and hardly prone to misinterpreting them. This UFO craze continued with minor fluctuations through the 1950s and well into the 1960s. Even future president Jimmy Carter would claim to have spotted one in October 1969 at a Lions Club meeting in Leary, Georgia. Was this a sustained period of mass hysteria? In this new age of celebrity and mass media, were people fabricating or embellishing sightings for a chance to appear in the newspapers?

Truth be told, many pilots and sky gazers in the southwestern United States had indeed seen UFOs. But rather than being alien spacecraft, they were actually U-2 and A-12 spy planes being test flown in the NTTR. Designed to fly at unprecedented altitudes and speeds, it is no wonder these craft were deemed otherworldly. In their earlier iterations, U-2s were silver, so light from the upper atmosphere reflected off their wings, creating the illusion of some form of extraterrestrial technology. Furthermore, Wernher von Braun, Ernst Steinhoff, Walther Riedel, and other former Nazi rocket scientists began launching *Hermes* missiles—the American name for V-2s—all over the southwest in early-1947, sometimes with disastrous results. That American UFO sightings would reach a crescendo in the mid-1950s that lasted through the '60s loosely covers the chronology of these missile launches, and the U-2 and A-12 test flights.

With their brains addled by stories of UFOs and aliens from another world, the American public overlooked the real conspiracies connected with Area 51, involving official cover-ups of the grievous effects of radioactive fallout from atomic bomb tests and the dire political consequences of clandestine spy plane programs.

———

It was not long before "Dennis" from S-4 revealed his true identity as 30-year-old Bob Lazar. He claimed to have a MS in Physics from MIT and a second in Electronics from Caltech. Investigative reporter George Knapp decided to look into the prospect of filming a series of follow-up news interviews with the lanky scientist.

"I spent the eight months between May and November trying to verify Bob's background to see if we could solidify the case, to see if we could find out if he was telling the truth," Knapp stated. "The plan was to unleash [the news series] in November, which is what we did . . . It was the highest-rated news special that ever aired in Las Vegas. And then it really exploded, it went all over the world. Bootleg copies of tapes were being sold and shown in movie theaters. You had media interest from all over the world." [4]

According to Lazar, he had been hired by Dr. Edward Teller, the physicist responsible for coinventing the thermonuclear bomb, in 1988. Lazar claimed to have first captured Teller's attention in 1982 when he famously assembled a Honda jet car that could reach speeds of 200 mph (320 kph). At the time he was living in Los Alamos, New Mexico, and the story made headlines in the *Los Alamos Monitor*—"LA man joins the jet set—at 200 miles an hour"—and "This is a real hot rod" in the *Alamogordo Daily News*. The articles described the eccentric inventor as a physicist at the Los Alamos Meson Physics Facility who had "worked with another researcher in the National Aeronautics and Space Administration [NASA] on the technology."[5] Fortuitously, Lazar had bumped into Teller while he was leaning against a wall reading the story outside, sparking a genial conversation between the two. Six years later, after a stint in Las Vegas, Lazar sent his resume to Teller who reciprocated by providing him with a contact at defense contractor EG&G special projects. After a couple of interviews, Lazar was offered a job working on an advanced propulsion system in an undisclosed remote location. He accepted and was assigned to S-4 near Groom Lake on the Area 51 compound. Lazar described S-4 as "a very interesting building. It's got a slope of probably about 30 degrees which are hangar doors. And it has textured paint on it, but it looks like sand. It's made to look like the side of the mountain . . . whether it's to disguise it from satellite photographs or what."[6]

Amid the stack of documents Lazar was required to review and complete on his first day, was a briefing explaining that the technology was developed by extraterrestrials from the third planet in the Zeta Reticuli binary star system. "One or two autopsy photographs I saw dealt with . . . heads, shoulders, and chest of an alien . . . [The] chest was cut open, teeth ashen, and one single organ was removed . . . From that photograph it looked like what you see in UFO lore as a typical 'Gray.' How tall it was . . . I couldn't tell because I only saw a portion of the photograph. But if everything else you see is correct, I'd imagine it was three-and-a-half or four feet tall."[7] The briefings went on to say that these "Grays" had genetically altered our simian ancestors to the tune of "65 or 63 corrections or additions to the genetic makeup that finally resulted in a human creature."[8] Lazar was later told that in 1979 there were live aliens at S-4. "At one particular point there was an area where some security personnel went to enter. And apparently because . . . [of] the bullets in the sidearms . . . if they would've entered the area the bullets would have detonated. And supposedly one of the creatures tried to stop the security personnel from entering the area and a fight ensued and . . . the security personnel . . . were all killed and they died of head wounds."[9] In a

2019 interview, Lazar said he originally dismissed this as disinformation, which in the event of a leak, could be used to trace and ascertain the identity of a rogue employee. Standard practice in highly-classified operations.

Though accounts of the chronology vary, Lazar claimed that one day he arrived at S-4 to find the hangar doors open. "I went into the hangar door and in the hangar door was the disk: the flying saucer that I worked on . . . It had a little American flag stuck on the side and I thought *oh my God this finally explains all the flying saucer stories, this is just an advanced fighter . . . this is . . . hilarious*, so as I went by I slid my hand alongside it. I got reprimanded immediately for touching the thing."[10] An armed guard ordered him to keep his eyes forward and arms at his side.

Eventually, Lazar met his lab partner, known only as "Barry." This loquacious character was eager to discuss the craft's technology. When Lazar examined the reactor, he realized that he was dealing with extraterrestrial technology. The device consisted of a basket-ball-sized sphere resting on a metal plate and produced a gravitational field—something far beyond known human scientific capabilities. At Barry's urging, Lazar attempted to touch the sphere, only to find his hand pushed back by an invisible force, as if he were trying to join two magnets. The reactor, which contained no wiring to connect its components, could be turned on and off by removing the sphere from a small tower at the center of the plate.

In the coming months, the two men continued to tinker with the reactor. They speculated that the metal plate was akin to a cyclotron, and that the device was fueled by a hitherto unknown element—Element 115—which Lazar described as coppery in color and somehow capable of producing its own gravity. However, though they loosely identified some of the reactor's processes, the technology was simply beyond their comprehension. Lazar concluded it was a riddle S-4 had been trying to solve for some time, and Barry even hinted that at least one of his previous lab partners had been killed when a plasma cutter had been used to saw into an operational reactor. Of their work on the propulsion and power systems, Lazar likened the experience to Victorian scientists encountering a modern portable nuclear reactor and attempting to take it apart to see how it worked. The Victorian scientists, who were completely ignorant of radiation and its effects, would have quickly died, along with all who came to attend to them. Lazar said he was concerned that their own meddling at S-4 might similarly open a Pandora's Box of unintended consequences.

Over the course of many interviews, the bespectacled physicist revealed more and more about his strange experiences while at S-4. On one occasion, Lazar claimed that he might have seen an extraterrestrial: "I walked down the hallway one time I was working out there, and there were doors . . . the doors that go to the hangars. The smaller doors from the corridors have a 9-inch or 12-inch square window with little wires running through it, just about head level. And as I was walking by I just glanced in and I noticed . . . two guys in white lab coats facing me toward the door, and they were looking down and talking to something small with long arms. Now, I was just surprised as I walked by, and I only caught a glimpse. But I don't know what on earth that was."[11]

Lazar has repeatedly asserted that on one occasion all of the hangars were open, allowing him to spot nine spaceships of various shapes and sizes. He was allowed to enter one of the craft—a dark pewter-colored saucer—but was restricted to observing only the bottom two levels. He described being inside as "very ominous."[12] Although he has provided considerable detail regarding the interior of the craft elsewhere, his most pertinent observation were the little seats, which would have perfectly accommodated a being the size of the alien.

In the end, Lazar alleges he was unexpectedly suspended from work without explanation for a lengthy period of time. Bored and aware that S-4 pilots conducted test flights of the spaceships over Papoose Lake every Wednesday, he invited some friends out to the location to watch and videotape the craft with his camcorder. After getting away with this for three Wednesdays in a row, he was finally ambushed at his regular vantage point by guards and taken the following morning to Indian Springs Air Force Base to be debriefed. Although he was released that evening, Lazar alleges he was subsequently placed under constant surveillance, his house raided, and that somehow his entire educational and work history was completely erased. In fact, he had chosen to come forward and reveal his identity purely to protect himself: "The only reason that [I'm] getting this on tape is insurance . . . Insurance is the true motivation behind this."[13] Unsurprisingly, when skeptics looked for proof of Lazar's employment at Los Alamos National Lab [LANL] or to verify his credentials, they found nothing. This led to accusations that he was a pathological liar and fraud.

Those who believe Lazar's story, including George Knapp and filmmaker Jeremy Corbell, point to his anachronistic knowledge of Element 115—which was synthesized by Russian and American scientists at the Joint Institute for Nuclear Research in 2003—along with pieces of information that only a person employed at Area 51 could have possessed.

These include the existence of the S–4 facility, a name completely unknown to Americans until Lazar first mentioned it in 1989. Knapp had had to telephone the public information office at Dallas Airforce Base to specifically ask about S–4 in order to confirm its existence.

Lazar also described a security system at S–4 involving a plate-like device that measured an employee's finger bones to grant them access to various areas of the facility. In the 2010s, a newspaper article on security at NTTR confirmed the use of an identical biometric hand scanner.

Does this prove Bob Lazar actually worked at S–4 after all? Before even reaching the facility, Lazar would have to have been apprised that EG&G—"the most powerful defense contractor in the nation that no one had ever heard of"[14] and gatekeeper to Area 51—was hiring personnel.

Furthermore, according to Corbell, Lazar's assertion that a Vegas-based federal investigator named Mike Thigpen searched his home during the standard background check into prospective S-4 employees, has been verified. Corbell located Thigpen, now living on the East Coast, who reportedly confirmed that he had been employed in this capacity and even remembered meeting Bob Lazar. Knapp and Corbell both insist that Lazar simply could not have known there was a Fed named Mike Thigpen whose job it was to investigate potential S-4 workers. And why would Thigpen recall meeting Lazar if a meeting had not occurred?

George Knapp believes that the strongest evidence to support Lazar's claims is the fact that he took his friends out to Papoose Lake to watch the "flying saucers" on three consecutive Wednesday nights, documenting the UFOs with his video camera. How else could he have known when and where these strange aircraft would appear with such reliability? Perhaps surprisingly, some of the footage Lazar shot survived; however it is grainy and of little help in pinpointing the location of what could be lights in the sky.

Finally, though LANL denied ever having employed Lazar, Knapp managed to locate a 1982 Los Alamos National Lab phone book that listed his name.

One of Lazar's most notable detractors, the nuclear physicist and UFO researcher Stanton Friedman, points out that while Lazar was indeed listed in the LANL phone book, which supplied names and numbers of employees with the Department of Energy *and* external contractor Kirk Meyer, Lazar's entry had "K/M" beside it, indicating that he worked for Kirk Meyer *not* the Los Alamos National Lab. Friedman contacted the personnel department at LANL who found no mention of a Robert Lazar in their employment records, but willingly confirmed one of Friedman's former colleagues had worked there.[15]

Checking Lazar's high-school records in New York State, Friedman discovered the purported physicist had only taken a single science course, chemistry, and had graduated in the bottom-third of his class. This would have disqualified Lazar from entry into both MIT and Caltech—a far more convincing explanation for his lack of records at these institutions than a government conspiracy to discredit him by eliminating his past and credentials.[16]

Today Bob Lazar maintains his life has been destroyed by multiple FBI raids, and often regrets his decision to have blown the whistle in 1989. He has also run afoul of the law on two occasions: In 1990 he served 150 hours of community service for his part in a prostitution ring; and in 2006 he and his wife, Joy White, pleaded guilty to illegally transporting hazardous chemicals used for making fireworks across state lines. Lazar says he no longer wishes to talk about Area 51, but he continues to do so. He participated in Jeremy Corbell's 2018 documentary *Bob Lazar: Area 51 & Flying Saucers* and appeared on The Joe Rogan Experience podcast in June 2019. The show has to date garnered 11.5 million views on YouTube.

The Men In Black

During the decades-long Cold War with the Soviet Union, the US became fertile terrain for the growth of an elaborate UFO/extraterrestrial mythology. Among the first characters to take root in the popular imagination was a sinister group of operatives known as the Men In Black . . .

The Men in Black (MIB) became infamous during the Cold War era for interrogating, harassing, and threatening UFOlogists and witnesses. Their name derives from their dark clothing—usually a business suit and hat or turtleneck—as well as their penchant for traveling in hulking old black cars, particularly Cadillacs. Broadly, there are two main schools of thought regarding the nature and origins of the MIB. The first is that they are CIA, military, or FBI agents pretending to be extraterrestrials as part of a disinformation campaign. The second directly contradicts the first: The MIB are actually space aliens doing a poor job of posing as government agents, or humans in other professions.

Those who have come into contact with Men in Black soon discover that they are nothing like the wisecracking heroes of the blockbuster movie franchise. They often describe MIB as physically slender with East Asian features and swarthy complexions. Often operating in groups of three, their MO is to arrive suddenly and unexpectedly at a subject's home or workplace in the days following a UFO sighting or research breakthrough. They frequently reveal knowledge that only the subject could possess and exhibit strange speech patterns and behaviors, giving the impression that they are somehow alien to this world.[1] Typically, they claim to be government agents, though their credentials are fraudulent and the organizations they profess to work for invariably deny all knowledge of them. While the MIB may sound frivolous or cartoonish when compared to other conspiracy theories, officials as powerful as J. Edgar Hoover, director of the FBI from 1935 to 1972, launched formal investigations into the phenomenon. According to UFOlogist and author Gray Barker, the FBI director first became aware of the MIB in 1958, when he received the following letter from a citizen in Oklahoma City: "Recently, many rumors have been printed in UFO periodicals, concerning reports that Special Agents of the Federal Bureau of Investigation have discouraged certain saucer investigators, particularly Mr. Albert Bender of Bridgeport, Connecticut, from further research into the secret of these elusive disks. Since you are the director of the FBI, I would like to know whether or not these reports are factual, or whether they are just rumors."[2]

Hoover took the citizen's query seriously, and responded that a local Special Agent would be in contact. He sent a memo to the lead SA at the Oklahoma City office asking him to rendezvous with the letter writer and obtain copies of the UFO literature referred to, which turned out to be *The Saucerian Bulletin*. After perusing the periodical, the agent relayed its contents to Hoover. Apparently, three men in black suits claiming to be agents from the FBI, Air Force Intelligence, and the CIA had terrified prominent UFOlogist Albert Bender to the point where he refused to discuss matters related to flying saucers or extraterrestrials ever again, causing an uproar in the UFOlogist community. Perplexed, Hoover decided to investigate further.

Thirty-one-year-old Albert K. Bender, a US Army veteran and factory clerk, had formed The International Flying Saucer Bureau (IFSB) in 1952 to gather and organize information related to UFOs. The organization aimed to understand the nature of flying saucers and lay the groundwork for amicable relations with their extraterrestrial pilots in the event that they made contact. The IFSB was an overnight success, with branches in 48 US states and attracting UFO researchers and enthusiasts from around the world. Beginning in October 1952, the IFSB began publishing a quarterly journal, *Space Review*, to report on its activities. Four months later, they created a Department of Investigation at their headquarters in Bridgeport, Connecticut, to analyze evidence of UFO sightings and photographs.

The IFSB members were unaware that Bender had been experiencing strange instances of harassment. On July 30, 1952, he had answered his phone only to be greeted by silence. Yet, his mind was suddenly flooded by warnings—as if from some telepathic source—to discontinue his UFO researches and the IFSB organization. A bizarre pulsing sound then emanated from the earpiece. Three months later, while Bender was walking home from the cinema, blue light flashed across the sky and his head started to throb. He experienced a feeling of being lifted off the ground as a disembodied voice ordered him once again to abandon the IFSB. Later that month, while seated in the same movie theater, he turned to see a man in the neighboring seat gazing at him with eyes "like flashlight bulbs"[3] burning through him. The throbbing in his head returned, and he closed his eyes in pain—only to find the figure gone when he reopened them. Unnerved, he moved to another area of the cinema, only to sense the man with the strange eyes seated behind him. Bender fled the auditorium and told the manager what had occurred, but when the manager swept the seats with a flashlight, there was nobody there.

These incidents continued with alarming frequency. In February 1953, Bender heard footsteps upstairs while he was in the kitchen. He was the only person home. Climbing the stairs to the second floor to investigate, he encountered a blue glow framing a face with blazing eyes. When he screamed, the entity vanished, leaving only a lingering stench of sulfur behind.

Meanwhile, the IFSB had become fully operational, and on March 15, 1953, its membership decided to try an unprecedented global experiment: At 6 pm EST, every member able to participate would simultaneously attempt to will a psychic invitation to the "space people"[4] to land on Earth in peace.

Back in Bridgeport, at the appointed time of 6 pm, Bender lay down in his darkened bedroom and concentrated his thoughts on the skies. Suddenly, the air filled with a sulfuric stink, and a chill ran through his body. Blue lights began dancing around the room as he levitated from his bed. Somehow, Bender could see his body lying inert on the bed 3 ft (less than a meter) below him. He heard a menacing voice inside his head say, "We have been watching you and your activities. Please be advised to discontinue delving into the mysteries of the universe. We will make an appearance if you disobey . . . We have a special assignment and must not be disturbed by your people . . . We are among you and know your every move, so please be advised we are here on your Earth."[5] The next thing he knew, Bender was back on his bed, and the room was flooded by a yellowish mist. He felt ill—both physically and mentally.

Nevertheless, Bender ignored these uncanny threats, and wrote in the next issue of *Space Review* that a "startling announcement"[6] would be forthcoming in the July issue. He subsequently returned home from a two-week summer holiday to find his radio mysteriously turned on and a pervading stench of sulfur. Later, as he prepared to go to bed, a blue light appeared in his bedroom and three men in black attire and wearing Homburg-style hats emerged. Their eyes began to glow, bringing on one of Bender's thumping headaches. The Men in Black communicated telepathically that they knew he was determined to discover the truth about flying saucers, but that his endeavors could result in great harm, and nobody would believe him. They insisted that his interference would not curtail their plans, and that others had been terminated for being overly curious. The MIB explained that they had concealed their spacecraft somewhere on Earth and passed him a small metal disk which he was to use to contact them in two days by turning on the radio, squeezing the disk, and speaking the name of their planet "Kazik."[7]

Forty-eight hours passed, and the time finally arrived. Bender followed their instruction and was teleported to a circular glass dome in their mothership at the South Pole, where he learned all about Kazik and the extraterrestrials' biology, culture, and goals. Specifically, they were extracting a valuable mineral from the Earth's oceans. This process left a residue that they had initially dumped on the planet's surface, before adopting the more secretive strategy of depositing it back into the sea. Bender learned that the aliens had infiltrated the Pentagon with spies, so they would always know what was going on.

After this harrowing experience—met with extreme skepticism by a close friend Bender chose to confide in—Bender resolved not to publish the "startling announcement" he had planned for the July issue of *Space Review*. Instead he announced in print: "The mystery of flying saucers is no longer a mystery. The source is already known, but any information about this is being withheld by orders from a higher source. We would like to print the full story in *Space Review* but, because of the nature of the information, we are sorry that we have been advised in the negative. We advise those engaged in saucer work to be very cautious."[8] Bender also announced that effective from January 1, 1954, the IFSB would be restructured, renamed, and switch focus from UFOlogy to a more generalized study of various "questions of the universe."[9] The members of the IFSB eventually concluded that Bender had been silenced by an insidious government agency, and prominent UFOlogist Gray Barker pointed the finger at the FBI in his *The Saucerian Bulletin*. Bender did not reveal the entirety of the story and the role in it of the so-called Men In Black until many years later, in 1963.

—

Although Albert Bender's alleged ordeal popularized the MIB phenomenon, it actually began years earlier with pilot Kenneth Arnold's alleged sighting of nine flying saucers near Mount Rainier, Washington, in June 1947. Within a month of the incident, Harold Dahl and Fred Crisman, two harbor patrollers at nearby Maury Island 3 miles (5 km) off the Tacoma coast, sent pieces of a strange mineral to Ray Palmer, the founder of *Fate,* a magazine devoted to covering unexplained phenomena. Dahl and Crisman claimed that on June 21, 1947, donut-shaped aircraft had dumped the mineral substance onto Dahl's boat, breaking his son's arm and killing their dog. Dahl added that he had taken photographs of these flying saucers. Aware that content involving UFOs was popular with readers, Palmer contacted Kenneth Arnold and offered to pay him $200—approximately $2,300 at the time of this writing—to fly from Boise, Idaho, to Tacoma, Washington, to investigate Dahl's and Crisman's story.

When Arnold arrived in Tacoma, he found all the hotels were booked up with the exception of the city's finest: the Winthrop. Though Arnold had informed nobody other than his wife about his travel plans, on approaching the front desk, he found that a reservation had already been made anonymously for a "Kenneth Arnold." Unable to find a rational explanation for this, he concluded that he was being followed.[10]

Arnold invited Harold Dahl to his hotel room, and the harbor patrolman recounted his UFO experience, before moving on to relate the even eerier events that occurred afterward. According to Dahl, the morning after the sighting, a man in a dark suit knocked on his front door and asked to take him to breakfast. Once they were seated in a diner, the Man in Black referred in detail to Dahl's UFO encounter. He then warned Dahl that he had seen something he wasn't supposed to, and that if he cared about his family, he should keep his mouth shut.

The following day, Fred Crisman corroborated the UFO part of Dahl's story. Feeling in need of some assistance and moral support, Arnold contacted a friend, Captain E. J. Smith, a pilot for United Airlines, asking him to come to Tacoma to help investigate Dahl and Crisman's account. Within hours of Smith's arrival at the Winthrop, Arnold received a telephone call at the hotel from Ted Morella, the news director of the United Press in Tacoma. Morella said that he had received calls from an unknown informant who claimed to have verbatim knowledge of everything Arnold and Smith had just discussed in Arnold's hotel room. Morella repeated what this informant had said and asked if Arnold would confirm it. The revelation that everything they had said about Dahl's and Crisman's UFO encounter had been overheard prompted the pilots to scour the room for electronic bugs. They found nothing.

Arnold then remembered two USAF officers, Lieutenant Frank M. Brown and Captain William Davidson of A-3 military intelligence, who had interviewed Arnold following his UFO sighting near Mount Rainier. They were good men, and might help. Arnold called them, and within a few hours, Brown and Davidson joined them at the Winthrop. They spoke briefly with Crisman and Dahl, but dismissed their UFO claims, and were soon boarding a B-52 back home.

Dahl and Crisman proved unable to provide any photographs of the flying saucers to Arnold despite their earlier claims to have taken some. Moreover, the vessel they claimed was battered by UFO debris was clearly not the same as the one they described. A "Major Sander," purportedly from Army Intelligence, then showed up at the Winthrop Hotel room and confiscated all of the mineral fragments Dahl and Crisman had given to Arnold. The whole endeavor seemed to fall somewhere between a pointless psi-op and a poorly constructed hoax.

Unbeknown to Arnold, once Brown and Davidson's B-52 was in the air, their plane started to malfunction, and Brown and Davidson were killed in the subsequent crash. Oddly, the survivors would later state that the USAF officers had had plenty of time to parachute from the aircraft.

—

The late Manhattan-based UFOlogist and author John Keel documented numerous Men in Black cases around the globe. Keel noted that a surge in MIB activity began in 1967. He interviewed a waitress at Max's Kansas City—an offbeat restaurant and nightclub at 213 Park Avenue South in New York City—who recalled a bizarre encounter she had had that summer. A gangly, bug-eyed man in an ill-fitting, outmoded black suit had entered the establishment. He seated himself at a booth, beckoned her over with a long, tapered finger, and muttered "something to eat."[11] She handed him a menu, but he seemed incapable of reading it, and merely said "food."[12] She suggested a steak. When the meal arrived, he stared at his knife and fork as if puzzled by them. She patiently showed him how to use them, and he wolfed down the steak. Curious, she asked him where he was from.

"Another world,"[13] he replied.

Keel wrote of similar instances involving strange, black-suited men in New York City. However, these proved to be just tasters for an explosion of MIB activity that would occur that winter in West Virginia.

At 5 pm on December 15, 1967, rush-hour traffic on the Silver Bridge connecting Point Pleasant, West Virginia, to Gallipolis, Ohio, was at a standstill. The sheer weight of vehicles caused a faulty eyebar to snap, collapsing the bridge, and plunging everyone and everything on it into the freezing waters of the Ohio River. All told, 46 people perished in the tragedy.

In the 13 months preceding the Silver Bridge Disaster, more than 100 people in the Point Pleasant area had reported seeing a large, dark humanoid with glowing red eyes and a 10-ft (2-m) wingspan. The creature soon became known as "Mothman," and some UFOlogists viewed its appearance as a harbinger of doom. At the same time there was a spike of UFO sightings in the area. These events were documented, separately but contemporaneously, by Gray Barker in *The Silver Bridge* and by John Keel in *The Mothman Prophecies*, published in 1970 and 1975 respectively.

Keel interviewed dozens of witnesses for *The Mothman Prophecies* including *Athens Messenger* reporter Mary Hyre. On the afternoon of Friday, December 22, 1967, police were still pulling cars and bodies from the murky Ohio River and newsmen from across the country had descended upon the once-sleepy little town. Mary Hyre was sitting in her office when two men wearing black overcoats walked in. They were so similar in appearance that she thought they might be twins. They were both short, about 5 ft 7 in (1.7 m), with dark, swarthy complexions.

"We hear there's been a lot of flying saucer activity around here,"[14] one of them declared. She confirmed that this was so and handed them a hefty folder full of reported sightings. The man briefly examined it, and passed it back to her. He asked her if anyone had instructed her not to publish the reports, and she shook her head. He then asked her what she would do if somebody told her not to write about flying saucers. She replied that she would tell them to go to hell. The two men exchanged glances, and when she next looked up from her work, they had gone.

Later in the afternoon, a similar-looking man wearing a black suit and tie entered the office. He introduced himself as Jack Brown, a UFO researcher. She noted he had unusually long and tapered fingers.

"What—would—what would you do—if someone ordered—ordered you. To stop printing UFO stories?" he stuttered. She asked him if he was with the two men whom she had spoken to earlier. He stammered that he was there alone and a friend of Gray Barker. Hyre then asked him if he knew John Keel.

"I—I used to think the world of K—K—Keel," he replied. "Then a few minutes ago I bought a—a magazine. He has an article in it. He says he's seen UFOs himself. He's—he's a liar."[15] When Hyre angrily countered that she had been with Keel when he saw the UFOs, "Jack Brown" wondered if she would show him where they had sighted them. She refused, but Jack Brown continued to stammer out questions before finally repeating: "I—I think he m—m—makes up all these stories . . . I'm a friend of G—G—Gray Barker."[16] Mary Hyre offered to give him the names of UFO and Mothman witnesses, so he could question them himself.

That evening, the man calling himself Jack Brown arrived at the home of Hyre's niece and Mothman witness Connie Carpenter and her husband, Keith, in nearby New Haven. The odd little man pulled into the driveway in a white sedan with a sputtering muffler, and knocked on the door. Introducing himself as a friend of Mary Hyre's, he began to ask Connie questions about a relationship between Hyre and John Keel, while Keith and her brother Larry looked on with increasing unease. There was something peculiar about his ears, his fingers, and his dark, mesmerizing eyes. Jack Brown wondered what Connie thought Mary Hyre would do if someone told her to stop writing about UFOs. "She'd probably tell them to drop dead," Connie replied.[17] The moment he left, Connie called her Aunt Mary to tell her about Jack Brown and learned that he had also paid her a visit.

—

Perhaps the most remarkable theory about the nature of the MIB was put forward by the aforementioned John Keel, who proposed that the MIB were age-old demons who had simply transmogrified into a twentieth-century form: "The Devil's emissaries of yester-year have been replaced by the mysterious 'men in black' . . ."[18]

Keel rejected the popular idea among UFOlogists that these strange visitors were extraterrestrials who had traveled to Earth in advanced spacecraft. Instead, he believed that "ultraterrestrials" from other dimensions have been manifesting on this planet for thousands of years and interacting with human beings. These ultraterrestrials conceal their true nature and intentions by deliberately creating frames of reference that correspond with human society's cultural and epistemological beliefs at any given time and place. Before the Industrial Revolution, ultraterrestrials appeared as angels, fairies, or other divine or magical beings, dictating myths and religious revelations to unwitting prophets who then relayed them to the rest of humanity. With the onset of rapidly advancing technologies, humans began to drift away from religious frames of reference toward a more scientific understanding of the world. Ultraterrestrials shape-shifted accordingly into Men in Black. Keel dubbed this mysterious strategy "Operation Trojan Horse."

———

Some UFOlogists and witnesses are convinced that the MIB are nothing to do with extraterrestrial machinations, but are a secret government agency determined to shut down all debate about UFOs.

Having grown up in the Kanawha Valley, only one hour's drive south of Point Pleasant, during the time of the Mothman and UFO sightings, author and photographer Andrew Colvin has no shortage of theories regarding the MIB. Colvin noted that several residents of the area, including himself, claimed to have seen Mothman in Mound[i] and Dunbar, West Virginia, between 1966-1967. On January 19, 1967, Tad Jones spotted a UFO on his way to work at the Union Carbide plant on Mound's Blaine Island, and was subsequently threatened and harassed by the MIB. The Union Carbide plant was known for isolating and purifying rare metals. According to Colvin, Geiger counters indicated that there were radioactive materials at the facility, as there were at a notorious TNT area in Point Pleasant, where numerous witnesses encountered Mothman.

Colvin has also asserted that "there is now credible evidence that Carbide manufactured some of the plastics and adhesives found at the scene of the Roswell UFO crash"[19] (see Chapter 4: Area 51), and that "pieces of the wreckage looked suspiciously Nazi-esque to initial USAF investigators, causing them to bring in German scientists to try and pinpoint the source."[20] These were the same Germans scientists smuggled into the United States under Operation

i Since renamed "North Charleston."

Paperclip.[21] Colvin went on to explain that Union Carbide shared patents with Nazi Germany during World War II, including one for synthetic rubber and oil manufactured at Mittelwerk[22]—where slave labor was used to create V-2 missiles under the supervision and direction of Major General Walter Dornberger, Dr. Wernher Von Braun, Arthur Rudolph, and Georg Rickhey. In light of this, Colvin proposed that Nazi Germany had begun developing flying saucer technology at Mittelwerk only to have those programs relocated to a Union Carbide plant in West Virginia immediately after the war. The Roswell UFO crash, then, was not extraterrestrial in origin, but a top-secret weapons technology produced by the USAF that went awry.[23] Given the alleged witness intimidation by the authorities following the Roswell crash, it is conceivable that the MIB played some role in the subsequent cover-up.

Incredibly, according to UFO conspiracy theorists, two of the men mentioned in this chapter—"harbor patrolman" Fred Crisman and Nazi "paperclip" Walter Dornberger—may have been involved in an incident that would shake the United States more than all of the preceding revelations combined: the 1963 assassination of President John Fitzgerald Kennedy.[24]

The Assassination of President John F. Kennedy

The assassination of President John F. Kennedy in November 1963 was a seismic event that rocked US society to its foundations and sent shockwaves around the world. The assassin was soon caught, but was Lee Harvey Oswald a genuine "lone wolf" or part of an insidious conspiracy? His subsequent murder left more questions than answers . . .

At 11:38 a.m. CST on Friday, November 22, 1963, President John Fitzgerald Kennedy, the First Lady Jacqueline Kennedy, Texas governor John Connally, his wife Nellie, and Senator Ralph W. Yarborough landed in Air Force One at Love Field Airport in Dallas, Texas. Three years earlier, Kennedy had achieved a narrow 50.52% victory in the "Lone Star State" during the presidential race with the Republican candidate Richard Nixon, largely thanks to the support of his Texan running mate Lyndon B. Johnson. However, Kennedy had only managed to secure 36.99% of the vote in Dallas. He was entering hostile territory.

Kennedy had traveled to Texas on November 21, 1963, to heal a rift between Connally, the conservative Democratic governor, and the liberal faction of the party under Yarborough. He had also met with local business leaders and planned public appearances in San Antonio, Dallas, Fort Worth, and Houston to lay the groundwork for his upcoming 1964 reelection campaign.

To date, JFK's presidency had generated both great praise and virulent condemnation. A young charismatic statesman, as well as the first Catholic to become President of the United States, Kennedy had won hearts by promising to put a man on the moon within ten years and for championing civil rights. However, in the early 1960s, his civil-rights position had made him many enemies. In addition, the president had appointed his brother Robert F. Kennedy—who openly vowed to crack down on organized crime—as Attorney General. It sounded good, but the reality was that Kennedy's presidential campaign had knowingly received support from Mafia mobsters, such as Sam Giancana, to deliver crucial union votes in key primaries. Not only were the Kennedys biting the hand that fed them, it was one with a well-founded reputation for pulling triggers.

Having "inherited" the Vietnam War from his predecessor, Dwight D. Eisenhower, President Kennedy was a firm believer in the Domino Theory, which held that the spread of Communism in Asia must be contained or the entire region would fall under the influence of the Chinese or Soviet Communist regimes. To bolster the defenses of the South Vietnamese government under Ngo Dinh Diem, between 1961-1962 Kennedy dispatched 11,000 Special Forces troops and military advisors to Saigon. However, when Diem declared martial law and began to violently suppress Buddhists in the spring of 1963—leading to the self-immolation of a monk that became an iconic photograph disseminated across the globe—everything changed. A military coup ousted Diem on November 1, 1963, and Kennedy began to reevaluate US support for South Vietnam. However, if it was discontinued, the country would fall to the combined forces of the Viet Cong and North Vietnamese Army, and the first domino would topple. Kennedy knew it, and more importantly, the CIA and military industrial complex knew it, too.

Undoubtedly, the biggest scandals of the Kennedy administration involved Cuba, from the botched Bay of Pigs invasion in 1961 to the resulting October Crisis of 1962, which saw the world teeter on the brink of nuclear annihilation. These military and diplomatic blunders had brought him into conflict not only with Cuban Prime Minister Fidel Castro, domestic Communists, and the

Soviet Union under Nikita Khrushchev, but also with Cuban expats, intelligence agencies, and high-ranking military men who thought he had gone too soft on the nation's Communist enemies in the USSR, southeast Asia, and the Caribbean. Before Castro's conquest of Cuba, the Mafia had enjoyed a firm and lucrative foothold in Havana—one which it sought to reestablish at nearly any cost.

Thus, by November 22, 1963, there was no shortage of powerful actors who had ample reason to eliminate President John F. Kennedy. According to JFK conspiracy theorists, more often than not, these individuals or organizations were working in tandem. And thanks to the *Dallas Times Herald* and *Dallas Morning News,* everyone knew exactly when the president would be in Dallas more than two months in advance.

—

After arriving at Love Field, the Kennedys and Connallys climbed into the presidential limousine—a 1961 navy blue Ford Lincoln convertible—with William R. Greer in the driver's seat next to fellow Secret Service agent Roy H. Kellerman, head of security. JFK and Jackie occupied the rearmost seats, with the First Lady on the left and President Kennedy on the right, while the Connallys where in the middle row, sandwiched between the Kennedys and Secret Service agents. The governor occupied the seat directly in front of the president and behind Kellerman. Nellie Connally was buttressed by Greer and the First Lady.

The presidential limousine was merely the centerpiece in an elaborate motorcade. Secret Service agents on motorcycles formed the vanguard, along with two automobiles—a "pilot car," manned by officers from the Dallas Police Department, a quarter mile (400 meters) ahead of an unmarked "rolling command car" driven by Police Chief Jesse Curry with Dallas County Sheriff J. E. Decker and two Secret Service agents in tow. The pilot car rode about four to five automobile lengths ahead of the Kennedy's. Four Secret Service agents on motorcycles flanked the presidential limousine, and many more followed. A 1955 Cadillac, the "presidential follow-up car," containing eight armed Secret Service agents brought up the rear, with presidential assistants Kenneth O'Donnell and David F. Powers seated in the middle row. Then came the vice-presidential automobile driven by Texas highway patrolman Hurchel Jacks and carrying Vice President Lyndon B. Johnson, his wife Claudia, Senator Yarborough, and Special Agent Rufus W. Youngblood. The "vice-presidential follow-up car" was next, containing even more Secret Service agents, driven by a Dallas policeman, and tailed by another slew of motorcycle cops. The remainder of the motorcade was comprised of vehicles carrying minor political figures, members of the president's entourage, and the press. A Dallas police cruiser brought up the rear.

At 11:52 a.m., the motorcade left Love Field and headed toward Dallas, stopping frequently on the president's orders, so he could meet and greet members of the public. As planned, it continued west on Main Street through downtown Dallas, turning right onto Houston Street and heading north one block toward Elm and Dealey Plaza. The streets were lined with adoring onlookers, prompting Governor Connally to crane his head back and proclaim, "Mr. President, you can't say Dallas doesn't love you."[1]

Reaching the intersection at 12:30 p.m., the motorcade slowed and turned left onto Elm, heading west toward a triple underpass. The presidential limousine was traveling at approximately 11 mph (18 kph) an hour when a gunshot rang out. Both Governor John and Nellie Connally claimed that the shot came from behind their right shoulders and turned to look in that direction. Unable to see the president, the governor started to turn to the left but felt a bullet tear through his back. He began screaming, "Oh, no, no, no! My God! They're going to kill us all!"[2] Jackie saw her husband clutching his throat, and leaned in closer, staring at his face. At that moment, a bullet struck the president's head.

Panicked, Mrs. Kennedy clambered onto the trunk of the limo where she encountered Secret Service Agent Clinton J. Hill who had immediately sprung into action, rushing to the back of the vehicle, and pulling himself up onto the rear of the car. Realizing that Mrs. Kennedy was in danger of falling from the car, Hill pushed her back into her seat, and lay across her to shield her from any additional bullets. Greer stepped on the accelerator and the Lincoln sped off. President Kennedy was pronounced dead at 1 p.m. at Parkland Hospital. Governor Connally survived gunshot wounds to his back, chest, wrist, and thigh; along with a broken rib.

Fortunately, Abraham Zapruder, a Kennedy supporter, had taken his Bell & Howell Zoomatic home-movie camera to film the president's ride through Dallas. According to Zapruder, "I got out . . . about a half-hour earlier to get a good spot to shoot some pictures. And I found a spot—one of these concrete blocks they have down near that park, near the underpass . . . And as I was shooting [film]— as the President was coming down from Houston Street making his turn; it was about a half-way down there—I heard a shot, and he slumped to the side, like this. Then I heard another shot or two—I couldn't say [if] it was one or two—and I saw his head practically open up, all blood and everything, and I kept on shooting [film]."[3] While open to seemingly endless interpretation, this 26.6-second, silent, 8-mm color footage, dubbed the "Zapruder film," is widely considered the most reliable and authoritative documentation of Kennedy's murder. It not only proved a crucial component in the Warren Commission's subsequent investigation, but also something of a Rorschach ink blot onto which conspiracists could project their own fanciful theories about what *really* happened at Dealey Plaza that tragic November afternoon.

With more books and articles penned about the JFK assassination than any other event in American history[4], to state that nearly every detail in the narrative has been debated is no exaggeration. What immediately follows is the official account of the murder as presented by the Warren Commission, along with the story of the alleged gunman: Lee Harvey Oswald.

—

While President Kennedy and Governor Connally were being rushed to Parkland Memorial Hospital, police were converging on the Texas School Book Depository, a seven-story building at the northwest corner of Houston and Elm. Steamfitter Howard Brennan had notified a policeman that, while seated across the street from the Depository, he had heard a gunshot from above. Glancing up, Brennan had spotted a brown-haired man with a rifle take another shot from the easternmost corner-window on the sixth floor. The man had then paused momentarily, as if deciding whether or not to take a third shot, before firing again. As Brennan was relaying these details to the policeman, two workers from the Texas School Book Depository approached the officer with more information. They had been watching the president from the southeast windows of the fifth floor when one of them, 25-year-old Harold D. Norman, had heard three gunshots ring out from overhead. Norman reported hearing spent cartridges ejecting onto the floor above him—a claim that seemed highly improbable until the Warren Commission recreated this scenario, and were able to hear the same thing.[5]

As Dallas policemen flooded into the warehouse, one officer spied a man standing by the lunchroom door with an inappropriately serene look on his face. The policeman questioned him briefly, and satisfied with his answers, moved on. No more than a minute later, this peculiar fellow walked out the front door of the Texas School Book Depository and disappeared.

Acting on information received from Brennan and Norman, Officer Gerald Hill and other Dallas policemen began searching the sixth floor. They found a dozen boxes stacked suspiciously around a corner: a perfect place for a crouching sniper to hide.

Concealed behind some boxes was a loaded 6.5x52 mm Mannlicher-Carcano Model 91/31 infantry rifle with a four-power scope—a cheap and clunky bolt-action firearm manufactured in Italy—along with three spent cartridges on the floor. By this time, the police had sealed off the Texas School Book Depository and released a description of a suspect: a white male standing approximately 5 ft 6 in to 5 ft 8 in (1.7 m) and weighing 160 lbs (72.6 kg), with brown hair. All of the employees scheduled to work at the depository that day were accounted for, save one: an "order-filler" named Lee Harvey Oswald.

While the officers were investigating the book depository, they received a call saying there had been another killing in the Oak Cliff neighborhood. This time the victim was one of their own. Officer J. D. Tippit had been shot four times outside his squad car on East 10th Street in front of seven people. Hill and other members of the Dallas police raced to the scene. Eye witnesses soon provided a description matching the suspect in the JFK assassination. Meanwhile, manager Johnny Calvin Brewer had spotted a brown-haired man hiding from police cars in the entryway of his business, Hardy's Shoe Store. Suspicious, Brewer followed the man down West Jefferson Boulevard where he saw him sneak into the Texas Theater cinema. Box-office attendant Julie Postal had been distracted by passing Dallas PD cruisers blaring their sirens. Brewer notified Postal of the intruder and she telephoned the police at 1:40 p.m. Convinced that the same man who had ducked into the Texas Theater was responsible for the killing of Officer Tippit, a squad of police officers descended on the cinema. As they entered the auditorium, the suspect reached for a .38 special, shouting, "Well, it's all over now!"[6] After a brief skirmish, the officers managed to subdue and arrest him as he screamed "police brutality."[7] In the back of the police car, the suspect refused to provide his name, a tactic which was easily circumvented when an officer yanked a wallet from his pocket. Inside were two IDs, a fake one in the name of "Alek James Hidell" and another revealing the suspect's true identity—24-year-old Lee

Harvey Oswald—the only employee unaccounted for at the Texas School Book Depository.

Back at Dallas Police Headquarters, Oswald was mobbed by reporters shouting out questions as camera bulbs flashed. "I don't know what dispatches you people have been getting, but I emphatically deny these charges," Oswald proclaimed, "They're taking me in because of the fact that I lived in the Soviet Union. I'm just a Patsy." Oswald's claim to be a fall guy would open the door to countless conspiracy theories, which still persist to this day. And, as we shall see, he had indeed lived in the USSR, from 1959 to 1962, even taking a Russian bride, Marina.

At 7:10 p.m. Oswald was charged with the murder of Officer J. D. Tippit. Just after 1:30 a.m. on November 23rd, he was arraigned for assassinating President John F. Kennedy.

Over two days, Oswald toyed with Detective Jim Leavelle, FBI Special Agent James Hosty, and Captain William Fritz in the interrogation room, seeming to revel in the game of cat and mouse. Meanwhile, investigators had linked the Mannlicher-Carcano rifle to the PO box of one Mr. A. Hidell (Oswald's alias) in Dallas. This was the address Oswald had used to purchase the weapon by mail. Handwriting analysis offered further evidence tying Oswald to the crime. When police recovered two black and white photos of Oswald posing with the gun in his backyard, he emphatically denied that it was him, proposing that his head had been superimposed on somebody else's body. Much like the "Patsy" statement, this assertion became a key point of contention among those who would later dispute the findings of the Warren Commission.

Whatever secrets Lee Harvey Oswald may have harbored were forever sealed during his transfer from Dallas Police HQ to the city jail on Sunday, November 24. As Detective Leavelle was handcuffing Oswald to him, he quipped, with remarkable prescience: "Lee, if anybody shoots at you, I hope they are as good a shot as you."[8]

"Nobody's going to shoot at me,"[9] Oswald replied.

Seconds later, at 11:21 a.m., as Leavelle was escorting Oswald through a crowd of reporters in the basement of police HQ, a figure in a gray fedora bounded into their path and fired a single shot from a .38 caliber revolver into Oswald's abdomen.

"You killed my president, you rat!" he snarled.

The gunman, who made no effort to resist, was arrested on the spot and immediately identified as strip-club owner Jack Ruby. Oswald died hours later in Parkland Hospital—the same facility he had sent President Kennedy and Governor Connally to only two days earlier.

"Any effort to explain what happened in Dallas must explain Lee Harvey Oswald," stated Chief Counsel of the House Assassinations Committee G. Robert Blakey, "and Lee Harvey Oswald is a mystery wrapped up in an enigma hidden behind a riddle. He is not . . . an easy man to explain."[10]

—

Lee Harvey Oswald's life got off to a rocky start and never recovered. His father, Robert, suffered a fatal heart attack two months before his birth on October 13, 1939. Oswald's mother, Marguerite, a single parent of three boys in New Orleans during the early 1940s, placed her two older sons in an orphanage and attempted to raise her newborn child. But by the time Lee reached the age of 3, she had similarly disposed of him. Compared to much of the rest of his life, Lee Harvey Oswald's nine years in an orphanage are poorly documented.

Eventually, Marguerite and her youngest son were reunited when Lee was 12. They moved across the country to a tiny apartment in the Bronx, where Marguerite worked in a dress shop from 7 a.m. to 7 p.m. Lee habitually skipped school to spend time at museums, the public library, and Bronx zoo, while obsessively memorizing the New York subway system. He remained friendless and stunted in his emotional development, struggling to develop a true sense of self.

That was until 1953, when he was handed a pamphlet protesting against the forthcoming execution of Julius and Ethel Rosenberg, an American couple who had been convicted of spying for the Soviet Union. Oswald began to voraciously consume Marxist and socialist literature at the library, rapidly developing a hatred for American capitalism. A psychological assessment carried out on May 1, 1953, by Dr. Renatus Hartogs resulted in a diagnosis of Schizoid Personality Disorder with passive aggressive tendencies, and highlighted his rich fantasy life, which centered around dreams of gaining omnipotent power.

After repeated run-ins with school truancy officers, resulting in court appearances by both Oswald and his mother, Marguerite returned with Lee to New Orleans, where they settled on the edge of the French Quarter. Though he continued to pursue his self-education in Marxism, on July 27, 1955, the 15-year-old Oswald enrolled in the Civilian Air Patrol (CAP) under the instruction of pilot David Ferrie, a rabid anti-communist. In 1956, aged 17, Oswald enlisted in the Marines where, contrary to the later assertions of conspiracy theorists, his exceptional marksmanship qualified him as a Sharpshooter.[11] Following his request to be a radar controller, he was stationed at the Naval Air Facility in Atsugi, Japan—a CIA base for U-2 reconnaissance missions over the Soviet Union—where he continued to learn Russian and preach Marxist doctrine to his fellow soldiers, all the while somehow receiving high-level security clearance. This stint led many conspiracy theorists to conclude that Oswald was actually a lifelong CIA agent who used his socialist leanings as a cover right up to the moment of his death.

On September 11, 1959, Oswald received a hardship discharge from active service, claiming his mother needed care and started planning to travel to the Soviet Union. Whether this was always in his mind, or a decision made on the fly following the collapse of his military career is open to debate. Skeptics of the official narrative wonder how Oswald could have arranged the trip alone, pointing to bank records showing that he only had $200 in his account. This contradicts Oswald's claim of saving $1,000 for this expedition while serving in the Marines.

Oswald arrived in Moscow by train on October 15, 1959, and approached the KGB saying he wanted to defect to the USSR owing to his Communist leanings and antipathy for American society. When the KGB rejected his request, Oswald attempted suicide by slashing his wrists in a hotel bathtub—though the sincerity of his effort has been questioned. He was successfully treated at Botkin Hospital and transferred to its psychiatric unit. At one point, the ward received a call from the KGB ordering them to hold Oswald until they arrived. Forty minutes later, three KGB agents descended upon the hospital and confiscated all documentation related to Oswald. According to an ex-KGB member, at this point they had briefly entertained the idea that the wannabe American defector could actually be of some use to them.

On October 31, Lee Harvey Oswald walked into the American Embassy in Moscow and told Consul Richard Snyder that he wished to revoke his US citizenship, as he had applied for a Soviet one. He then inexplicably disclosed that he was a former radar technician at Atsugi and intended to reveal everything he knew about American technologies to the Soviets. Frantic, Consul Snyder immediately relayed this information to the US armed forces, forcing them to change their radar codes. Despite the fact that the Russians claimed Oswald had told them nothing they didn't already know, American U-2 pilot Gary Powers, whose spy plane was shot down by a Soviet surface-to-air missile over Sverdlovsk on May 1, 1960, would later lay the blame for his capture squarely on Oswald.

While it is unlikely that Lee Harvey Oswald was responsible for Powers' arrest, nevertheless, Oswald's threat to divulge US military secrets nearly resulted in a major international incident between the two superpowers. As such, the KGB decided to let him remain in the USSR in order to prevent him from further endangering the already precarious peace. Oswald's tenure in the

Soviet Union later prompted numerous conspiracy theories that he had assassinated President Kennedy on orders from Moscow. Others hold that he was a double-agent, pretending to be a Soviet spy while working for the CIA, or vice-versa.

In January 1960, Oswald was assigned to work at a television and radio factory in Minsk, supposedly to get him out of the way. He was given a surprisingly luxurious apartment. Naturally, the suspicious American was subject to round-the-clock surveillance. Within a year, he had soured on life in the USSR's "socialist utopia," rather humorously writing in his diary: "I am starting to reconsider my desire about staying. The work is drab, the money I get has nowhere to be spent. No nightclubs or bowling alleys, no places of recreation except the trade union dances. I have had enough."[12] That year he married a beautiful young woman named Marina Prusakova six weeks after meeting her at a dance, and soon fathered a daughter, named June. The couple decided to move back to America. Following an 18-month period, in which both the governments of the US and USSR had to give their approval, they were finally granted permission.

Oswald apparently anticipated a great deal of media attention upon his return to the US on June 13, 1962, even preparing statements and rehearsing answers for the press. When the couple landed at Love Field in Dallas to find a complete absence of reporters, his disappointment was palpable. In fact, the only attention he got was from the FBI, who questioned the short-tempered ex-Marine about his activities in the Soviet Union. Strangely, the CIA later denied ever interviewing Oswald, despite their voluminous file on him (yet to be released to the public). An independent investigation by the Public Broadcasting Service's *Frontline* program, only uncovered one former CIA agent out of 30 interviewed off-record who admitted that Oswald had been subject to a standard debriefing.

The Oswalds moved into an apartment on Mercedes Street in Fort Worth, where Lee's mother and brother resided. Around this time, Oswald began to hit Marina. They had often quarreled in the past, but he had always refrained from physical abuse.

The couple were befriended by a group of White Russians—anti-Communists who had fled their homeland after the Bolshevik revolution—in particular, oil accountant George Bouhe, dental technician Elena Hall, and petroleum geologist George de Mohrenschildt and his wife Jeanne. Oswald's association with de Mohrenschildt is a curious one. Though hailing from a Slavic country, de Mohrenschildt had changed his name from the Germanic "von Mohrenschildt" when he moved to America in 1938. His brother, Dimitri, was a member of the OSS and harbored a burning hatred for Communism. Stranger still, de Mohrenschildt had allegedly known JFK's wife, Jacqueline Bouvier, when she was a little girl. In fact, their relationship was so close, little Jackie would regularly sit on his knee and refer to him as "Uncle George."[13]

According to the testimony of one Alexander Kleinlerer, the White Russian community cared far more about Marina, who was unable to speak English, than her rude, self-centered, and openly anti-American husband: "Oswald always acted toward her like a soldier commanding one of his troops. My overall impression of Oswald was that he was angry with the whole world and with himself to boot; that he really did not know what he wanted; and that he was frustrated because he was not looked up to; and that he was dissatisfied with everything, including himself . . . It seemed that he did not care what others thought about anything."[14] The description offered here is consistent with the profile of a classic violent lone-wolf offender. However, conspiracy theorists have argued there was more to Oswald's relationship with the White Russians, especially de Mohrenschildt, a line of inquiry which we will explore in greater detail later. What is known is that Marina told Elena Hall that she was scared of her husband, as was Kleinlerer, who sensed Oswald's capacity for violence. Marina added that she planned to leave Oswald once she had a greater grasp of the English language, a tongue in which he refused to converse with his wife.

For a time, Marina and their daughter stayed with Hall, while Oswald relocated to Dallas in search of employment. George de Mohrenschildt eventually found him a position as a photoprint trainee at the Jaggars-Chiles-Stovall graphic arts firm. Oswald began on the first weekend in October, and by early November, de Mohrenschildt's daughter and son-in-law, Alexandra and Gary Taylor, drove Marina and June to Oswald's Dallas apartment, their new home.

It was at Jaggars-Chiles-Stovall that Oswald forged his infamous fake Alek James Hidell ID. He also opened a PO box in Dallas which he used to receive leftist publications such as *The Worker* and *The Militant,* along with the Mannlicher-Carcano rifle and the .38 revolver used to kill Officer Tippit. Meanwhile, in domestic life, Oswald struck Marina with increasing frequency and force. Psychologically, he seemed to be coming apart.

At a February 1963 party, while conversing with German oil geologist, Volkmar Schmidt, Oswald learned of the openly racist retired general Edwin Anderson Walker. The previous year, Walker had campaigned to become governor of Texas, but lost the Democratic Primary election to John Connally. An anti-Castro conservative, Walker had been traveling the country rallying support for a Cuban invasion and spouting pro-segregationist rhetoric, which had sparked a 15-hour race riot at the University of Mississippi. Attorney General Robert F. Kennedy had ordered him confined to a mental hospital for 90 days of psychiatric examination in September 1962 owing to his role in the riots, though the American Civil Liberties Union and prominent psychiatrist Thomas Szaz had opposed this on ethical grounds, meaning Walker only spent five days in the institution.[15]

On the weekend of March 9, Oswald began to conduct a reconnaissance of the "fascist" Walker's Dallas home, photographing the residence and a spot where he planned to stow his rifle, and making elaborate maps of the area. Back at home he scribbled political screeds, presumably expecting somebody to pore over them in the near future.

One day, Marina was in the backyard hanging laundry when her husband stepped out of the house dressed in black and brandishing a rifle with a .38 pistol hanging at his hip. He encouraged her to photograph him posing with the firearms. These were the same pictures Oswald would later tell the Dallas PD were doctored; however, Marina admitted taking them, even identifying the Imperial Reflex camera she had used. A subsequent investigation linked the photos definitively to the camera, while analysis by a panel of photographic experts concluded that Oswald's face had not been "pasted" onto somebody else's body as he had claimed. They also debunked another favorite conspiracy theorist talking point—the supposed unrealistic shadows in the photo—an error which they attributed to a misunderstanding of optics. Oswald had even given a copy of the photo to his friend, George de Mohrenschildt. On the back, written in Russian in his own handwriting was an all-too-telling message: "Hunter of fascists hahaha - Lee Oswald."[16]

True to his word, Oswald crept up to Edwin Walker's residence on the night of April 10, 1963, and took aim at him while he was sitting at his desk. Oswald fired a single shot through the window from about 100 ft (30 m), shattering the glass, and just missing the general, riddling his arm with bullet fragments. Marina Oswald later confirmed her husband's role in this attempted assassination, saying that Oswald had returned home ghost-white at 11:30 p.m., trembling and confessing, "I shot Walker."[17] After the JFK assassination, the bullet recovered from the Walker crime scene was subject to neutron-activation analysis, which determined the probability that it was made by the same manufacturer as the bullets in the JFK assassination as "extremely likely."[18]

Inevitably, Oswald was fired from his photography job in early April 1963 for his generally contemptuous interpersonal style. Once again, he and Marina parted ways. Oswald headed back to his birthplace, New Orleans, on April 24 to look for work, while Marina moved to the Dallas suburb of Irving with her new friend Ruth Paine, a madrigal singer apparently eager to improve her Russian. Ruth's husband, Michael, was an engineer for a Bell Helicopter facility in Fort Worth. They had been introduced to the Oswalds at a party by George de Mohrenschildt—a piece of information that will prove particularly curious in light of subsequent events.

Perhaps the most suspicious and compelling era of Oswald's life transpired during his return to New Orleans. The city was a haven for anti-Castro Cuban émigrés, who had formed a paramilitary organization that routinely trained in the swamps and bayous in hopes of reconquering their mother island. These young firebrands, whom Castro derisively dubbed *gusanos* (worms) were headed by Carlos Bringuier, delegate of the *Directorio Revolucionario Estudantil* (Student Revolutionary Directorate) in New Orleans. Given the Bay of Pigs debacle and President Kennedy's repeated inability to oust Castro from Cuba, the DRE harbored a burning hatred for the 35th POTUS.

Once settled into a dwelling at 4907 Magazine Street, Oswald, ever the reckless contrarian, took to Canal Street to hand out pro-Castro leaflets to passersby. They read "HANDS OFF CUBA! Join the Fair Play for Cuba Committee. NEW ORLEANS CHARTER MEMBER BRANCH. Free Literature, Lectures LOCATION: L.H. OSWALD 4907 MAGAZINE STREET NEW ORLEANS, LA. EVERYONE WELCOME!"[19] On August 5, Oswald walked into Carlos Bringuier's clothing store and introduced himself as a former Marine adept in guerilla warfare who would like to join the struggle against Castro both by training *gusanos* and actively participate in the coming invasion. He returned the next day and handed the fervently *anti*-Castro Bringuier *A Guidebook for Marines* that contained diagrams and instructions pertaining to the creation of explosive devices and booby traps, along with information on how to conduct sabotage operations. A few days later, Bringuier bumped into Oswald handing out his pro-Castro pamphlets on Canal Street and an angry confrontation ensued. Curiously, this time the pamphlets featured a different address: 544 Camp Street.

Nearly three years after the Kennedy assassination, New Orleans District Attorney Jim Garrison—famously portrayed by Kevin Costner in Oliver Stone's Academy Award nominated 1991 epic *JFK*—realized that 544 Camp Street was the address of the same building that housed the office of Guy Banister, an FBI agent turned private investigator. Banister was instrumental in orchestrating the training of anti-Castro paramilitary organizations in "The Big Easy." Furthermore, Banister was close colleagues with anti-Castro former airline pilot David Ferrie—the *same* David Ferrie who had been Lee Harvey Oswald's instructor in the Civilian Air Patrol seven years earlier! In the years since, Ferrie had been ousted from the CAP for pushing right-wing political views on his students.

Even more astonishingly, both Banister and Ferrie were linked to New Orleans Mafia boss Carlos Marcello. On April 4, 1961, Robert Kennedy had ordered the US Justice Department to arrest Marcello, deporting him to Guatemala. Marcello had made his way back to New Orleans within two months, where he engaged in a prolonged legal battle to fight his deportation. Marcello's attorneys had hired Banister and Ferrie as private investigators to assist with his case. Marcello's hatred of the Kennedys was confirmed by illegal FBI audio surveillance, in which he was recorded in Sicilian verbalizing the idea of hiring a "nut" to "whack" the president—a descriptor that certainly fits Lee Harvey Oswald. Naturally, if such an assassin was caught, he would have to be quickly eliminated, in case he implicated Marcello, Banister, and Ferrie in the conspiracy. This anti-Castro-Mafia-Oswald conspiracy theory crystalized with the revelation that Carlos Marcello was connected to Jack Ruby through two of Marcello's lieutenants in Dallas, the Campisi brothers. The theory has formed the basis for numerous JFK conspiracy books, including *Fatal Hour* by Billings & Blakey, John

H. Davis's *Mafia Kingfish*, *Mob Lawyer* by Frank Ragano, and Lamar Waldron's *The Hidden History of the JFK Assassination*.

Convinced that Oswald was somehow connected to the CIA and a network of New Orleans coconspirators, DA Jim Garrison set his sights on local businessman, and playwright Clay Shaw. At Shaw's 1969 trial for conspiring to murder the president, Garrison relied primarily on the testimony of an insurance salesman named Perry Russo who claimed to have been at a party hosted by David Ferrie, where both Lee Harvey Oswald (using the alias "Leon Oswald") and Shaw (going by the name "Clem Bertrand") talked openly about assassinating the president using a triangulation of crossfire. Ultimately, Garrison's case was riddled with procedural errors, including the misuse of sodium pentothal, while Russo's story was proven to be unreliable. It took the jury less than an hour to acquit Shaw. However, during a civil lawsuit in the late-Seventies, former CIA director Richard Helms divulged that Shaw had been a part-time CIA contact, providing information from Latin America. To put this in context, over 100,000 other Americans had acted in a similar capacity. UFOlogist and Men In Black researcher Gray Barker observed that "when Clay Shaw was tried as a conspirator in New Orleans, I subscribed to *The Times-Picayune* in order to follow the case closely. Skimming over the myriad details the paper was reporting prior to the trial, I almost skipped a list of grand jury witnesses. But I glanced at it quickly and . . . I saw a name that rang a peculiar bell. That name was Fred L. Crisman!" [20] This was apparently the same Fred Crisman who was one of the harbor patrolmen that spoke with Kenneth Arnold following the 1947 Maury Island UFO incident, which culminated in the deaths of two USAF officers. Barker declared that Crisman was a self-described "disruption agent" who testified at Shaw's trial that he knew nothing of the JFK assassination. Stranger still, Crisman had been identified by a reliable eye witness as one of the MIB who had descended upon Point Pleasant, West Virginia between 1966–1967. Not only was Crisman a colleague of fellow CIA pilot David

Ferrie, but there was also a strong possibility that Ferrie had himself played a part in terrorizing Point Pleasant during the mothman era! At least, according to Gray Barker . . .

—

Returning to 1963, how do we reconcile Lee Harvey Oswald's flagrant espousing of pro-Castro beliefs on Canal Street while simultaneously volunteering his services to Carlos Bringuier and providing Banister's building address to pedestrians who were sympathetic to the Cuban Revolution? Was his pro-Castro stance merely a facade to collect information on potential Communists? Or was he attempting to infiltrate the *gusanos* in order to feed intelligence back to Havana and join the Cuban revolutionary cause?

In light of Oswald's subsequent September 25 bus journey to Mexico City, the second scenario seems the more likely: He entered the Cuban embassy with a portfolio of documents confirming his history of pro-Castro activities in an obvious attempt to ingratiate himself with the Cuban government and secure permission to fly to Havana. This pilgrimage ended when Oswald lost his temper with a Cuban consul and was ejected from the embassy. Dejected, Oswald traveled back to the US on October 3, returning to Dallas.

As fate would have it, Marina Oswald's generous friend Ruth Paine found him a job at the Texas School Book Depository on the corner of Main and Elm. Though it only paid $1.25 an hour, Oswald said he liked the thought of being around books all day. Marina continued to live with the Paines in Irving, while Oswald stayed at a rooming house in Oak Cliff, presumably trying once more to save money for a home for his pregnant wife and daughter. On November 20, 1963, Dallas newspapers published maps detailing President Kennedy's motorcade, which happened to be passing right by the very warehouse where Lee Harvey Oswald had recently stumbled into employment.

Was it simply another coincidence that Ruth Paine just happened to find an unhinged pro-Castro sharpshooter a job in a building right next to one of the most dangerous legs of the presidential motorcade? Men in Black conspiracy theorist Andrew Colvin has written that "the man who reportedly headed the Dora flying saucer production line [at Mittelwerk was] Gen. Walter Dornberger, who was brought into the country via Operation Paperclip [see Chapter 3] . . . eventually became an executive at Bell Aircraft in Dallas, supposedly a haven for military men who hated JFK."[21] Ruth Paine's husband Michael just happened to be an engineer at Bell Helicopters in Fort Worth.

In her January 1984 article "The Nazi Connection to the John F. Kennedy Assassination" for controversial publisher and free-speech activist Larry Flynt's magazine *The Rebel*, Mae Brussell, the self-styled "Queen of Conspiracy," proposed that the CIA; Mafia; and fanatical, former-Nazi "Paperclip" scientists colluded to bring about the president's demise. According to Brussell, when Lee and Marina Oswald left the USSR and settled in Dallas in June 1962, many of the anti-Communist White Russians they befriended either had ties to the Nazis or worked in the American oil and gas industries. One White Russian who met both criteria, George de Mohrenschildt, not only had ties to the CIA and Jackie Kennedy, but was actually accused of being a Nazi spy by the former CIA director Richard Helms. George de Mohrenschildt had also introduced Bell Helicopter engineer Michael Paine and his wife Ruth to the Oswalds.

—

This account has been merely a taste of the mountainous layer cake of interweaving and cross-pollinating conspiracy theories surrounding the JFK assassination. His November 22, 1963, murder is a route into a Byzantine labyrinth of conspiracy theories, which has confused countless JFK researchers. One way to help resolve this situation is to debunk some of the most common and pervasive arguments associated with the assassination.

Firstly, the official narrative's second shot, which struck JFK in the upper back before exiting through his throat, penetrating Governor Connally's back and chest, and following a downward trajectory to wound his wrist and thigh has been ridiculed as the "magic bullet" theory by its critics, who claim that such a feat is physically impossible. To begin, it is crucial to understand that Connally was seated 1 ft 6 in (0.5 m) in front of Kennedy and 3 in (7.6 cm) to the left. Thanks to computer modeling technologies, researchers have been able to digitally replicate the geographical setting, positions, speeds, and movements of the targets; and track the trajectory of the bullet in accordance with physical law. In the words of JFK conspiracy skeptic Gerald Posner, "Four government commissions all concluded it was a straight line right through the two men. There's no question that a single bullet could inflict all seven wounds on both the president and the governor and emerge in very good condition. As it slowed, as it moved through the two men, it moved fast enough to break bone but not fast enough to deform the bullet. The computer technicians used reverse projection to go from the wounds on Kennedy and Connally and determine where the assassin had to be located to inflict those wounds. And a cone is splayed out from the wound and shows that the only area almost centers on the southeast corner sixth floor schoolbook depository."[22]

Another common claim is that there was a second gunman on the infamous grassy knoll located to the southwest of the school book depository. This is based purely on eyewitness testimony, a form of evidence that has repeatedly been scientifically proven to be unreliable, especially when it concerns a fleeting observation. The grassy knoll was investigated almost immediately by Dallas police motorcycle officer Clyde Haygood, and unlike the Texas School Book Depository, which contained a veritable treasure trove of leads, no physical evidence of a second shooter was found there whatsoever—no firearm, no spent cartridges, no ammo or footprints.

Finally, there are those who argue that more than three shots were fired—including the House Select Committee on Assassinations, which relied on an audio Dictabelt recording of dubious origins that seemingly captured a fourth shot. However, when this recording was reviewed by the FBI's Technical Services Division and the National Academy of Science's Committee on Ballistic Acoustics (CBA), both the FBI and CBA found egregious errors in the scientific methodology, effectively debunking it. "There were only two shots that struck President Kennedy. Both came from the rear," Gerald Posner explains. "Four government investigations all came to the same conclusion. The Warren Commission in the Sixties. In 1968, the Clark Panel set by Attorney General Ramsey Clark. In the Seventies, the Rockefeller Commission, and finally in the late-Seventies the House Select Committee with the largest forensics panel reexamining the evidence."[23]

At the end of the day, Lee Harvey Oswald was seen walking into work on November 22 carrying a brown oblong paper bag which he claimed contained curtain rods. Oswald worked on the sixth floor of the Texas School Book Depository. Not only was his rifle the exact length and shape to fit into the bag, but both the brown bag and rifle were recovered from the sixth floor. Oswald's fingerprints were lifted from the boxes he had used to steady the rifle along with partials near the trigger guard and a full palm print on the barrel. By the time of Oswald's arrest, Marina Oswald had also found $175 her husband had left for her on the bureau—what little money he still had left in this world—along with his wedding ring.

—

Given the passage of time and loss of evidence, the most probable route to finding who killed John F. Kennedy lies in learning about the man who murdered Lee Harvey Oswald. In many ways, Jack

Ruby was an even more mercurial character. Nicknamed "Sparky" for his notorious hair-trigger temper, he had a reputation for throwing people down the stairs of the Carousel, his Dallas strip club, and using the establishment to ingratiate himself with cops and gangsters alike.

Initially, Ruby claimed he had murdered Oswald to "show the world that a Jew had guts."[24] But those who had contact with him in the days since Oswald's arrest described him as inconsolable: "Jack [Ruby] thought it was just horrible that weasel could kill the President of the United States . . . He was extremely upset that the President of the United States had been assassinated."[25] According to journalist Hugh Aynesworth, who knew Ruby and spoke to him on the phone after his arrest, "He said he just did it spur of the moment . . . He said, 'I didn't have it in mind.' "[26]

Delving into the conspiracy-verse, the most likely motive for Ruby gunning down Lee Harvey Oswald was that Ruby was acting on orders from his New Orleans mob associate, Carlos Marcello. In this scenario, Oswald was either a gunman hired by the Mafia (potentially in tandem with government and/or non-government anti-Castro elements) to kill Kennedy, or a fall guy who had been set-up to distract from Marcello's real assassins. Either way, he was a loose end that needed to be tied up, and Ruby had done the job perfectly. Ruby would begin dropping veiled hints of a wider conspiracy in 1965, though he contradicted this during a 1967 death-bed confession in which he reportedly admitted there was no conspiracy to kill Oswald, and he alone was involved.

The truth may lie somewhere in between. In a series of newspaper articles, Ruby wrote that he had no memory of what had happened in the time between reaching for his gun and realizing that the police had pinned him to the ground. A psychiatric assessment solicited by his legal defense team opined he had entered "a 'fugue state' with subsequent amnesia."[27] His attorney, Melvin Belli, referred to this as "a blank spot in [Ruby's] memory"[28] into which motives for his crimes "had been poured like water into the vacuum in his pathologically receptive memory and, once there, had solidified like cement."[29] In other words, Belli thought it was utter folly to try to ascertain Ruby's motives, as the gunman did not know them himself. Any reasons he gave were therefore, necessarily, confabulations. For instance, Ruby agreed to go along with his defense team's suggestion that he had murdered Oswald so that Jackie Kennedy would not have to endure witnessing Oswald's trial, even though this was not true.

When Ruby was found guilty of murder, he was stunned. He fired his attorney and turned to psychiatrist Dr. Hubert Winston Smith, who also boasted a law degree, as representation during the appeals process. Smith immediately recognized the need for another psychiatric assessment, and knew just the man for the job: a hypnotist and truth-serum expert named Dr. Louis Jolyon West. From the earliest news of the Oswald assassination, "Jolly" West had petitioned Ruby's judge, Joe R. Brown, to be involved with the case, albeit unsuccessfully. Allegedly he had been "asked" by an unnamed party.

On April 26, 1964, West flew into Dallas to examine Jack Ruby. After leaving Ruby's cell, West announced to the world that Ruby had suffered "an acute psychotic break"[30] within the last 48 hours. In a short time, "Sparky" the strip club owner had gone from a one-time amnesiac to a full-blown madman, raving that Jews were being massacred all over America because of what he had done.

Was Jack Ruby simply a crazed killer, with his murder of Lee Harvey Oswald simply representing a murderous episode on his incremental slide into madness? Or, considering that every mental health practitioner *before* West had declared Ruby sane, and everyone *after* West had diagnosed him as utterly delusional, what if there was something more to this "Jolly" doctor? What if he was a far stranger, more nefarious character than Oswald and Ruby combined . . .

"Them"

German philosopher and mystic
Adam Weishaupt, founder of
the subversive Illuminati.

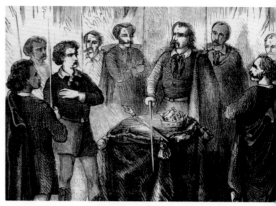

A 19th-century French print, showing
the initiation of an Illuminati member.

A depiction of a masonic ritual,
New York, c.1900.

An artistic
impression
of "grays,"
often cited
in eyewitness
accounts
of close
encounters
with alien
lifeforms.

The Eye of Providence: alleged
masonic iconography features on
the back of the US dollar bill.

Operation Grey Wolf

This propaganda image of Hitler's corpse did little to dissuade conspiracists that he might have escaped Nazi Germany.

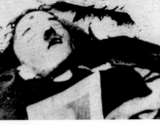

EXTRA THE STARS AND STRIPES **EXTRA**

HITLER DEAD

Fuehrer Fell at CP, German Radio Says; Doenitz at Helm, Vows War Will Continue

Banner headlines greeted news of Hitler's suicide on April 30, 1945.

Martin Bormann, Operation Grey Wolf mastermind.

Images produced by the US Office of Strategic Services in 1944 show five disguises Hitler might employ if escaping.

Eva Braun and Hitler with their dogs Wulf and Blondi, Berghof, Germany, 1942.

A Red Army soldier indicates the spot where Hitler and Eva Braun's bodies were burned after their joint suicide.

Nazi Ratlines

Nazi war criminal Adolf Eichmann on trial in Jerusalem, Israel, June 1961.

Eichmann's false Red Cross passport, which enabled him to enter Argentina in 1950.

Fleeing Nazis tried to merge with legitimate refugees.

Bishop Hudal, who helped Nazis escape justice.

Brazil, 1985: a doctor displays Mengele's exhumed skull.

Nazi Medical Officer Josef Mengele, (above), and allegedly with friends in Brazil in the 1970s (right).

Prominent Nazi war criminals that escaped using Bishop
Alois Hudal's "Ratlines" network included (left to right)
Franz Stangl, Gustav Wagner, and Alois Brunner.

Pope Pius XII, accused by some
commentators of pro-Nazi
sympathies, but exonerated by others.

Cardinal Siri (left) with Pope John XXIII was
implicated in the Nazi Ratlines network.

December 15, 1962: former Gestapo chief
Walter Rauff is arrested in Chile.

Nazi hunter Simon
Wiesenthal displays photos
of Rauff and an ambulance
used to execute Jews.

A sign warns any potential Area 51 trespassers of dire consequences.

A satellite image of Area 51 taken on July 20 2016.

Conspiracy theorist Bob Lazar during a Q&A session at a screening of the documentary *Bob Lazar: Area 51 and the Flying Saucers*.

A puppy sports a tinfoil hat as "protection" from disturbance by possible UFO activity.

The devastation wrought by V2 rockets in East London, in the final months of World War II.

Former Nazi Wernher von Braun, smuggled to the US as part of Operation Paperclip as a missile expert.

The weapon that established von Braun's reputation: the V2 rocket.

Pilot Gary Powers, shot down and captured by Soviet troops in 1960, at the height of the Cold War.

A U-2 spy plane similar to that flown over Soviet airspace by Powers.

During the 1950s, atom bomb tests in the Nevada desert became a popular spectacle.

The Men in Black

An ad for a 1956 book by conspiracy theorist Gray Barker.

FBI Director J. Edgar Hoover, who launched investigations into Men in Black reports.

The poster for the 1997 movie that presented the MIB as heroes.

The Assassination of President John F. Kennedy

The president's motorcade, moments before the fatal shots were fired.

Kennedy's assassination shocked the world.

Assassin Lee Harvey Oswald (center)
under arrest, November 22, 1963.

Images of Oswald posing in
a backyard with a rifle
seemed to confirm his guilt.

Jack Ruby poses with burlesque
performers from his Carousel night spot.

Oswald's passport with
incriminating items found in
the Texas Book Depository.

Ruby's police
mug shot
following the
murder of Lee
Harvey Oswald.

November 24,
1963: Ruby
shoots Oswald in
the basement
of the Dallas
city jail.

MK-ULTRA

The CIA's MK-ULTRA program is one of the most insidious conspiracy theories. For 20 years this government agency used psychedelic drugs and cruel brainwashing techniques to bend vulnerable minds to do its bidding. The consequences of these sinister, mind-controlling experiments were horrifying and far-reaching . . .

A rmchair skeptics who turn up their noses at the suggestion that the CIA might have been involved in the Men in Black phenomenon or the assassination of President John F. Kennedy will also likely balk at the notion that the agency conducted illegal and harmful psychotropic mind control experiments on thousands of unsuspecting American and Canadian citizens. Yet, in 1975, inquiries by both The Church Committee under Senator Frank Church, and the Rockefeller Commission, spearheaded by Vice-President Nelson Rockefeller, reported that such a program had indeed existed.

Commencing in 1953 and lasting 20 years until the Watergate Scandal—which prompted CIA director Richard Helms to destroy countless incriminating documents—Project MK-ULTRA was not only real, but also, paradoxically, the progenitor of both the peace and love psychedelic era of the 1960s and a slew of high-profile homicides.

MK-ULTRA was rooted in 1949's Operation BLUEBIRD, in which inmates at American federal and military prisons were involuntarily administered narcotics and subjected to a barrage of unethical experimental procedures. The CIA's main drug of choice was lysergic acid diethylamide, commonly known as LSD or simply "acid."

LSD was first synthesized in Basel, Switzerland, by chemist Albert Hofmann on November 16, 1938. Hofmann had been attempting to create a less-uterotonic analeptic but LSD-25 received little interest from physicians and pharmacologists and was shelved for five years. Hofmann eventually returned to investigate this mysterious compound on April 16, 1943, and accidentally got some of the substance on his fingertips. Once absorbed into his system, he was amazed by its potent effects: "Remarkable restlessness, combined with a slight dizziness ... a not-unpleasant, intoxicated[-]like condition, characterized by an extremely stimulated imagination ... In a dreamlike state, with eyes closed ... I perceived an uninterrupted stream of fantastic pictures, extraordinary shapes with intense, kaleidoscopic play of colors."[1] Three days later, Hofmann decided to voluntarily imbibe LSD and experienced the world's first full-blown "acid trip"—reportedly, a fairly horrific one. For six years, LSD was used purely in medical and psychological settings, until, in 1949, it came to the attention of the CIA's Operation BLUEBIRD.

This program was a true expression of the US's Cold War mentality, in which mind control was considered a hair's breadth away from Soviet groupthink: a pandemic of cognitive conformity that seemed poised to sweep the globe. Only by scientifically getting ahead of the Soviets in this realm, the CIA reasoned, could they hope to defend the country against the ideological zombification of Communism.

Interestingly, the word "brainwashed" only entered the English lexicon in 1950 with the onset of the Korean War—a direct translation of the Mandarin term *xi nao*. American pilots who had been captured by Communist forces began appearing on Korean radio to "admit" that they had illegally scattered biological weapons over the peninsula: something both the US military and CIA knew they had certainly *not* done. As such, the US authorities attributed these false claims to brainwashing, and subsequently subjected 56 freed American prisoners of war to "deprogramming" under the supervision of Cornell University psychiatrist Dr. Louis J. West. (This was the same Dr. West who, years later, would examine Jack Ruby, the killer of President Kennedy assassin Lee Harvey Oswald.) West's efforts were successful: Not only did he manage to undo *xi nao*, paving the way for the men to reenter American society, but his methods also led the former POWs to retract their previous statements. Overnight, Jolly West was invited into the inner circles of the CIA.

By 1951, the defensive Operation BLUEBIRD had morphed into the offensive Operation ARTICHOKE—a joint CIA, FBI, and military project—which focused primarily on the use of hypnosis, isolation, and narcotics to brainwash subjects into perpetrating assassinations. As one January 1952 memo speculated: "Can we get control of an individual to the point where he will do our bidding against his will and even against fundamental laws of nature, such as self-preservation?"[2] These puppets of the state would later become known as "Manchurian Candidates," a term derived from a 1959 novel by Richard Condon—filmed in 1962—in which US soldiers return from the Korean War having been brainwashed to become fanatical communists.

Author and journalist Stephen Kinzer has called the supposed Cold War origins of American mind-control programs into question, noting that Nazi scientists had already begun researching this area during the Second World War. In particular, he pointed to two individuals: Dr. Kurt Blome, former Deputy Health Minister of the Reich, and General Walter Schreiber, the Nazi army's surgeon general.

As the Third Reich's director of research into biological warfare, Dr. Kurt Blome had conducted bacterial, viral, and chemical experiments upon the inmates of Nazi Germany's most notorious concentration and death camps, arguably making Josef Mengele's efforts seem almost tame by comparison. Most pertinent here, however, was Blome's use of mescaline and other psychoactive drugs in an attempt to control or destroy his subjects' minds. His knowledge was considered so valuable that he was one of only seven defendants acquitted at the Nuremberg Trials: seemingly the result of American gerrymandering so they could pick his brain afterward.

General Walter Schreiber had approved hideous experiments, including those involving mind control, at Auschwitz, Dachau, and Ravensbrück during the war. Having slipped away from Soviet captivity, he had escaped to the American prison of Camp King where he was eager to share his knowledge in exchange for an expedited "paperclip" contract to the USA (see Chapter 3: Nazi Ratlines). Arrangements for his transfer were immediately made. Dr. Kurt Blome had started a medical practice in Dortmund after narrowly escaping the noose at Nuremberg, when he learned that his old *Kumpel* Schreiber was moving to America. Offered a "paperclip contract" himself in 1951, he leaped at the opportunity. Unfortunately for Blome, Schreiber's arrival in the US did not go unnoticed and erupted into a scandal, which resulted in the rescinding of his "paperclip" contract. Realizing the need to avoid drawing undue attention to Operation Paperclip, the CIA similarly cancelled Blome's contract. But where Schreiber resettled in Argentina, Blome stayed in West Germany, taking over his position as staff doctor at Camp King. From there, he resumed his mind-control experiments using all manner of drugs, while enjoying the protection of the CIA, and even advised on their interrogations in other countries.

—

Born to Jewish Hungarian parents in The Bronx, NYC, future chemist and CIA mastermind Sidney Gottlieb's brilliant mind was initially offset by deformations to both of his feet. He only walked for the first time at the age of 12, with the aid of braces. Though he improved substantially, he would continue to limp slightly all his life (he died in 1999). He also lisped. Despite being ridiculed by his peers, Gottlieb excelled academically, managing to claw his way up from his working-class immigrant beginnings to earn a doctorate in biochemistry from the California Institute of Technology in 1943.

After a few years of conducting standard research for pharmaceutical and agricultural chemicals, Gottlieb was recruited into the CIA's Operation BLUEBIRD in 1951. Deputy Director for Plans Allen Dulles had realized that the program was stagnating owing to too much input from CIA bigwigs, and saw Gottlieb as an innovative genius who could revitalize it. A month after his appointment, BLUEBIRD became ARTICHOKE, and Gottlieb was given the title Chief of the Chemical Division of the Technical Services Staff. By the end of 1951, the unconventional Gottlieb asked CIA physician Harold Abramson to administer LSD to him, and observe him closely during his first "trip." The experience culminated in an epiphany—*this* was the miracle mind-control drug upon which the CIA should focus. Come April of 1953, Sidney Gottlieb had drawn up a novel and ambitious research plan that necessitated a $300,000 starting budget and the ability to autonomously begin subprojects without having to ask permission or fill out paperwork. Dulles approved, and on April 13, Operation ARTICHOKE became MK-ULTRA. Around the same time, the CIA deputy director allegedly spent $240,000 to buy up the global supply of LSD. The agency began to distribute its psychedelic stockpile to the Sidney Gottliebs and Jolly Wests of the world—archetypal "mad doctors."

Gottlieb had scouted a new talent to oversee his operations, a narcotics officer and former Office of Strategic Services (OSS) prodigy with a reputation for sampling contraband. George Hunter White has been described as "a big powerful man with a completely bald head. Not tall, but big. Fat. He shaved his head and had the most beautiful blue eyes you've ever seen."[3] For the most part, Gottlieb's projects involved offering or tricking people into taking LSD and other narcotics, and then observing them in a controlled setting.

Under Gottlieb's instruction, White added sex to the mix in 1955 with the onset of MK–ULTRA subproject 42: Operation Midnight Climax. Acquiring an apartment at 225 Chestnut Street at San Francisco's northernmost tip, White had the bedroom decked out with mirrors, red curtains, and a cache of pornography and sex toys. He then hired sex workers to escort their clients back to this safehouse and slip them LSD before sex. Seated on a portable toilet next door, White would sip a pitcher of Martinis and observe what took place via a one-way mirror. Hidden audio-recording devices secretly documented these trysts. White's colleague, Ira Feldman, was responsible for recruiting sex workers, offering them 50 to 100 dollars per client. They were also given a phone number connected to George Hunter White, who guaranteed he would spring them from custody if they were arrested for soliciting by the police. Often these sex workers would be paid to pick up specific individuals in bars and bring them back to 225 Chestnut to glean information from them—a well-established "honey-trap" technique of intelligence agencies all over the globe. In fact, a major protocol of Operation Midnight Climax was to see if the addition of LSD could enhance this form of information gathering. Another was to see how the male clientele reacted to different combinations of drugs and sex acts.

Both White and Feldman were amazed how loose the men's tongues became after sex, especially if the women remained in their company for some time. Seemingly, the combination of LSD and intimacy was vastly superior to torture as an interrogation technique: "Now, with these drugs, you could get information without having to abuse people."[4] In addition, White frequently invited Sidney Gottlieb and local narcotics officers to 225 Chestnut Street to indulge in sex and drugs, too.[5]

—

A number of clandestine MK–ULTRA subprojects entailed the administration of LSD to volunteers at hospitals and clinics across North America.

At a 1954 American Psychological Association conference, the CIA became aware of mind-altering experiments conducted by Dr. Donald Hebb at McGill University in Montreal, sponsored by the Canadian army. Hebb paid student volunteers to be blindfolded and ear-plugged, with their hands and feet tied together and stuffed into foam-rubber mitts. They were then locked into a soundproof chamber, where the majority suffered a breakdown within days. None were able to endure more than a week of such treatment. Perhaps most pertinent was Hebb's observation that after a few hours their thoughts became disjointed, indicating "direct evidence of a kind of dependence on the environment that has not been previously recognized."[6]

Hebb's ruthless experiments led the CIA to discover the even more extreme work of fellow McGill faculty member Dr. Ewen Cameron at the Allan Memorial Institute, Montreal. In a 1956 research paper, Cameron had noted that his subjects reacted in a manner similar to "the breakdown of the individual under continuous interrogation"[7]: a discovery the CIA found particularly appealing. Impressed, Sidney Gottlieb recruited him as a contractor for the MK-ULTRA program—though it would be quite some time before Cameron learned who was really financing his experiments. In order to maintain plausible deniability, Gottlieb sent Maitland Baldwin of the National Institute of Mental Health (NIMH)—a CIA front that researched the effects of LSD—to Montreal to encourage Cameron to apply for funding from the Society for the Investigation of Human Ecology, another shell organization, to work on Subproject 68. He would receive $69,000 in funding over the next few years to support his efforts.

In experiments that were later judged "comparable to Nazi medical atrocities,"[8] Cameron isolated volunteers in small cells, coupled LSD and other narcotics with hypnosis to induce a clinical coma, and exposed them to endlessly repeating phrases. Cameron believed rapid changes to a subject's attitudes and beliefs could be elicited by exposing them to specific stimuli or depriving them of any stimuli whatsoever for prolonged periods. As such, he took people suffering from minor mood disorders and subjected them to intense heat and powerful electroshock "treatments." In one experiment, he attempted to "repattern" a subject's neurological pathways by exposing them to eight hours of red light every day for months.

Ultimately, Cameron would report that though he had succeeded in obliterating his patients' minds, he had been entirely unsuccessful in replacing them with new, functioning personalities. To provide a picture of one of his "achievements," we need look no further than Cameron's own writings: "The shock treatment turned the then-19-year-old honors student into a woman who sucked her thumb, talked like a baby, demanded to be fed from a bottle, and urinated on the floor."[9]

—

Another prominent MK-ULTRA facility was the Menlo Park Veterans Administration Hospital, located some 33 miles (53 km) south of San Francisco in Paolo Alto, California. There, in 1959, Ken Kesey, an aspiring novelist completing a fellowship in creative writing at Stanford University, had his first encounter with LSD. Enamored with this paradigm-shifting substance and its creative possibilities, Kesey used the royalties from his successful 1962 novel *One Flew Over the Cuckoo's Nest*—inspired by observing patients, who were often under the influence of psychoactive drugs, at Menlo Park—to purchase a log house in La Honda. There he regularly hosted "acid tests," introducing musicians, writers, and Hells Angels to this glorious new mind-altering, life-changing hallucinogen. The beat poet Allen Ginsberg, too, was profoundly shaped by LSD after volunteering for the Menlo Park VA Hospital psychological experiments, along with fellow poet and future Grateful Dead lyricist, Robert Hunter, who had previously been dosed with

LSD, psilocybin (magic mushrooms), and mescaline by the MK-ULTRA financed program.

Eventually, Kesey and his cohorts, known as The Merry Pranksters, bought a school bus they dubbed Furthur [sic], outfitted with a sound system, and painted with an array of psychedelic designs. Stocking it with a bountiful supply of LSD, 500 Benzedrine pills, and a shoebox of marijuana joints, the Merry Pranksters left La Honda on June 17, 1964. In a journey later memorably chronicled by the writer Tom Wolfe in *The Electric Kool-Aid Acid Test*, Furthur was driven by none other than Neal Cassady—aka Dean Moriarty in Jack Kerouac's 1957 best-selling beat novel *On the Road*. The charismatic, wildly eccentric Cassady somehow ferried Kesey and the Merry Pranksters through southern California and Arizona to Texas, New Orleans, and Florida, before heading up the eastern seaboard to New York City, which they reached on June 29. The bus then made its way back to La Honda through Canada, arriving in August. While the official purpose of the trip was to promote and celebrate the publication of Kesey's second novel *Sometimes a Great Notion* and attend the 1964 World's Fair in NYC, in reality, the trip also aimed "to turn America on to this particular form of [psychedelic] enlightenment,"[10] and to see what would happen when a subculture of impulsive, hallucinogen-abetted weirdos collided with the cautious and conservative conformity of middle-America. Along the journey, The Merry Pranksters freely dosed hundreds of Americans with then-legal LSD mixed with orange Kool-Aid. The trip has been credited with sowing the seeds of the hippie movement that would be in full bloom two years later. Carolyn "Mountain Girl" Garcia, wife of the late–Grateful Dead frontman Jerry Garcia and mother to Kesey's daughter Sunshine, summarized it thus: "They didn't know they were starting the '60s, obviously, but they knew they had a big secret and they were going to exploit it to the fullest."[11]

That secret was LSD.

—

Having inadvertently employed narcotics to create the kind of left-wing insurgency they had specifically sought to counteract in the first place, the FBI and CIA launched Operation COINTELRPO and Operation CHAOS, respectively. The point of these programs was to sow discord and incite violence among various elements of the fast-growing hippie counterculture.

CIA mindbender Jolly West surfaced in San Francisco in 1966, and set up a "laboratory disguised as a hippie crash pad"[12] in a Victorian house on Frederick Street, two blocks south of Haight. West's Haight-Ashbury Project (HAP) experiment involved recruiting six graduate students to pose as hippies to entice young "flower children" back to this apartment. These subjects were welcome to stay indefinitely, as long as they acquiesced to grad students documenting their behavior. HAP was receiving financial support from the Foundations Fund for Research in Psychiatry, Inc. which investigative reporter Tom O'Neill has alleged was a front for the CIA, based on its startling similarities to Operation Midnight Climax. The crash-pad opened in June 1967, San Francisco's so-called "Summer of Love."

Coincidentally or not, that same month, David Elvin Smith, a 26-year-old postdoctoral student at the University of California San Francisco, opened a complimentary health care facility at 558 Clayton Street, one block west of the intersection of Haight and Ashbury. The Haight-Ashbury Free Medical Clinic (HAFMC) offered treatment for drug-related afflictions, malnutrition, and venereal disease, along with psychological counseling to hundreds of hippies a day. Though the HAFMC did not demand monetary compensation from its patients, there was certainly a cost.

Before opening the HAFMC, David Smith had conducted experiments injecting rodents with LSD and amphetamines and placing them in overcrowded spaces. He was particularly interested in the efficacy of LSD in enhancing suggestibility and of amphetamines on aggression. Much of this research was funded by NIMH.

The NIMH also offered financial support for research carried out by another mysterious Smith (no relation). Roger Smith was a doctoral student in criminology at University of California, Berkeley, and was similarly interested in the effects of drugs on human behavior. A self-described "rock-ribbed Republican," Roger Smith was considered an expert on gangs and narcotics after conducting undercover "participant-observer" research with several such groups in Oakland, California. He had concluded that drug use more often caused violent behavior than ameliorated it.

Though purportedly hailing from different backgrounds and locales, Roger Smith, Jolly West, and David Smith would all have offices in the HAFMC during the Summer of Love. West used the space mainly to recruit subjects for the house on Frederick Street. And, given the amount of funding his presence generated for the clinic, the two Smiths were more than willing to assist him in his poorly-defined experiment.

Stranger still, Roger Smith was Charles Manson's parole officer.

—

Charles Manson lived in the Haight-Ashbury area from late-spring 1967 to June 1968. Here he recruited wayward teens into his so-called Family by plying them with psychotropic drugs, especially LSD, and admonishing them to forget every "lie" they had ever been told by society. The 32-year-old Manson had been released from LA county's Terminal Island prison on March 21, 1967. A psychopathic criminal through-and-through, he had immediately violated parole by relocating 375 miles (600 km) to Berkeley, near San Francisco. Though Manson was required to remain in Los Angeles under threat of automatic reimprisonment, he simply called the San Francisco Federal Parole Office and was placed under the supervision of Roger Smith. Manson's transfer into Smith's care was facilitated by an experimental parole program which also received funding from the NIMH. While Smith at one time had a pool of 40 clients, in 1967 it was suddenly reduced to just one: Charles Manson. Smith's research assistant at the time, Gail Sadalla, was certain that Manson and Roger Smith had known each other previously. Tom O'Neill offers this as evidence to explain Manson's suspiciously seamless vault from LA to San Francisco. Rather than absconding, he had been sent into parole officer Smith's care. Once Manson arrived in the San Francisco area, Roger Smith instructed him to move to Haight-Ashbury for a healthy dose of peace and love—a strange suggestion considering his own academic conclusions regarding the relationship between narcotics and violence.

Or was it?

Manson was frequently and repeatedly arrested while serving parole under Roger Smith. Time and time again he was mysteriously freed without conviction; almost as if someone was pulling strings for him behind the scenes. The same treatment was extended to members of his Family. According to Tom O'Neill, "Once I was absorbed in the Family's origin story, I found evidence everywhere of a curious leniency, always helped by a hand from the outside."[13]

In one of many examples, Manson had decided he needed to recruit more young men into the cult. He asked female members, Susan Atkins, Patricia Krenwinkel, Ella Jo Bailey, Stephanie Rowe, and Mary Brunner—some of whom were already on parole—to find and seduce suitable candidates. Their MO was to lure boys into an all-girl orgy featuring a buffet of narcotics. The girls did as Charlie commanded, enticing three teenage males into a sex party in Ukiah where they gave them marijuana laced with LSD. Their plans quickly went south when one of the young men, the 17-year-old son of a Mendocino County Deputy Sheriff, fled the bacchanalia for home, hallucinating wildly. Though all five women were arrested and charged with felony drug possession along with contributing to the delinquency of minors, all it took was a phone call to Roger Smith and they walked free. Law enforcement officers all over California recalled similar events.

By this time, Manson had isolated his Family at Spahn Ranch, a set for the cowboy films of old in LA's Santa Susana Mountains, and was no longer a client of Roger Smith. Nevertheless, the two men continued to see each other—with Smith affectionately referring to him as "Charlie." Smith and his wife had even acted as foster parents for Manson and Brunner's child, "Pooh Bear."

—

On August 9, 1969, Family members Susan Atkins, Patricia Krenwinkel, and Charles "Tex" Watson, high on amphetamines, entered 10050 Cielo Drive in Benedict Canyon at night, armed with a .22 revolver, ropes, and knives. Watson shot Steven Parent, the groundskeeper's visitor, four times near the front gate, killing him. Once inside the home, the trio rounded up and, in a series of manic assaults, murdered all four occupants of the house—amateur screenwriter Wojciech Frykowski, 32; his girlfriend and coffee heiress Abigail Folger, 25; celebrity hairstylist Jay Sebring, 35; and 26-year-old actress Sharon Tate, who was eight-and-a-half months pregnant.

The following night, the Cielo Drive murderers accompanied Charles Manson and family members Steve "Clem" Grogan and Leslie Van Houten into a bungalow at 3301 Waverly in Feliz, where homeowners Leno and Rosemary LaBianca were brutally slaughtered. Tom O'Neill points to the CIA's stated objectives, the nature of the research conducted by Roger and David Smith, and their connection to Manson, along with a wealth of other evidence, to argue that the Tate-LaBianca murders were part MK-ULTRA experiment, part CHAOS operation. Though the Manson Family were chemically driven to slay by amphetamines, commonly known as "speed," the American public were led to believe that their crazed violence was the product of LSD. Clearly, acid was not only an agent of peace and love, but also homicidal hatred. Historians of the 1960s often cite the Manson murders as a major death blow to the burgeoning, hippie movement, with its peace and love idealism, support for civil rights, and, most galling to the authorities, profound opposition to the US's ongoing involvement in the Vietnam War. If Tom O'Neill is correct, Operation CHAOS was a roaring success. When O'Neill asked forensic psychologist Alan Scheflin, coauthor of *The Mind Manipulators*—a seminal, 1978 book on MK-ULTRA—if the murders committed by the Manson Family had been an MK-ULTRA experiment gone wrong, he replied, "No . . . an MK-ULTRA experiment gone right."[14]

Not only had the agency created a group of brainwashed killers, they had seriously undermined the liberal, leftist movement to which they had accidentally given birth.

—

Another infamous mass murderer tentatively linked to MK-ULTRA, was Theodore John Kaczynski. From 1978-1995, Kaczynski sent 16 bombs by mail, chiefly to professors, computer stores, and airline officials across the United States, resulting in three deaths and 23 injured, and earning him the moniker the UNABomber (University and Airlines Bomber). In June 1995, letters from the UNABomber arrived at *The New York Times* and *Washington Post* offering to halt his terrorist activities if either publication printed his enclosed 35,000-word manifesto *Industrial Society and Its Future*. After consulting with federal authorities, the *Washington Post* agreed to publish the piece in its entirety. On September 19, it was included as an eight-page supplement to their regular paper.

When Kaczynski's brother, David, read its contents he noticed striking similarities between the UNABomber's Luddite philosophy and the ideas espoused in letters from his brother Ted, a former professor at University of California, Berkeley, who had left suddenly in 1969 and spent the last 25 years living in the Montana wilderness. David reluctantly notified the authorities and Ted

Kaczynski was arrested in his rustic cabin on April 3, 1996, and in 1998, convicted on three counts of murder.

As a child, Theodore John Kaczynski had been blessed and cursed with a 167 IQ. After skipping grades at both Evergreen Park Central Junior High School and Evergreen Park Community High School in Illinois which isolated him from his peers, he graduated at age 15 and was offered a scholarship to study mathematics at Harvard. In 1958, 16-year-old Ted Kaczynski moved into an old house called the Annex 8 Prescott Street on the Harvard Campus.

Kaczynski soon became acquainted with renowned psychologist Dr. Henry Murray, best known for co-developing the Thematic Apperception Test (TAT) test with his wife Christiana D. Morgan. During World War II, Murray had worked with the OSS to formulate a situation test to screen an applicant's abilities to "stand up under pressure, to be a leader, to hold liquor, to lie skillfully, and to read a person's character by the nature of his clothing . . . "[15] According to LSD guru Dr. Timothy Leary, who had also been working as a psychologist at Harvard at the same time, Murray had monitored brainwashing experiments for the US military.

Murray also contributed to the famous *Analysis of the Personality of Adolf Hitler* for Major General William "Wild Bill" Donovan which predicted that Hitler would commit suicide when faced with defeat (*see* Chapter 2: Operation Greywolf). Murray was genuinely concerned about the threat posed to the world by atomic weapons, and believed that if humanity was to survive, people would have to undergo "transformations of personality such as never occurred quickly in human history; one transformation being that of National Man into World Man."[16] To put these ideas in terms we can understand today, Murray believed people would have to be socially engineered away from tribalism and toward globalism to avert nuclear war.

Murray had already resumed Multiform Assessments of Personality Development Among Gifted College Men, a series of highly unethical psychological experiments he had begun before the

Second World War. Among the 22 Harvard undergraduate students chosen to participate in the program was teenage prodigy, Ted Kaczynski. Ironically, Kaczynski was assigned the pseudonym "Lawful." Beginning in the fall of 1959, Murray's research program entailed intensive interrogation—what Murray himself called "vehement, sweeping, and personally abusive attacks." These verbal assaults were deliberately calculated to demolish subjects' egos and most-cherished ideals and beliefs. These character assassinations persisted on a weekly basis until spring 1962, and were essentially a continuation of the mock interrogations Murray had practiced for the OSS.

After Kaczynski's incarceration, author and academic Alston Chase, who had corresponded extensively with Kaczynski, approached the Henry A. Murray Research Center of the Radcliff Institute for Advanced Study at Harvard University and requested to view the records of Murray's experiments. Though he was refused access to Kaczynski's file, as his pseudonym "Lawful" had already been leaked to the press, making anonymity impossible, Chase was nevertheless able to confirm the prisoner's claims of being subjected to Murray's experiments. As a result of former-CIA Director Richard Helms' destruction of countless documents, whether or not the Harvard experiments were an extension of the MK-ULTRA program remains purely speculative; however, Dr. Henry Murray's connection to both the CIA and mind control is indisputable.

—

Following the Watergate Scandal of 1972, President Richard Nixon looked to the CIA for help, only to be turned down by director Richard Helms. When Nixon fired him in February 1973, Helms realized he had lost a powerful ally and was suddenly vulnerable. As a result, he discontinued MK-ULTRA, though conspiracists and serious researchers alike argue that government mind-control research programs continue to this day, cloaked by different codenames.

The destroyed lives of many innocent young Americans and the creation of killers such as Manson and Kaczynski may not have been the only bitter fruits of the CIA's MK-ULTRA program. When Senator Robert Francis Kennedy was gunned down in the kitchen of the Ambassador Hotel in June 1968, many believed that his assassin, Sirhan Sirhan, was a "Manchurian Candidate," a puppet programmed to kill . . .

The Assassination of Senator Robert Kennedy

Robert Kennedy was elected Senator for New York in 1964. During his four years in power, he advocated stricter gun control, cracked down on organized crime, and spearheaded urban redevelopment initiatives. In a horrific instance of history repeating itself, his liberal values made him, like his brother, the target of an assassin's bullets.

When Senator Kennedy visited South Africa in 1966, he gave what is often hailed as his greatest speech, his "Day of Affirmation Address" on June 6. Delivered at the University of Cape Town, this was a bold and courageous statement—a passionate attack on South Africa's apartheid regime. During the ensuing months Kennedy focused on the injustices he perceived plaguing his homeland. He spoke powerfully of alleviating the plight of the poor and underprivileged, working closely with civil rights leaders Dr. Martin Luther King, Jr., César Chávez, and Dolores Huerta. Both privately and publicly, Kennedy advocated scaling back the war in Vietnam, which continued to escalate under the administration of President Lyndon Johnson.

Finally, after meeting and breaking bread with Chavez, who was 25 days into a hunger strike, Kennedy decided to challenge both Johnson and fellow nominee Senator Eugene McCarthy for leadership of the Democratic Party. Kennedy announced his presidential campaign on March 16, 1968, four days after Johnson won the important New Hampshire primary, narrowly defeating McCarthy. McCarthy was running on an anti-Vietnam War platform, so

Kennedy's entry into the race split this voter bloc, and resulted in fierce criticism from McCarthy's supporters.

On March 31, 1968, President Johnson shocked America by announcing he was suspending his reelection campaign: "I have concluded that I should not permit the Presidency to become involved in the partisan divisions that are developing in this political year. With America's sons in the fields far away, with America's future under challenge right here at home, with our hopes and the world's hopes for peace in the balance every day, I do not believe that I should devote an hour or a day of my time to any personal partisan causes or to any duties other than the awesome duties of this office—the Presidency of your country. Accordingly, I shall not seek, and I will not accept, the nomination of my party for another term as your President."[1]

Four days later, Martin Luther King, Jr., was shot dead in Memphis, Tennessee, prompting Kennedy to make his iconic and prescient "On the Mindless Menace of Violence" speech in Cleveland, Ohio.

On April 27, Johnson was replaced by his vice-president Hubert Humphrey in the race to become the Democratic candidate. While Humphrey used "favorite sons" to scoop-up delegates in Florida and Ohio, Kennedy and McCarthy fought neck-and-neck, with the former winning primaries in Indiana (May 7) and Nebraska (May 14), and the latter taking Wisconsin (April 2), Pennsylvania (April 23), Massachusetts (April 30), and Oregon (May 28).

After Kennedy's loss to McCarthy in Oregon, his only hope of remaining in the Democratic presidential contest hinged on victory in California, with its 174 delegates. When a June 1 television debate with McCarthy failed to have the impact Kennedy had hoped, on June 3—the day before the primary—he embarked on a last-minute, 1,200 mile (1,931 km) barnstorm through San Francisco, Long Beach, Watts, San Diego, and then back to his campaign base in Los Angeles. Exhausted, he spent the night at the waterfront home of the film director John Frankenheimer in Malibu. Coincidentally, in light of future events, one of Frankenheimer's best known films was 1962's *The Manchurian Candidate,* starring John F. Kennedy's friend Frank Sinatra as Major Bennett Marco who is brainwashed into becoming a political assassin.

On June 4, Kennedy slept late, before rising to converse on the beach with political journalist and historian Theodore H. White and swim in the Pacific Ocean with his family. Foreshadowing what was to come, Kennedy nearly drowned saving his son David when a large wave suddenly engulfed the child. He spent the rest of the day watching CBS News with White, campaign manager Fred Dutton, and Richard N. Goodwin, a speechwriter and aide, as the results of the California primary slowly rolled in. Early signs were that he would emerge victorious.

—

Fred Dutton drove Kennedy to his campaign headquarters at the Ambassador Hotel, 3400 Wilshire Boulevard. They entered the building at 7:15 p.m., where Kennedy went to his bedroom at Suite 511, and took a phone call from Senator George McGovern. He informed Kennedy that he had defeated both McCarthy and Humphrey in South Dakota. Still, it would be California that would make or break the RFK campaign.

By this time, a number of people had gathered in the hallway of Suite 511, along with approximately 1,800 revellers in the Embassy Room, an overspill directed downstairs to the Ambassador Ballroom by security. There were two professional groups charged with looking after the senator's well-being that evening. The first were the Ambassador's own unarmed guards under the supervision of William Gardiner, while the second were gun-toting hirelings supplied by Ace Guard Services and commanded by Fred Murphy, a former LAPD Lieutenant.

From around 9 p.m., Kennedy periodically left his bedroom to fraternize with the assembly in the hallway, before sitting down for an interview with Roger Mudd of CBS News. In the meantime, Murphy allegedly directed Ace security guard Thane Eugene Cesar to guard the double doors on the west side of the downstairs "pantry"—in reality a small room for drinks and *hors d'oeuvres.*

Just before midnight, Jesse Unruh, Speaker of the California State Assembly, summoned Senator Kennedy downstairs to deliver his victory speech. Not wishing to muscle his way through the crowd, Kennedy asked if there was another option than the main elevators, and was taken via the freight elevator to the ground-floor kitchen. He was escorted south through the kitchen doors and into the pantry, then continued right, through another door that exited onto the stage. It was now 12:10 a.m. on Wednesday, June 5.

As Kennedy approached the dais next to his beloved wife Ethel, the room was filled with chants of "We want Kennedy!"[2] Smiling, the Senator expressed his gratitude to the men, women, and communities who had supported and worked with him throughout his campaign. He then added, "What I think is quite clear, is that we can work together . . . And that what has been going on within the United States over the period of the last three years, the divisions, the violence, the disenchantment with our society, the divisions, whether it's between Blacks and Whites, between the poor and the more affluent, or between age groups or on the war in Vietnam, that we can start to work together. We are a great country, an unselfish country, and a compassionate country. And I intend to make that my basis for running over the period of the next few months . . ."[3]

The crowd erupted with cheers, whistles, and applause, continuing as Kennedy flashed a peace sign, and began to exit stage right, before being redirected to the left. Fred Dutton had determined the Senator's next stop would be the Colonial Room where throngs of reporters awaited. This entailed heading directly back through the pantry. Unfortunately, Kennedy's personal bodyguard, William Barry, was waiting stage right, where the Senator had originally headed, and had to push through a mass of people in an attempt to reach his charge. Protocol necessitated that Barry should always walk in front of the Senator. Instead, Ambassador Hotel *maître d'* Karl Uecker took Kennedy's right hand and led him back into the pantry. As Kennedy passed through the double doors, Thane Eugene Cesar took the Senator's right elbow and helped him through the crowd of over 75 people, pushing them gently away. Bodyguard Rosey Grier followed closely behind, with Ethel trailing him. Robert Kennedy proceeded at a snail's pace, routinely stopping to shake the hands of the staff members who reached out to him. As Kennedy passed an ice machine on his right and steam table on his left, he stopped to shake the hand of Juan Romero, a busboy. Uecker took his arm again.

At once, a young dark-haired man with a vacant smile lurched into Kennedy's path and pointed a gun.

"Kennedy, you son-of-a-bitch!"[4]

Suddenly, the pantry was filled with "pops," flashes, and screams. Kennedy raised his hands, slipping from Uecker's grasp, and stumbled, twisting in a counterclockwise direction. Before anybody knew what was happening, his back hit the floor. Springing into action, William Barry hit the gunman twice in the face, as bodyguards Rafer Johnson, Rosey Grier, and journalists Jimmy Breslin and George Plimpton pushed the shooter against the steam table and repeatedly slammed his hand. He continued firing. Eventually, he relinquished his grip on the revolver. Yet, despite being pinned down by an Olympic decathlete and former defensive line, the attacker managed to wriggle free and grab hold of the pistol once more. His gun was empty. Within seconds, he was securely restrained.

During the confusion, a bullet had struck Schrade in the forehead, dropping him. Others hit ABC associate director William Weisel in the abdomen, reporter Ira Goldstein's left hip, the left shin of campaign volunteer Irwin Stroll, and grazed the hairline of Democratic activist Elizabeth Evans.

With the assailant pinned, William Barry tucked his jacket under Senator Kennedy's head to stop the bleeding. Panicking, young Juan Romero cradled Kennedy's bloodied body and pressed a rosary into his palm, winding it around his right thumb.

"Is everybody okay?" the Senator murmured.

"Yes," Romero replied, "everybody's okay."

Turning away, Kennedy tried to reassure him, "Everything's going to be okay."

Twenty-six hours later, at 1:44 a.m. PDT on November 7, Robert F. Kennedy was pronounced dead at LA's Good Samaritan Hospital. An autopsy confirmed he had suffered three bullet wounds in an indeterminate sequence. The fatal shot had been fired within 3 in (7.6 cm) of his right ear leaving powder burns on the skin and sending a bullet through his right posterior auricular region. This slug had already been removed during an emergency craniotomy. A second bullet had entered through the right posterior chest (upper back), traveling upward at a 67-70-degree angle, before becoming lodged in the subcutaneous area at the base of the neck. It was later removed. The entry wound for bullet number three was located in the posterior right axilla (armpit) but the projectile itself had traveled at a 59-degree angle and exited near the right clavicle.[5]

In short, there were:

- three gunshot wounds, all of which originated behind the victim.
- one .22 caliber bullet retrieved, along with fragments of a second.
- powder burns behind the victim's right ear, meaning the muzzle of the firearm must have discharged within three inches of the entry wound.

A hole in Kennedy's coat indicated a fourth shot had missed his body but penetrated his clothing. Later, this was said to have been the same bullet that struck Paul Schrade in the head.

The LAPD created Special Unit Senator (SUS) to investigate the assassination.

—

The alleged gunman was 24-year-old Palestinian Sirhan Bishara Sirhan.

Born an Arab Christian in Jerusalem on March 19, 1944, Sirhan had witnessed countless acts of Israeli-on-Arab violence while growing up in the West Bank, including the accidental death of his brother, who was crushed by a military vehicle.

In January 1957, the 12-year-old Sirhan immigrated to California in the US with his family, where he attended Eliot Junior High School in Altadena, John Muir High School in Pasadena, and eventually Pasadena City College. His father, reportedly a stern man given to beating his sons, moved back to the Middle East, leaving his family in the US to fend for themselves.

At 5 ft 5 in (1.7 m) tall and 120 lbs (54.4 kg), Sirhan used his diminutive figure to his advantage, relocating to Corona to work as a horse jockey. Following an equestrian accident in 1966, he sustained a head injury, and found himself unemployed and disillusioned with horse racing. At this time, Sirhan's family claim to have noticed a change in the young man—he became irritable and wished to be left alone. He then moved into the home of his brother, Munir, in a working-class neighborhood of Pasadena.

Like Lee Harvey Oswald before him, Sirhan seemed lost in life, repeatedly changing churches from Lutheran to Baptist to Seventh-Day Adventist. He even became a Rosicrucian, and claimed to have learned self-hypnotism from literature supplied by his connections in this esoteric order. One technique was "The candle experiment, where you would concentrate on seeing the flame in the candle. And any color that you wanted it to become. You just look at the flame and think red, for instance, long enough and you will see a red flame. And then a green flame. And then a yellow flame. And then you get to the point where you see any color you want."[6] He would also spend an inordinate amount of time gazing at his own reflection in the mirror, another technique to facilitate autohypnosis.

One day in early 1966, Sirhan asked Munir if he would get him a pistol. Sirhan was not yet a US citizen, and therefore could not legally obtain one himself. Believing his brother simply wished to go sport shooting, Munir purchased an eight-shot Iver Johnson Cadet .22 revolver from a workmate and gave it to Sirhan.

Sirhan later said that he became obsessed with killing Robert Kennedy after learning that, during a speech in Oregon, Kennedy had pledged to give 50 military aircraft to Israel. Sirhan elaborated on this statement during a 1989 interview with British television personality David Frost: "It erupted soon after the 1967 [Arab-Israeli] war where the Arabs had lost, and the Israelis had won—my anger at the American people's reaction to the loss of the Palestinians and the Arabs . . . I was young. I was immature. I was wild. I really didn't have the ability to sit back and reflect on it as just one speech—perhaps one pandering speech—to a potential bloc of voters whom he was appealing to. And now of course I realize that, and I wish I could reverse all my actions concerning Robert Kennedy . . . To me he was my hero. He was my champion. He was the protector and the defender of the downtrodden and the disadvantaged. And I felt that I was one. And to have him say that he was going to send 50 Phantom jets to Israel to deliver nothing but death and destruction on my countrymen, that seemed as though it were a betrayal . . ."[7]

Beginning on February 12, 1969, Sirhan Bishara Sirhan stood trial for the murder of Robert Francis Kennedy. Against his wishes, his attorneys pursued a legal defense of not guilty by diminished capacity. Sirhan Sirhan was convicted on April 17 and sentenced to die in the gas chamber. His sentence was commuted to life in 1972 following the temporary abolition of capital punishment in

California. In the years since, he has unsuccessfully applied for parole on 15 occasions.

At least, that's the *official* version of events.

—

Although it has received a fraction of the attention afforded the JFK assassination, from an evidentiary perspective, the murder of Robert F. Kennedy is equally intriguing.

Like Lee Harvey Oswald, Sirhan Sirhan was labeled a "patsy" by conspiracists—either an unwitting pawn of greater forces *or* the least powerful player in a far-reaching conspiracy. Observing his claims to have no memory of the shooting, many concluded that Sirhan had been a victim of mind control. This speculation gained traction in the mid-1970s with the revelations of the MK-ULTRA program, particularly a 1954 CIA document that detailed attempts to induce a subject "to perform an act, involuntarily, of attempted assassination against a prominent [redacted] politician or if necessary, against an American official"[8] with a recommendation that the unwitting assassin be "surreptitiously drugged through the medium of an alcoholic cocktail at a social party."[9]

This MK-ULTRA angle fit perfectly with one of the most persistent and exotic threads in the RFK assassination conspiracy theory: the mysterious "girl in the polka dot dress."

The day after he was sentenced to death, Sirhan Sirhan sat down with NBC's Jack Perkins for a televised interview. The conversation quickly turned to the events of June 4–5, 1968. Sirhan claimed that he had gone to the Ambassador Hotel to attend the party. After drinking four Tom Collins gin cocktails, he realized he was too drunk to drive home, and needed to sober up.

"I started searching for coffee," he explained. "That was all I wanted to do. And I found some . . . I don't remember where I saw it, but I remember getting the cup. It was a shining . . . urn. And there was a girl there."[10]

"She was a pretty girl?"[11]

"I thought she was."[12]

"Did you think you might try to pick her up?"[13]

"Why not?"[14]

"Did you know Senator Kennedy was in the hotel that night at that time?"[15]

"Sir, I did not know that."[16]

"After you poured coffee for the girl, then what happened?"[17]

"Then I don't remember much of what happened after that other than the choking and commotion [after Kennedy had been shot] . . ."[18]

"The last thing you have a distinct recollection of, you say, is pouring coffee for a girl in the hotel . . . You remember nothing in between [emphasis added]?"[19]

"If I do, sir, I don't know it . . . It's totally out of my mind, so obviously, I don't remember it."[20]

When Perkins brought up a litany of disturbing "RFK must die" scribblings found in Sirhan's diary, he received a similar answer.

"I know, sir, that they are my writings. It's my handwriting; they are my . . . thoughts. But I don't remember them, sir."[21]

"Well, did you only write them when you were in great fits of anger?"[22]

"I must have been, sir. I must have been. They are the writings of a maniac, sir."[23]

Conspiracists latched on to Sirhan's statements—conveniently overlooking the more poignant ones about Kennedy's promise to send Phantom Jets to Israel—and concluded that he was a "Manchurian candidate" programmed to kill by the CIA's MK-ULTRA program.

"This girl kept talking about coffee. She wanted cream. Spanish, Mexican, dark-skinned," Sirhan elaborated in another interview. "When people talked about the girl in the polka-dot dress . . . maybe they were thinking of the girl I was having coffee with."[24]

This enigmatic *femme fatale* was supposedly seen at the Ambassador

Hotel by more than a dozen witnesses, including waiter Vincent DiPierro and Kennedy campaign volunteer Sandy Serrano.

DiPierro's attention had been drawn to Sirhan because he was being followed through the pantry by a "good-looking girl in the crowd there . . . it looked as if she was almost holding him."[25] Sirhan reportedly turned to say something to her, but rather than replying, she had simply smiled back. Though the woman was "very shapely,"[26] DiPierro noted "when she first entered, she looked as though she was sick also."[27] He described the mysterious beauty as a Caucasian in her early-twenties, with brown hair "puffed up a little"[28] and clad in a "white dress with—it looked like either black or dark violet polka dots on it and kind of a [bib-like] collar."[29]

While the girl's proximity to and familiarity with the man who would shoot Robert F. Kennedy minutes later did raise a red flag, subsequent observations made by Sandy Serrano set it ablaze.

According to Serrano, earlier that night, she had observed a person whom she later believed to be Sirhan Sirhan in the company of a man in a gold sweater and a young brunette sporting a bouffant hairstyle and white dress with dark polka dots. They had ascended the fire escape of the Ambassador Hotel. Serrano pegged the girl as being Caucasian, in her mid-twenties, and approximately 5 ft 6 in (1.6 m) tall. Then, after midnight, while Serrano was lingering outside on the same fire escape, the girl and man in the gold sweater suddenly hurried down the stairs, almost stepping on her.

"We've shot him! We've shot him!"[30] the girl declared excitedly.

"Who did you shoot?"[31] Sandy replied.

"We shot Senator Kennedy!"[32]

Writing in *Probe Magazine*, journalist Lisa Pease proposed that the LAPD convinced both DiPierro and Serrano to "admit" that they had only heard about the girl from one another. However, in reality, the department seemingly spent a great deal of time trying to locate this mysterious young woman.

Another favorite of RFK conspiracists is the apparently irreconcilable discrepancy between the autopsy reports and the testimony of dozens of eyewitnesses in the pantry. Both LAPD criminologist DeWayne Wolfer and medical examiner Dr. Thomas Noguchi had concluded through powder tests that the bullet wounds were from "contact shots": The muzzle was either pressed against Kennedy's skin or fired at a maximum distance of 1 in (2.5 cm) away. However, according to Lisa Pease, at least three of the five witnesses best positioned to see Sirhan attack Kennedy in the pantry—Frank Burns, Martin Patrusky, Jesus Perez, Juan Romero, and Karl Uecker—stated that Sirhan was between 18 in to 4 ft (46 cm to 1.2 m) away from his target.[33] This minimum distance was also supported by less reliably placed witnesses such as Richard Aubry, Vincent DiPierro, Pete Hammill, Richard Lubic, Edward Minasian, Valerie Schulte, and Lisa Urso.

Author Mel Ayton In his 2018 article "Who Killed RFK? Sirhan Sirhan Did It" for *History News Network*, disputes this claim, stating, "others, like Vincent DiPerro who was 5 ft (1.5 m) behind the Senator, were certain Sirhan had placed the gun directly at RFK's head."

Furthermore, Pease contests the official conclusion that Sirhan fired all eight shots, emptying his Iver Johnson .22 Cadet revolver, without any additional bullets being discharged in the pantry. This argument relies, to an extent, on Sirhan and Kennedy's relative physical positions, the autopsy reports, and the implausible trajectory of the bullets. Firstly, according to the LAPD, five innocent bystanders—Schrade, Weisel, Goldstein, Stroll, and Evans—were struck with separate bullets, while Kennedy was hit by three. This accounts for all eight possible shots that could have been fired by Sirhan's .22. However, as Sirhan was facing west and Kennedy was walking east with his entourage, including Paul Schrade, who was trailing him, Pease proposed that it was physically impossible for any bullet fired at Kennedy's back to hit Schrade, for the simple reason that Schrade was behind him. Such a feat would have necessitated the bullet making a 180-degree turn in midair, and soaring back over Kennedy's shoulder to strike Schrade's head.

According to Pease, the LAPD also claimed a bullet had been fired into a ceiling tile, rebounded off an unspecified object on the other side, exited through another tile, and struck Elizabeth Evans's head on its descent. This seems highly improbable.

Less convincingly, Pease casts doubt on the possibility of an errant bullet which tore through Ira Goldstein's pant leg, ricocheted off the concrete floor, and struck Irwin Stroll in the left shin.

As further proof of investigative chicanery, RFK assassination conspiracists offer photographs of LAPD members running strings through bullet holes in the ceiling tiles to establish trajectories, along with a picture published by the Associated Press on June 5 that showed Sgt. Charles Wright and Sgt. Robert Rozzi examining what appeared to be a bullet hole in the door frame accompanied by the headline "Bullet Found Near Kennedy Shooting Scene."[34] Later, the famous prosecutor Vincent Bugliosi would track Wright and Rozzi down, and ascertain that the two investigators were not only looking at a hole, they were actually inspecting a bullet embedded in it. According to Bugliosi, when he told Wright that Rozzi had said he was "pretty sure" the bullet was removed, Wright replied, "There is no pretty sure about it. It definitely was removed from the hole, but I don't know who did it."[35] Rather than absconding with a bullet, the LAPD actually removed the doorjambs and ceiling tiles as evidence.

Robert Wiedrich, a reporter for the *Chicago Tribune*, who was in the pantry when the doorjambs were taken away, quite innocently wrote of "a crime laboratory technician's probe [removing] two . 22-caliber bullets that had gone wild."[36] At the time, Wiedrich had no idea of the significance of his observations. Citing two additional eyewitnesses, along with FBI documents that confirmed the presence of two bullets in the center doorframe, Pease declared, "Bullets do not create bullet holes in wood frames behind victims, exit those holes in the reverse direction, and then circle around to enter victims from the front! . . . Two bullet holes in the doorframe would make ten bullets overall *at a minimum*."[37] If true, there can be no other explanation for the presence of nine or more bullets in the pantry other than two guns having been fired, which suggests a conspiracy.

Some conspiracists proclaim Sirhan was unknowingly firing blanks to prevent the "real" assassin from being shot. Witnesses had apparently described a lengthy flame emanating from the muzzle of his revolver as well as paper falling to the floor: allegedly telltale signs of blanks being fired. However, when combined with the "more than eight bullets" claim, this assertion becomes laughable. It would have entailed at least two hidden gunmen with .22 revolvers, in addition to Sirhan, making the pantry a veritable OK Corral for seemingly invisible cowboys.

Unfortunately, the ceiling tiles and doorjambs were no longer available for inspection as early as June 27, 1969, when the LAPD ordered their destruction. Other key items that were lost or destroyed included Sirhan Sirhan's blood test, which would have included his toxicology results, and three rolls of film taken by 15-year-old Scott Enyart for a high school newspaper, allegedly depicting the melee inside the pantry. In the minds of those skeptical of the official account, this missing evidence amounted to further proof of a cover-up.

—

Conspiracists propose that security guard Thane Eugene Cesar, who had drawn his revolver in the pantry—a fact he had personally confirmed, along with at least nine eyewitnesses—was better positioned to fire the shot behind Kennedy's ear. Strangely, nobody from the LAPD asked to see his revolver, which Cesar claimed was a Rohm .38. When questioned later about an H&R .22 pistol he also owned, Cesar said he had sold it before the assassination, but lost the receipt. Nevertheless, police were able to recover a receipt proving that Cesar had actually sold the gun to a friend *after* the assassination.

Adding to their suspicions, Thane Eugene Cesar had only been hired by Ace Guard Services a week before the Kennedy killing, and was moonlighting on the night of the assassination. His primary job was as a plumber at Lockheed's "Skunk Works" in Burbank, California—the same CIA-affiliated facility that manufactured the U-2 and A-12 spy planes flown at Area 51. According to Cesar, he was granted the second-highest level of security clearance granted by the Department of Defense. This placed Thane Eugene Cesar right in the intelligence agency/military industrial complex nexus—powerful organizations that had more than a few axes to grind with Bobby Kennedy.

Cesar, an admirer of pro-segregation presidential candidate Governor George Wallace, had a history of making disparaging remarks about the Kennedys and espoused far-right views, even after the assassination: "I definitely wouldn't have voted for Bobby Kennedy because he had the same ideas as John did, and I think John sold the country down the road. He gave it to the commies. He gave it to whoever else you want him to . . . He literally gave it to the minority. He says 'here, you take over. I'm giving it to you. You run the White man.' Nobody should be run. I'm not saying that the Whites should be the slaves of the Black or Black the slaves of the White. But he turned the pendulum too far the other way."[38]

Regarding the events of the RFK assassination, Cesar simply stated, "When the shots fired, I reached for my gun and got knocked down. I got back up, and I had my gun out, but they already had him [Sirhan] restrained."[39]

Over the years, Thane Eugene Cesar has become such a prominent alternate suspect in the RFK assassination that hours after his death in the Philippines on September 10, 2019, Robert Kennedy, Jr., announced his belief that Cesar, *not* Sirhan Sirhan, had murdered his father: "Cesar waited in the pantry as my father spoke in the

MK-ULTRA

A 1994 portrait of Swiss chemist Albert Hoffman, accidental discoverer of lysergic acid diethylamide (LSD).

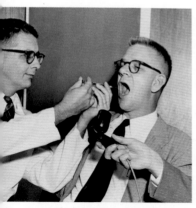

An early medical experiment on the effects of LSD, carried out at Emory University, Georgia, in 1955.

Murderous cult leader Charles Manson (left) used LSD to control his Family.

The Merry Pranksters' bus at Woodstock, August 1969.

LSD can take you places you never dreamt of.

A 1970 poster aimed at the young warns of the grave dangers of experimenting with LSD.

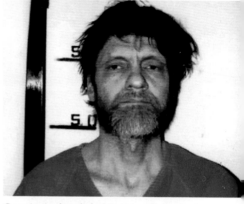

Conspiracists have linked American domestic terrorist Theodore John Kaczynski, aka the Unabomber, to the CIA's MK-ULTRA brainwashing program.

The Assassination of Senator Robert Kennedy

Joyful Democrat supporters mob presidential hopeful Robert Kennedy. Soon, joy would give way to despair.

Busboy Juan Romero kneels beside the dying candidate.

Assassin Sirhan Sirhan is seized: Conspiracists claimed that the lone-wolf killer was a victim of mind control.

Robert F. Kennedy's state funeral, June 8, 1968.

Denied parole: Sirhan Sirhan at a hearing in 1986.

Evidence photographs of the handgun used by Sirhan Sirhan.

The Moon-Landing "Hoax"

Apollo 11 lifts off from NASA's Kennedy Space Center, July 16 1969.

The Apollo 11 crew (from left): Neil Armstrong, Michael Collins, Buzz Aldrin.

Conspiracists questioned whether the image of Armstrong's first step on the moon was genuine.

This iconic picture of Buzz Aldrin saluting the American flag has provoked much speculation among conspiracy theorists.

Is the Earth Really Flat?

Flat Earth fans in Orange County,
California, March 25, 2017.

This 17th-century print celebrates
numerous famous mariners who had
circumnavigated the globe.

Samuel Shenton,
founder of the
International Flat
Earth Research
Society, pictured
in 1967.

Samuel Rowbotham's
1864 flat-Earth map
shows land masses and
oceans enclosed by
walls of ice.

Environmental Modification Weapons

Conspiracists have linked disasters, such as the 2010 earthquake in Haiti to US government weather interference.

The sky trails left by jet aircraft have led to increased speculation that they contain dangerous chemicals.

The HAARP facility, Alaska, blamed for numerous strange phenomena, including the "Windsor Hum."

Mary Rich, mother of Seth Rich, pleads for information about her son's death at a press conference in August 2016.

Julian Assange, the controversial founder of WikiLeaks.

DNC chairman Debbie Wasserman Schultz praised Seth Rich for protecting voters' rights.

July 31, 2018: Conspiracists hold up placards at President Trump's "Make America Great Again" rally.

The Mysterious Life and Death of Jeffrey Epstein

Virginia Roberts Giuffre, whose testimony helped expose Epstein's sex-trafficking operation.

Billionaire businessman and convicted sex criminal Jeffrey Epstein, pictured in 2013.

Linked to Epstein: media mogul Robert Maxwell with daughter Ghislaine and wife Elizabeth in 1990.

Epstein's lavish Palm Beach mansion, just one of his many homes.

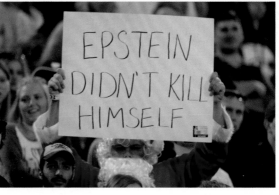

Suicide or murder? Conspiracy theories followed Epstein even after his death.

COVID-19

The "wet markets" of Wuhan, China, a possible source for the Coronavirus pandemic.

A shrine outside Kings College, Cambridge, UK, pays tribute to Dr. Wenliang, villified by the Chinese authorities for alerting the world to COVID-19.

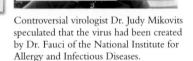

Controversial virologist Dr. Judy Mikovits speculated that the virus had been created by Dr. Fauci of the National Institute for Allergy and Infectious Diseases.

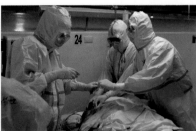

Doctors in full PPE battle to save a patient in intensive care, San Salvador, Spain, August 2020.

July 2020: after initially downplaying the virus, President Trump began appearing in public wearing a mask.

Regent Street, London, deserted during government lockdown, March 2020.

ballroom, then grabbed my father by the elbow and guided him toward Sirhan . . . Sirhan fired two shots toward my father before he was tackled. From under the dog pile, Sirhan emptied his 8 chamber [sic] revolver firing 6 more shots in the opposite direction, 5 of them striking bystander [sic] and one going wild . . . By his own account, Cesar was directly behind my dad holding his right elbow with his own gun drawn when my dad fell backwards on top of him. Cesar repeatedly changed his story about exactly when he drew his weapon . . . According to coroner, Dr. Thomas Noguchi, all 4 shots that struck my father were 'contact' shots fired from behind my dad with the barrel touching or nearly touching his body . . . Cesar sold his .22 to a coworker weeks after the assassination warning him that it had been used in a crime. Cesar lied to police claiming he'd disposed of the gun months before the assassination . . . Cesar was a bigot who hated the Kennedys for their advocacy of Civil Rights for Blacks . . . The LAPD Unit (SUS) that investigated my dad's assassination was run by active CIA operatives. They destroyed thousands of pieces of evidence . . . Sirhan's appointed lawyer was Johnny Rosselli's personal lawyer, Grant Cooper. Roselli was the mobster who ran the assassination program for the CIA against [Fidel] Castro. Cooper pressured Sirhan to plead guilty so that there was no trial . . . Sirhan, to this day, has no memory of the assassination."[40]

Author Dan Moldea, who spent many hours interviewing Thane Cesar, asked him if he would agree to be hypnotized or take a lie-detector test in 1994 regarding the events surrounding the RFK assassination. Cesar agreed. After sitting down with the esteemed Los Angeles polygraph examiner Edward Gelb to answer questions, Gelb informed Cesar, "These charts are so clear and so blatant that I can tell you right now that you had absolutely nothing to do with the Kennedy assassination. I can see the way the scores are adding up right now, indicating you didn't fire a weapon, you didn't shoot at Kennedy, and that you weren't part of any plan to assassinate Robert Kennedy."[41]

In keeping with this, RFK conspiracy theory skeptic Mel Ayton has cited new ballistics evidence that Ayton says proves Cesar did not discharge his Rohm .38 that night. Ayton observed that, if Cesar had indeed sold his H&R .22 pistol in the aftermath of the RFK assassination to distance himself from the murder weapon, why did he wait three months to do so?

Ayton also challenged the whole "second gunman" theory by demonstrating how conspiracists have manipulated statements by initial witnesses Marcus McBroom, Sam Strain, and Dr. Fred S. Parrott; while continuing to promote the previously debunked accounts of Patricia Nelson and Dennis Weaver as evidence; and ignoring photographic evidence and retractions or clarifications by witnesses Booker Griffin, Evan Freed, and Don Schulman.

Regarding the issue of Sirhan's alleged lack of proximity to Kennedy, Ayton points to research by Dan Moldea that reveals that the majority of the eyewitnesses only observed Sirhan's position during his first shot—which was at a distance—and failed to see subsequent maneuvers that allowed him to place the muzzle of the revolver right against the Senator's head. Among the notable exceptions are journalist George Plimpton's wife, Freddy, who, according to Moldea, "saw an arm go up toward Senator Kennedy's head, but did not see a gun, heard shots and it was obvious to her that Senator Kennedy had been shot . . . She saw Sirhan very clearly. She saw his arm up toward Senator Kennedy's head . . ."[42] and DiPierro who clarified that Sirhan "was 3 ft [90 cm] away but the muzzle of the gun (in his outstretched arm) couldn't be more than 3 to 5 inches [7.6 to 12.7 cm] away from his head."[43] Likewise, Kennedy's posterior wounds are easily explained by the fact that the senator had turned at least 90-degrees to shake busboy Juan Romero's hand seconds before the shooting, exposing the right side of his back and head to Sirhan.

Finally, Ayton torpedoes the girl-in-the-polka-dot-dress narrative. He posits that no rational actor involved in a highly sophisticated murder would flee the crime scene loudly boasting of their involvement. He does, however, allow for the possibility that a woman shouting amidst the chaos may have been misheard or taken out of context—for instance, given the rash of assassinations in the 1960s, the "we" in "we shot Kennedy" could potentially represent hotel attendees, the Democratic Party, the American people, or even humanity as a whole.

Ayton also debunks the popular notion that dozens of eyewitnesses had seen a girl wearing a polka-dot dress. He notes that the two most oft-cited "polka-dot girl" witnesses, Sandy Serrano and Vincent DiPierro, had been together at the police station after the shooting. Ayton recounts how DiPierro told a Sgt. Hernandez, "[Sandy Serrano] stated that there was this girl that was wearing a polka dot dress [who] came running down, I guess it was the hallway, saying that 'We shot him,' and . . . she . . . you know, we started asking each other questions about the girl, and evidently I went along with what she said as being a person that I imagine that I saw."[44] As for Serrano, her story crumbled once she was subjected to a polygraph test. Conspiracists typically respond to this by alleging the police must have browbeat her into recanting. Another favorite speculation is that certain officers actually worked for the CIA. If true, this ever-widening ring of conspirators would have included Fire Department Captain Cecil R. Lynch. He had inspected the fire escape Serrano was supposedly sitting on alone for 50 minutes while Senator Kennedy was addressing the crowd, but found no evidence she had ever been there.

Finally, Ayton concedes there were multiple young women wearing polka dot dresses, or similar attire at the Ambassador Hotel at the time—after all it *was* the 1960s—but the LAPD were ultimately able to account for all of them. Not only have studies shown that eyewitness testimony is notoriously unreliable, especially during chaotic events, but there were obviously countless male and female voices shouting about the terrible fate that had befallen Senator Kennedy. Given the magnitude and disorder of the situation, it would have been impossible to confidently recount the exact words of any screaming individual.

As for Sirhan Sirhan being a mind-controlled patsy, conspiracists often allude to what they consider a nonsensical outburst he made during his trial, in which he insisted on pleading guilty, stating "I killed Robert Kennedy willfully, premeditatedly, with 20 years of malice aforethought . . ."[45] They argue that Sirhan could not have possibly entertained assassinating Kennedy for a period of 20 years as the Palestinian would have been five-years-old and Kennedy was still unknown at the time. Thus "mind control." In doing so, the conspiracists conveniently overlook a crucial clarification made by Sirhan in 1989: "[With that courtroom statement] I tried to really show that the Palestinian problem did not just suddenly erupt with the shooting of Bobby Kennedy. That there was a history to it that dated back to 1947 or 1948, when the state of Israel was created forcibly on the Arabs and when the Palestinian Arabs were forced to evacuate and to be expelled from their homes and lands to accommodate the new . . . Jewish arrivals in Palestine."[46] The year of Kennedy's assassination was exactly 20 years after 1948.

Still, the bizarre bullet trajectories and proposition that more than eight shots were fired are not as easily dismissed. Ayton admits that most of the more than 75 victims had no idea how many shots they had heard, but provides the names of 30 who all placed the number at eight or less. These include Hamill, Unruh, Aubry, Grier, Freddy Plimpton, Breslin, Perez, and Johnson.

Nevertheless: how does a bullet make a sudden radical change of direction in mid-air?

———

Today, many historians see the RFK assassination as the first of a series of violent engagements between the Arabic world and United States, a tragic and bloody dialogue that sadly persists.

After years marred by the suspicious assassinations of a forward-thinking president and his fearless, even more progressive brother, it is hardly surprising that many in the world responded with doubt when an American man finally reached the height of human achievement on July 20, 1969, by walking on the moon. By the end of the 1960s, the West had entered a state perhaps best described by the era's most popular music group: *nothing* is real . . .

The Moon-Landing "Hoax"

On July 21, 1969, at 2:56 am UTC, an estimated 600 million people gathered around television sets all over the globe to watch in awe as Commander Neil Armstrong stepped out of the Lunar Module *Eagle* and onto the moon's dusty surface. But not everyone believed what they were seeing, and theories of an official conspiracy slowly began to gather pace . . .

"It's one small step for man," Armstrong's voice crackled authentically over the feed, "one giant leap for mankind." No one seemed to notice or care that Armstrong, one of three American astronauts on the *Apollo 11* voyage, had flubbed his lines, saying "man" instead of "*a* man," the magnitude of the achievement overwhelmed such petty concerns. Eight years after President John F. Kennedy's promise to reach the moon by the end of the 1960s, National Aeronautics and Space Administration (NASA) had finally done it! Besides honoring the word of a beloved statesman, cut down by a sniper seeking recognition not in creation, but in destruction, this staggering achievement redeemed the hopes of a generation—one that had seen profound social change, sometimes for the better, all too often for the worse.

Nineteen minutes later, Colonel Edwin "Buzz" Aldrin—who had piloted the *Eagle* from *Apollo 11* to the moon—joined Armstrong in a 21-hour, 36-minute lunar romp that included planting the US flag on the surface. The event marked not only the height of human technological accomplishment, but ingrained the names Armstrong and Aldrin as heroes and aspirational figures in the fabric of history.

Thirty-three years later, Americans chuckled in nihilistic bemusement as clips of a 72-year-old Aldrin decking "documentary" filmmaker Bart Sibrel with a right cross aired on *CNN International*, *The Tonight Show With Jay Leno*, and *The Late Show With David Letterman*. Sibrel had approached Aldrin outside the Luxe Hotel in Beverly Hills, badgering him to swear on the Bible that he had walked on the moon. Despite the best efforts of the bellman to dissuade Sibrel from harassing Aldrin, the conspiracist persisted. Aldrin remarked, "You really like attention, don't you?" prompting Sibrel to reply, "You're the one who said you walked on the moon when you didn't. Calling the kettle black . . . you are a coward, and a liar, and a th—"[1] His final insult was cut short by Aldrin's fist connecting with his mouth.

Although many applauded the astronaut's no-nonsense manner of handling Sibrel, it was in many ways a sad reflection of what the nation had become. By 2009, polls in the US, UK, and Russia revealed that 25 percent of people believed that the Moon Landing was a hoax.[2] How did it come to this?

—

The first book to call the Moon Landing into question was William Kaysing's *We Never Went to the Moon: America's Thirty Billion Dollar Swindle*, published in 1976. It is likely no accident that this book gained traction in the mid-1970s, a time when the American public's mistrust of government was at an all-time high. The Watergate Scandal, in which spies working for President Richard Nixon attempted to break into the headquarters of the Democratic National Committee in Washington, D.C., had finally concluded with Nixon's resignation on August 9, 1974, after two years of continuous cover-ups. To make matters worse, his successor, President Gerald Ford, pardoned Nixon on September 8, revealing that there was seemingly no bottom to this abyss of government corruption. The following year, the CIA sheepishly admitted the existence of the MK-ULTRA program, and Saigon fell to Vietnamese Communist forces, despite the wasteful loss of more than 58,000 American lives. In no time, a Moon-Landing conspiracy theory was full blown; it waned in the '80s, only to regain credibility with the birth of the internet.

Moon-Landing conspiracists point out that by 1967 NASA showed little prospect of ever fulfilling Kennedy's dream. The Soviet Union had already put the first man into space, cosmonaut Yuri Gagarin, on April 12, 1961, beating the American Alan Shepard by almost a month. And while American rocket technology was sufficient to put a large vessel into orbit, thanks largely to the genius of the former Nazi scientist Wernher Von Braun (awarded the National Medal of Science by President Ford in 1977), NASA still struggled mightily with auxiliary tasks, such as guiding a manned spacecraft and determining how to safely land it on the moon and bring its occupants safely back to Earth. Even the nation's most beloved astronaut, Virgil "Gus" Grissom, one of the first Americans in outer space, was openly critical of the program, complaining that NASA was racing to meet a deadline at the expense of astronauts' safety. Of particular concern was the amount of flammable Velcro in the cabin. Earning the nickname "Gruff Gus," on April 1, 1966, Grissom and two fellow crew members photographed themselves gathered in mock prayer around a model capsule. On August 19, they presented the photograph to Apollo Spacecraft Program Office manager Joseph F. Shea bearing the humorous inscription: "It's not that we don't trust you, Joe, but this time we've decided to go over your head."[3] Grissom even hung a lemon from the flight simulator at Cape Kennedy to express his frustration regarding the unreliability of the existing technology.

Though clearly cognizant of the danger, Command Pilot Grissom and fellow astronauts Ed White and Roger Chaffee boarded Apollo command and service module #012 at Cape Kennedy on January 27, 1967, for a launch rehearsal test in preparation for a lunar mission scheduled for February 21. Tragically, at 6:31 pm, the cabin burst into flames, instantaneously immolating the three men. While most people regarded the demise of the Apollo crew as a horrific accident—though, arguably, one that should have been prevented—certain Moon-Landing conspiracists interpret it as a ruthless and calculated act of murder.

Given the well-documented inadequacy of the Apollo program in 1967, "moon truthers" believe that NASA and other government officials, specifically the CIA, had come to terms with the fact that it would be impossible to reach the moon by the end of 1969, Kennedy's deadline. These authorities also recognized that the *perception* that Americans had accomplished this landmark feat was more important than the *reality* of accomplishing it. This was true from both a public and international relations perspective. If the Soviet Union *believed* the US had pulled ahead of them in the space race, this disinformation would nevertheless serve as a useful deterrent against Russian aggression. Similarly, the illusion that America had overtaken their Communist rival and made good on Kennedy's promise would provide a much-needed boost to national morale. In other words, rather than actually landing on the moon, it would be far easier and less costly to simply fake it. Of course, a true scientist and patriot like Gus Grissom, America's favorite astronaut, would never agree to participate in such a deception on any level. Therefore, Grissom had been eliminated, with White and Chaffee written off as collateral damage, in order to make room for those who prioritized fame and glory above truth.

This supposed "Moon Landing," conspiracy theorists say, must have been filmed in a circular studio about the size of an airport fuel tank, allowing photographers to film convincing 360-degree panoramic footage. Many conspiracists have presented Area 51 as the location where this propaganda was secretly created.

In fact, there was a genuine connection between the Apollo program and the Nevada Test Site (NTS) that houses Area 51. According to the Pulitzer Prize finalist Annie Jacobsen, Neil Armstrong, Buzz Aldrin, and subsequent Apollo astronauts were all flown into Areas 7, 9, 10, and 20 of the NTS to hike across its rugged terrain, circumvent massive boulders, and climb through vast subsidence craters created by previous nuclear explosions. Traversing the NTS's decimated desert wasteland proved to be invaluable practice for walking on the moon.

—

There is no shortage of evidence purportedly proving that the Moon Landing was a hoax. The most common, and one of Kasing's central theses, is that in photographs taken by astronaut Neil Armstrong, using a 70mm lunar surface camera, the American flag appears to be flapping, despite the fact there is no atmosphere—and hence no wind—on the moon. In this case, the scientific rebuttal actually stems from the same soil as the criticism. Aware that the lack of wind would cause the Star-Spangled Banner to droop, producing underwhelming photographs, NASA designed US flags embedded with extendable rods to ensure the flag appeared fully unfurled. However, when the time came, Armstrong and Aldrin struggled to extend the rod all the way, which created the illusion of rippling fabric in their still photographs. In video footage, the flag can also be observed moving when the astronauts are twisting it into the ground. Space historian Chris Riley has since pointed out that, once you make a flag swing in a vacuum, it will continue to do so because there is no air to slow it down.

Another "gotcha" put forth by Kasing and other Moon-Landing conspiracists is that the photographs show a complete absence of stars in the pitch-black firmament. This is easily explained. Owing to their white space suits and the brightly illuminated lunar surface, the Apollo astronauts were using daylight exposures rather than the longer shutter speeds needed to capture the relatively dim stars. This can easily be verified by taking a quick-exposure camera onto your back porch at night, flipping on the lights, and snapping pictures of the heavens. Even though you can still see the stars with your naked eye, the camera will be unable to document them for the aforementioned reasons.

Kasing's final bone of contention with the astronauts' Moon-Landing photos is that they do not show a blast crater where the *Eagle* supposedly landed. However, this is because the typically concentrated exhaust jet from a rocket engine flares into a conical shape when operating in a vacuum, lessening the pressure in the exhaust and causing very little disturbance to the dusty earth below.

Beyond Kasing's criticisms, a popular talking point among conspiracy theorists involves the overabundance of light compared to shadow, along with the fact that this light appears to be electrical in origin rather than solar, and seemingly emanates from multiple sources. These criticisms can be accounted for by uneven topography, subtle changes in gradation, and the very different manner in which light bounces off the surface of the moon compared to Earth, once again, due to the absence of an atmosphere.

Conspiracists have also noted that there are objects still visible on the moon even though they are clearly in shadow, arguing this would not be possible if the sun was the only source of light. They argue that this is more reminiscent of the unnatural lighting one observes in a Hollywood film. However, according to Dr. Rick Fienberg, press officer for the American Astronomical Society: "Sunlight is being scattered or reflected off the ground every which way, and some of it—a small fraction but enough to be able to see—scatters into the shadows."[4]

Among the weaker rebukes is that there were no independent witnesses to confirm the event. From the moment *Apollo 11* took off until the astronauts returned to Earth, the only source of information on the mission was NASA, the alleged hoaxer itself! Yet, approximately 400,000 Americans worked on the Apollo project in some capacity. Even if we reduce this number to hundreds, the notion that so many people *could* or *would* successfully conspire to deceive the global population without a single reliable whistleblower emerging stretches credulity to breaking point. Furthermore, even if there were independent witnesses, they would have had to receive extensive training by NASA in order to survive in space, at which point conspiracy theorists would likely conclude they had been similarly compromised and thus could no longer be considered "independent witnesses."

Perhaps the most powerful argument for a Moon-Landing hoax comes from *Nexus Magazine UK* publisher Marcus Allen, who finds the quality of the photographs far too good, considering they were taken by men "wearing armored gauntlets through which you couldn't actually feel anything"[5] using a camera without a viewfinder. Further complicating matters, Armstrong and Aldrin would have had to manually set the aperture and shutter speed on their cameras under seemingly impossible conditions. Chris Riley has addressed this by pointing out that the astronauts likely received extensive training in photography under difficult circumstances, long before ever launching into space. Moreover, Armstrong and Aldrin took far more pictures than are generally presented to the public, including many that were poorly framed or out of focus. These did not find their way into the mass media for obvious reasons—they were aesthetically dreadful. Funnily enough, Allen's criticism directly contradicts another favorite "silver bullet" of the conspiracists that the images of Armstrong and Aldrin were deliberately shot in black and white and made fuzzy to obfuscate the scene. Here we have a clear example of confirmation bias: good quality photographs indicate a cover-up; likewise, if the photographs are of poor quality.

—

A further point made by conspiracists is that the Moon-Landing footage bears a startling resemblance to scenes in film director Stanley Kubrick's 1968 classic *2001: A Space Odyssey*, released just one year before the *Apollo 11* mission. Author and filmmaker Jay Weidner believes that *2001* was actually a research and development project to prepare Kubrick for the task of filming sham Moon-Landing footage in collaboration with the US government. Claiming to have spoken with "Hollywood special-effects people from the '60s and '70s who were front-screen projection experts,"[6] Weidner confidently proposes that the Moon-Landing footage was produced using front-screen projection: a process that combines performances in the foreground with previously filmed background footage. To support his case, he points to the fact that the bottom of the screen is always concealed in both the relevant *2001* scenes and lunar footage, adding that every time an Apollo image has a visible background, a line separating the foreground set and the screen is clearly visible. Weidner also cites the observations of the author Richard C. Hoagland who discerned strange light reflections in the Moon-Landing footage's black sky. Hoagland interpreted these reflections as emanating from a gargantuan glass city built by extraterrestrials—one of many alternative lunar-related "rabbit holes"—but Weidner explains these supposedly anomalous reflections as coming from little beads on the Scotch light screen used in front screen projection.

Convinced that Kubrick was the mastermind behind the Moon-Landing footage, Weidner began to scour his subsequent films for clues that the notoriously controlling and symbolically-inclined director might have planted. Weidner seemingly found some in *The Shining*.

Released in 1980, *The Shining* is based on Stephen King's novel of the same name, and stars Jack Nicholson, Shelley Duvall, and child actor Danny Lloyd as the ill-fated Torrance family. When novelist Jack Torrance (Nicholson) accepts a position as winter caretaker at the isolated and snowbound Overlook Hotel in Colorado, the Torrances find themselves trapped in a seemingly haunted building with a violent and sordid past. Initially viewing his stint at the Overlook as an opportunity to work on his novel, Jack begins to slip into madness and entertain thoughts about hacking his wife, Wendy, and 6-year-old son, Danny, into pieces with an axe.

Watching the film, Weidner spotted a smattering of references that could potentially be related to the Moon Landing; however, he remained aware that he could simply be seeing what he wanted to see. One example was an oversized can of TANG orange drink powder in the Overlook pantry, a beverage mix famously used by astronauts, including the Apollo 11 crew, and actually present in some of the Moon Landing shots. Then, nearly an hour into the film, Weidner struck conspiracy-theory gold.

In a particularly eerie scene, Danny is seated alone at the end of a hallway, playing with his toy trucks. Then, silently and inexplicably, a ball rolls along the carpet, and comes to rest directly in front of him. When Danny rises to look where the ball has come from, he is wearing a blue sweater depicting a rocket blasting into space. On the side of the rocket are the words "Apollo 11 USA." Walking tentatively down the hall, Danny sees the door to room 237—which he has been warned never to enter—ajar. A key dangling from the lock bears the words "ROOM No 237." Curious, Danny enters the room, only to emerge later in the film with his sweater torn and unexplained bruising around his neck.

The Apollo 11 sweater needs no explanation other than to show that Kubrick may be leading the viewer to think of the Moon Landing. However, Weidner notes that of the text on the room key, only the letters R O O M and N are capitalized. These letters, he claims, can be rearranged to spell only two words: "moon" and "room." According to Weidner, Room 237 therefore represents the Moon-Landing set—a forbidden space that contains knowledge of Kubrick's secret involvement in the lunar-landing hoax.

In Stephen King's novel, the forbidden room is 217. Kubrick claimed to have changed this to 237 at the request of the owners of the Timberline Lodge in Mount Hood, Oregon, where exterior shots of the Overlook Hotel were filmed. Kubrick added that the owners were concerned guests would be frightened to be assigned room 217, so he simply changed the room number in his movie to 237, which did not exist at the Timberline. However, when Weidner contacted the Timberline Lodge, he learned that there was no Room 217 at the establishment. Why would Kubrick have lied? Pondering the possible significance of the number 237, Weidner claimed that most science textbooks at the time stated that the moon was located approximately 237,000 miles (381,415 km) from Earth!

In addition, according to Weidner, the pattern of the hallway carpet bears a striking resemblance to launchpad 39a at Cape Kennedy from where most of the US's manned space missions blasted off.

Later on in *The Shining*, Wendy nervously suggests to Jack that they should leave the Overlook. He responds furiously: "Have you ever thought for a single solitary moment about my responsibilities to my employers? . . . Does it matter to you at all that the owners have placed their complete confidence in me, and that I have signed a letter of agreement, a contract, in which I have accepted that responsibility?"[7]

Shortly afterward, Wendy sneaks into Jack's study and, thumbing through his stack of typewritten pages, is horrified to discover that instead of writing his novel, her husband has spent the last few months hammering out "All work and no play makes Jack a dull boy," over and over again.

Weidner interprets these scenes of conflict between Jack and Wendy Torrance as representing Kubrick's own tempestuous experience of hiding the *Apollo 11* hoax from his beloved wife, Christiane, only to have her discover the true nature of his work anyway. The employers at the aptly named "Overlook" represent the US government officials that placed their trust in Kubrick to handle the job competently and in complete secrecy.[8]

Film analyst Rob Ager took a critical view of Weidner's Apollo-Kubrick-*Shining* theory. Firstly, he observed that, contrary to Weidner's assertion that you can only make the words "moon" and "room" out of the letters R O O M N, there is also the possibility of "on"; "or"; "moor"; "norm"; "rom"; "moo"; and perhaps most fittingly "moron"—the sole word that uses all five letters. Ager also consulted numerous scientific sources, but failed to find a single mention of there being 237,000 miles (381,415 km) between the Earth and moon, though the number 239,000 (384,633 km) did come up. Checking the Timberline Lodge website, Ager also learned they had once had a Room 217 but changed the number owing to *The Shining*'s fame.[9] These revelations would seem to invalidate Weidner's claims, even though the Kubrick conspiracist has hinted that he has received "visitations" and has allegedly been surveilled.[10]

—

Surprisingly, America's most prominent conspiracy theorist, InfoWars host Alex Jones, rejects ideas that the Moon landing was a US government hoax altogether. Instead, Jones views NASA's very real space-exploration missions as part of a public relations campaign to distract from the primary projects and goals of their "shadow government." These are to establish a rogue "break-away civilization" and conduct interdimensional meetings with "little three-foot-tall gray creatures with green hats . . . "[11] called the Clockwork Elves. According to Jones, after World War II, Nazi "paperclip" scientists such as Wernher Von Braun informed US intelligence that the Third Reich had been using narcotics and child murder to pierce the veil of reality and interface with alien beings. It was largely through such interactions that Nazi Germany was able to obtain various technological advantages during the war.

Jones maintains that the existence of the Clockwork Elves has been recorded by "every culture from Japan to Latin America, Meso-America to Ancient Europe to the Norse . . . "[12] Histori-cally, these entities were contacted during psychotropic shamanic rituals "usually at ancient sites . . . like Stonehenge or the pyramids in Egypt, the pyramids of Mexico, or pyramids in Peru—these sacred sites, because of the magnetic lines of the huge mercury nickel core of the earth—and it's shooting out all this stuff that opens up gates . . . "[13] The human sacrifices that took place during these ceremonies were made to attract the Clockwork Elves, "like chumming for sharks in the ocean, putting blood out. The sharks start showing up, they're going to get fed."[14]

Acting upon this Nazi-derived knowledge, the American establishment/elite/globalists—allegedly including politicians, prominent Silicon Valley leaders, and celebrities—have been attending psychedelic rituals presided over by black magicians in attempts to communicate with the elves. At the main project centre in San Francisco, Jones asserts there are "astronaut-level people taking super hardcore levels of drugs and going into meetings with these things and making intergalactic deals"[15] by mind-melding to obtain advanced technologies.

Despite their initial, fairly harmless-seeing appearance, the Clockwork Elves are malevolent and "have horns when they show you who they really are . . . but they don't contact you unless you contact them, and then they are almost not even concerned with what you're doing."[16] In the past, these interdimensional aliens were conceived of as demons, thus the communion rituals often take on the character of devil worship.

—

In many ways, the ardor and persistence of moon truthers like the previously mentioned Bart Sibrel—who posed as a History Channel interviewer to confront and provoke Apollo astronauts—barely seems worth the effort. Even if the Apollo missions *were* faked, the decades since the last moon landing have shown us that, beyond serving as Cold War propaganda, landing on the moon ultimately had little or no effect on our collective wealth, well-being, or lives. However, Sibrel's insistence that astronauts "swear on the Bible"[17] that they walked on the moon may betray a more fundamental and dangerous belief: the Flat-Earth conspiracy theory. All at once, the moon truthers' struggle transforms from simply exposing a scientific deception to waging a Biblical information war: a divinely sanctioned mandate to discredit the lunar missions at all costs . . .

Is the Earth Really Flat?

One of the most longstanding conspiracy theories is the belief that Planet Earth is really flat, rather than imperfectly spherical. Despite overwhelming scientific evidence to the contrary, "flat-earthers" refuse to admit defeat. Though ridiculed by many, the conviction that the Earth is flat does have its disturbing implications.

Christopher Columbus might have discovered America in 1492, but he was far from the first fellow to prove the world was round. In 240 BCE, the Greek mathematician Eratosthenes was head of the library in Alexandria, Egypt. One day, he learned that no vertical shadows were cast at noon on the summer solstice in Syene (now Aswan), a city to the south. Eratosthenes conducted an experiment to see if this was also the case in Alexandria. When the solstice arrived on June 21, he jammed a stick into the earth, stood back, and waited. Upon observing a vertical shadow measuring seven degrees, he realized that if the sun's rays were coming from the same angle at the same time of day, this must mean that the Earth has a curved surface—a hypothesis put forth by the mathematician Pythagoras 260 years earlier. Not yet satisfied with this astounding revelation, Eratosthenes hired a man to walk from Alexandria to Syene, and learned the distance between the two was 5,000 stadia, or 497 miles (800 km) in modern measurement. Armed with this data, Eratosthenes was able to use mathematics to calculate the Earth's circumference: 24,855 miles (40,000 km).

The notion that almost everybody on Earth believed it to be flat until Columbus "sailed the ocean blue" is also a widespread myth. The *globus cruciger*—an orb with a cross on top of it—is a symbol of authority in Christendom dating back to the Early Middle Ages (5th-10th century CE) and can be seen in the clutches of statues and portraits of the emperors Charlemagne, Frederick I Barbarossa, and Charles II of Naples and Hungary, to name a few. All these images pre-dated Columbus' voyages. Furthermore, ancient mariners were able to spot the sails of a distant ship gradually emerging over the horizon, and had long concluded that the world was, at the very least, not flat. In fact, the esteemed science historian Stephen Jay Gould has argued, "There never was a period of 'flat earth [intellectual] darkness' among scholars (regardless of how many uneducated people may have conceptualized our planet both then and now). Greek knowledge of sphericity never faded, and all major medieval scholars accepted the earth's roundness as an established fact of cosmology. [King] Ferdinand and [Queen] Isabella [of Spain] did refer Columbus's plans to a royal commission ... composed of both clerical and lay advisers ... All assumed the earth's roundness. As a major critique, they argued that Columbus could not reach the Indies in his own allotted time, because the earth's circumference was too great."[1]

—

Contrary to popular understanding, flat-earth theory only bloomed in the late-19th century. In part, this was due to conflict thesis—an imperfect academic historiography concerning the so-called "battle" between religion and science—promulgated by John William Draper and Andrew Dickson White, along with the heavily romanticized *A History of the Life and Voyages of Christopher Columbus* by author Washington Irving, who more famously penned *The Legend of Sleepy Hollow*.

The man who truly got the flat-earth theory rolling was Samuel Rowbotham, a religiously-disposed English inventor who apparently "confirmed" the world was flat in 1838, in accordance with scripture, after the first Bedford Level experiment. In this experiment,

Rowbotham entered the Old Bedford River carrying a telescope 8 in (20 cm) above the water. Using the device, he observed a boat— the flag on its mast positioned 3 ft (91 cm) higher than the water—row away from him. It remained constantly in sight for 6 miles (9.7 km). Rowbotham reasoned that if the Earth was indeed curved, the top of the mast would have been 11 ft (3.4 m) beneath his sight line. Rowbotham's error, exposed by Alfred Russel Wallace in 1870, was in failing to account for the effects of atmospheric refraction.

Eleven years after the Bedford Level experiment, using the pseudonym Parallax, Rowbotham published his findings anonymously in a 16-page pamphlet, *Zetetic Astronomy*. In 1864, he expanded his tract into a book under his own name. Rowbotham's *The Earth Not a Globe* cites more than a dozen such experiments to conclude that the "whole mass [of the Earth], land and water together constitute an IMMENSE NON-MOVING CIRCULAR PLANE. If we travel by land or sea, from any part of the earth in the direction of any meridian line, and towards the northern central star called 'Polaris,' we come to one and the same place, a region of ice, where the star which has been our guide is directly above us, or vertical in our position. This region is really THE CENTER OF THE EARTH and recent observations seem to prove that it is a vast central tidal sea, nearly a thousand miles in diameter, and surrounded by a great barrier wall of ice, eighty to a hundred miles in breadth in every direction *human ingress is barred by unsealed escarpments of perpetual ice* [emphasis added], extending farther than eye or telescope can penetrate, and becoming lost in gloom and darkness."[2]

Rowbotham also provided an overhead diagram of the flat earth's surface in *Earth Not A Globe* (reproduced in this book's second 8-page photographic section).

Samuel Rowbotham's convoluted geography provided the prototype upon which the vast majority of subsequent flat-earth theories were modeled.

Rowbotham's works were published by the English printer William Carpenter, who became his disciple. In 1879, Carpenter immigrated to the United States and settled in Baltimore, where he continued printing and disseminating flat-earth literature consistent with Rowbotham's assertions. Meanwhile, back in England, Rowbotham founded the Zetetic Society in 1883, but it quickly dissolved after his death the following year. On September 21, 1892, the nondenominational Universal Zetetic Society (UZS) was founded by John Williams of Southwark. At the first UZS meeting at his home, the founders created the following set of rules:

OUR MOTTO
For God and His truth, as found in Nature and taught in His Word.

OUR OBJECT
The propagation of knowledge relating to Natural Cosmogony in confirmation of the Holy Scriptures, based upon practical investigation.

RULES
1. Everything extraneous to "Our Object" to be avoided.
2. The so-called "sciences," and especially Modern Astronomy, to be dealt with from practical data in connection with the Divine system of Cosmogony revealed by the Creator.
3. Every honest opponent to be treated with respect and consideration.
4. Members *to subscribe not less than six shillings a year, which entitles them to two copies of The EARTH (not-a-globe) REVIEW each issue, and a copy of every paper issued by the Society. Such will be also eligible to be voted to serve on Committees, to vote on motions, to write articles (subject to editorial approval) for the Earth Review, and to propose (subject to Rule 8.) any alteration thought to be beneficial to the Society.*
5. Associates *to subscribe not less than two shillings and sixpence per year, which entitles them to a copy of every publication issued by the Society.*

6. All subscriptions to the Society to be paid in advance (quarterly if desired) and to the Secretary.

7. The financial year to commence on September 21st.

8. Three months notice to be given in writing to the Secretary, before any alterations, or additions to the Rules can be made. The Secretary to bring any suggested alteration or addition before the whole of the Committee, to vote on the final decision.

9. Every meeting of the Society to be opened with prayer and the reading of some portion of the Holy Scriptures.

10. The Society's meetings to be held (pro. tem.) at 32, Bankside, Southwark, London, S.E.

Though it was already present, these rules codified confirmation bias—"The tendency to test one's beliefs or conjectures by seeking evidence that might confirm or verify them and to ignore evidence that might disconfirm or refute them"[3]—into the very fabric of the organization. Never financially viable in itself, the UZS was kept afloat by funding from wealthy divorcee Lady Elizabeth Blount of Bath, who oversaw the publication of the society's *Earth: a Monthly Magazine of Sense and Science* from 1901-1904.

Twenty-one years after Blount's death, professional sign writer Samuel Shenton of Dover, UK, created the International Flat Earth Research Society to continue the work of the UZS. He attributed satellite images showing the planet's curvature to a deliberate trick using a wide-angle lens to deceive the public. After Shenton died, his library was passed across the Atlantic to mechanic Charles K. Johnson, who presided over the International Flat Earth Research Society of America from 1972 until 2001. Under Johnson's leadership, the society became unabashed in its religious fundamentalism, reportedly growing to 3,500 members and publishing the quarterly *Flat Earth News*.

By the time of Charles K. Johnson's demise, the Internet was already pumping information into homes across the developed world. Given this technological marvel, it did not take long for flat-earth conspiracy theories to make an unexpected and powerful return.

—

The multiplicity of flat-earth media, groups, and conspiracists in the Internet age is so great it is impossible to fully chronicle them here. Naturally, any modern belief in a flat earth must entail support for the moon-landing hoax, along with varying degrees of skepticism regarding satellites. It must also reject the authenticity of satellite imagery. Therefore, NASA is unavoidably complicit in the alleged global scientific cover-up.

The first 21st-century flat-earth conspiracist to make an impact on YouTube seems to have been Math Powerland, a pseudonym for Matthew Boyland. In his video "NASA Insider Exposes the Flat Earth!," Powerland claimed to be a former contract artist for NASA. While attending a party in the Hamptons with NASA's elite, he was laughingly informed that GPS systems do not work in Antarctica because the Earth is flat.

Having viewed Powerland's video along with alleged suspicious flight patterns in the southern hemisphere, conspiracist Mark Sargent began to look into flat-earth theory, supposedly to debunk it. According to Sargent, after nine months of research, at 3:30 a.m. on February 10, 2015, he woke up with an epiphany—the world *is* flat. His first video, "FLAT EARTH Clues Introduction," received enough positive responses to encourage him to continue making more. Sargent became "King of the Flat Earthers."

"FLAT EARTH Clues Introduction" purports that, "for the first 4,000 years of our civilization we believed that the Earth is a flattish disk surrounded by a solid dome barrier called the firmament. All of the five major religions had their own version of this, and the churches enforced the belief. Then, around 1514, a man named Copernicus . . . stated that if the Earth was spinning around 1,100 miles an hour [1,770 kph] and circling the sun at 60,000 miles an hour [96,560 kph] the world was then round . . . The new world view was promoted and took hold. The religions adapted to handle the new reality, and life moved on."[4] As the opening paragraphs of this chapter shows, Sargent was factually incorrect in a number of these assertions.

To support his theory, Sargent stated that he watched the Plane Finder global map for more than 45 days, unsuccessfully trying to find a nonstop flight crossing the South Pacific or Indian Oceans from the southern hemisphere. Whether Sargent was lying or merely incompetent, at the moment of this writing, the website shows a half-dozen planes doing exactly that.

Sargent, who by his own admission is an avid fan of cinema, proposes that "You are actually in a giant planetarium/terrarium/soundstage/Hollywood backlot that is so big that you, and everyone you know, and everyone you've ever known, never figured it out."[5] Essentially, he has taken the skeleton of the Moon Landing Footage Hoax—a much stronger conspiracy theory as it entails a deception perpetrated in a tiny, remote area—and applied it to every aspect of the material reality we inhabit on an ongoing basis. He is convinced that the Earth and sky are encased in a dome, and that the sun and moon are merely lights in the sky. Approximately 70 percent of [21st]-century flat-earth theorists believe in the dome, while 30 percent subscribe to an alternative hypothesis.

—

Naturally, if there is a far-reaching conspiracy to conceal the true nature of the universe from humankind, the questions "Why?" and "By whom?" arise. One of the most prevalent answers to the former revolves around an anti-Christian agenda. Flat-earth conspiracist Nathan Thompson has articulated a version of this: "The Biblical cosmology is a geocentric cosmology . . . they don't want anyone to know anything . . . so they can inject them with their vaccines, and their public schooling and this heliocentric model, which is basically forced sun worship."[6] Thompson also believes "they" made up dinosaurs to convince people the world is older than it actually is.

According to Patricia Steere, the former host of a conspiracy YouTube channel entitled "Flat Earth and Other Hot Potatoes," conspiracists have implicated "the Jews, Masons, Rothschilds, Rockefellers, Jesuits, Satanists, [and] the Vatican"[7] in this deception, to name a few. Math Powerland has named NASA, the FBI, CIA, and National Security Agency (NSA). A not-uncommon misconception circulating in the flat-earth community is that NASA—when pronounced "nasha"—is a Hebrew word meaning "to deceive."

Powerland also proposes that his competitor Sargent is actually "Dennis Luka,"[8] a Warner Brothers executive operating in "an intelligence fashion."[9] Powerland believes this entertainment company has a deal with a number of government agencies.

Many flat-earth conspiracists also suspect Patricia Steere of being a CIA "honeypot." The clues are apparently evident in her name: PatriCIA who uses her physical attractiveness to "steer" male flat earthers in the government-sanctioned direction and away from the truth. Steere also claimed that she has been accused of being a blood-drinking member of the so-called Reptile elite (*see* Chapter One). In a fleeting moment of lucidity, she confessed, "I wonder if in their hearts, if people who do that know they're lying or are they so conspiratorial [sic] that they actually believe it? Then it makes me worry about maybe things I believe in. Am I like another version of them?" before quickly adding, "but I know I'm not."[10]

In mid-2019, Steere abruptly canceled her YouTube channel and walked away from social media. Her account of what prompted her sudden departure, *Everything That Was Beautiful Became Ugly: Escaping Flat Earth* by author Noel Hadley became available for purchase on Amazon that summer.

—

That the flat-earth conspiracy theory has gained any traction whatsoever is patently absurd. Looking back at the JFK and RFK assassinations, and to a lesser extent, Operation Greywolf, it is understandable why the public would seriously question the official narratives. In fact, in the first two cases, it is almost equally delusional to state that one believes the investigators' conclusions with 100 percent certainty—there are far too many peculiarities and loose ends not to leave a shred of doubt. In other cases, such as the Nazi Ratlines and MK-ULTRA, what were once conspiracy theories have since been confirmed as conspiracies that legitimately took place. That said, by no means every aspect put forth by conspiracists turned out to be accurate. But would we seriously expect them to repeatedly hit the bullseye? Even the UFO sightings around Area 51 turned out to be real. However, they were classified military and surveillance technologies, rather than extraterrestrial spacecraft. It is at least plausible that the most sensible theories concerning the Men In Black visitations (FBI or CIA agents etc.) and the Moon Landing (actually happened, but footage faked) may have been accurate.

Flat-earth theory is altogether different. One merely has to think logically in order to debunk it, or rely on the countless epistemological eviscerations the scientific community has offered up.

A good place to begin when assessing the potential merit of a given conspiracy theory is to ask two questions: (1) how many people would need to be complicit, and (2) of that number, what percentage would be civilians with no meaningful ties to intelligence agencies or the military industrial complex? A conservative estimate of the number of conspirators needed to maintain the illusion that a flat earth is really round would be hundreds of millions—many sailors, all long-distance pilots (and, arguably, air-traffic controllers), every politician above the municipal level in countries all over the world, practically the entire scientific community, and countless explorers. Clearly, they cannot all be in the pockets of a "them" or intimidated into silence. Not only would this have to be true of people operating in these professions in our own lifetimes, but also throughout history.

A second devastating blow to flat-earth theory is the simple empirically-validated fact that one can sail or fly a plane consistently in one direction and arrive back at the location of departure without having to perform a 180-degree turn. This simply could not happen on a flat-earth without the vessel crashing into an alleged ice wall, or in its absence, falling off the edge of the planet.

On September 20, 1519, the legendary Portuguese explorer Ferdinand Magellan departed from Spain with a fleet of five vessels, and sailed west. The ships passed through the South American strait which would later be named for him, and into the Pacific. Upon reaching the Philippines, Magellan was killed in the Battle of Mactan, but his crew continued westward under the command of Juan Serrano and Duarte Barbosa, finally arriving in Spain on September 6, 1522.

The first pilot to fly around the world was Hugo Eckener who left Lakehurst, New Jersey, on August 8, 1929, heading east in the *Graf Zeppelin* with journalists Lady Grace Drummond-Hay and Karl von Wiegand, explorer Hubert Wilkins, and cameraman Robert Hartmann. It continued in this direction for three weeks until landing back at Lakehurst on August 29. Less than two years later, on June 23, 1931, American pilot Wiley Hardeman Post and his Australian navigator Harold Gatty flew east in *Winnie Mae*, a single-engine monoplane, from Roosevelt Field on Long Island, New York. Having traversed the globe, they landed back at Roosevelt Field eight days later on July 1.

Mark Sargent's critique of astrophysics is equally myopic: "You think you're on a globe spinning at 1,000 miles an hour [1,609 kph]. That globe is spinning around the sun at 60,000-plus miles an hour [96,560 kph]. That solar system is flying sideways through the galaxy at half a million miles an hour [804,672 kph], and that galaxy is going through the rest of the universe at millions of miles an hour. And you feel *nothing*?"[11] Here Sargent overlooks an important consideration. As human existence evolved on Earth and every human being, with the exception of those astronauts who have actually visited space, has only ever been on Earth, there is no point of comparison that would allow us to discern a difference. For example, if someone were to hypothetically spend all of their time in an arid climate, they would never know what dankness felt like, because they would never have experienced it. This does not negate the existence of humidity.

If, for some unfathomable reason, these rebuttals are insufficient, the celebrity astrophysicist Neil deGrasse Tyson—literally "He-Who-Shall-Not-Be-Named"[12] in the vocabulary of flat earth conspiracists—offers countless mathematical and scientific counterarguments debunking the conspiracy theory on YouTube.

—

It is a strange paradox that the resurgence and popularity of flat-earth conspiracy theories in the 21st century have been almost entirely the result of "improvements" in information technologies. Despite its many benefits, the Internet has not only connected once-isolated conspiracists, but has also ensnared mankind in a digital web of lies, errors, and misinformation. As a response, the credibility of the mainstream media, obliged to compete for audience share, has suffered. Every conspiracy theory in the remaining chapters has been born of or borne by the internet. While, socially we are coming together, at least superficially, psychologically, we appear to be falling apart.

Environmental Modification Weapons

The godlike ability to control weather has long been an aspiration for the world's superpowers. But has secret US government tech achieved this seemingly impossible, disturbing goal, endangering people's health and even the entire planet?

On November 13, 1946, Vincent Schaefer, a chemist for General Electric, flew over the Berkshire Mountains in upstate New York. After depositing 6 lb (2.7 kg) of dry ice in a cloud, resulting in snowfall in west Massachusetts, he became the first man in history to successfully "cloud seed."

In the 75 years since, governments around the world have regularly practiced cloudseeding, generally to cause precipitation. Beginning in 1955, the US conducted a series of airplane missions to drop chemicals, usually lead and silver iodides, into hurricanes in an attempt to weaken them. In 1962, this led to the establishment of Project Stormfury, supported by the US Navy and Department of Commerce. This was subsequently considered a scientific failure and abandoned in 1983.

One CIA-sponsored weather modification project kept hidden from both the public and high-ranking government officials was Operation Popeye. During the Vietnam war, the North Vietnamese Army circumvented the provisions of the 1954 Geneva Accords by secretly smuggling supplies and manpower into South Vietnam using the so-called Ho Chi Minh Trail—a series of footpaths, hidden structures, and tunnels running through the jungles of eastern Laos and northeast Cambodia. Between 1967 and 1972, Operation Popeye saw the US Air Force seed clouds all over Indo-China in an attempt to extend the monsoon season. Operating under the motto "make mud, not war," the pilots of the 54th Weather Reconnaissance Squadron aimed to transform the Ho Chi Minh Trail into a sludge pit, bogging down the enemy's trucks, creating landslides, and flooding river crossings. Reportedly the brainchild of National Security Advisor Henry Kissinger and Robert McNamara, neither disclosed Operation Popeye to McNamara's successor, Secretary of Defense Melvin Laird. Because he had never authorized the operation, Laird unknowingly denied the existence of military weather-modification programs to Congress and was forced to apologize in 1974. Journalists had been reporting on the use of weaponized cloud seeding in Vietnam since 1971; finally, two days after an article on Operation Popeye was published in the *New York Times* on July 3, 1972, the project was suspended. It remains the first known use of militarized weather in history.

As with the Nazi escapee reports and the MKULTRA operations, the revelation of a top-secret, joint CIA/USAF weather modification operation laid the groundwork for future conspiracy theories. These have typically focused around the HAARP research center and the reported presence of "chemtrails" in the skies.

—

In the early 1990s, BAE Advanced began constructing a scientific research facility in Gakona, Alaska: HAARP. Resembling a super-villain's base in a 1980s action film, the High-frequency Active Auroral Research Program station consists of an Ionospheric Research Instrument (IRI) and a suite of other scientific and diagnostic instruments. The IRI is comprised of 180 dipole antennae clustered in 12 to 15 unit arrays spanning a 33–acre (13.4-hectare) area. A number of transmitters located in trailers feed power to the antennae from the main building.

According to Bob McCoy, director of the Geophysical Institute at the University of Alaska Fairbanks, the HAARP program was designed to conduct "active experiments in the ionosphere . . . at

100 kilometers up . . . We can do experiments. We can create bubbles. We can heat small sections. We can create waves. We can excite plasma residences . . . We can transmit signals all around the world. We can study the effects of the ionosphere. It basically makes the ionosphere a laboratory. And we can do experiments that no one else can do. It's a laboratory without walls."[1]

Yet author Nick Begich insists HAARP is being used for far more sinister purposes. Begich and co-author Jeane Manning's 1997 exposé *Angels Don't Play This HAARP: Advances in Tesla Technology* accuses HAARP of both environmental warfare and mind control. The opening pages state that HAARP will be used for "Earth-penetrating tomography" (looking through layers of the Earth to locate underground facilities or minerals)[2] and "communications with submarines."[3] These claims have been confirmed by the Pentagon.[4] However, Begich and Manning cite a patent (#4,686,605 with the USPTO) assigned to ARCO Power Technologies Incorporated (APTI) which supposedly mapped onto HAARP's proposed transmission of energy into the ionosphere. In the author's view, this technology could be used to disrupt communications systems over large areas of Earth to destroy, deflect, or confuse missiles and aircraft; and for weather modification by altering solar absorption, and increasing concentrations of ozone and nitrogen in the atmosphere.

While this patent *does* exist and is quoted in *Angels Don't Play This HAARP*, the authors admit they cannot confirm whether or not APTI was actually using the patent in conjunction with HAARP. In addition, the US military denies there has ever been any link between HAARP and these patents.

According to the Geophysical Institute at the University of Alaska Fairbanks, who now runs the facility, HAARP is unable to control or manipulate the weather because the radio waves it transmits are not absorbed by the troposphere or stratosphere. Moreover, even the sun's ionospheric storms barely affect the weather, let alone HAARP with its far more limited capacity.[5]

However, many conspiracy theorists find it difficult to believe that a facility and program formerly managed and administered by the Air Force Research Laboratory (AFRL), Office of Naval Research (ONR), Naval Research Laboratory (NRL), and *particularly*, the Defense Advanced Research Projects Agency (DARPA) has not been—and is perhaps still being—used for more sinister purposes.

DARPA was founded in 1958 by President Dwight D. Eisenhower, just a year after the Soviet Union had terrified the governments of the Western world by sending the world's first man-made satellite *Sputnik* into orbit around the Earth.[6] Known as ARPA until 1996, DARPA began its long and checkered career with Operation Argus. Between August 27 and September 9 , 1958, three nuclear missiles were launched from the South Atlantic 300 miles (480 km) into space, detonating in the magnetosphere. The aim was to create a long-lasting belt of high-energy electrons that would theoretically cause future intercontinental ballistic missiles to malfunction. Ultimately, Argus was a total failure, recklessly perpetrated by a cabal of scientists who should have been well aware that it could have triggered an apocalyptic cataclysm. Only two weeks earlier, a group comprised of many of the same "masters of war" had sent the nuclear warhead Orange on Werner von Braun's Redstone rocket 28 miles (45 km) into the air at Johnston Atoll, Hawaii, risking blowing a hole in the ozone layer![7]

DARPA also played a part in Operation Ranch Hand, the scandalous Vietnamese War operation in which US airplanes sprayed the herbicidal defoliant Agent Orange over the jungles of Indo-China, causing horrific injuries and illnesses to as many as 3 million Vietnamese. More recently, DARPA has been dabbling in military artificial Intelligence reminiscent of Skynet from James Cameron's *Terminator 2,* and even bio-weaponized insects. Naturally, these programs have been presented to the public as defensive and benevolent, though the potential for them to go seriously awry or to be used aggressively is obvious.[8]

Given DARPA's track record of careless and dangerous environmental projects, it is no wonder that its involvement in HAARP was viewed with extreme suspicion. While Nick Begich's assertions about HAARP's weather control capabilities are up for debate, it is difficult to argue with his assessment that Americans "need to have a debate about how HAARP is used and what are the applications. And in the Congress right now we have no scientists to speak of. There's no one to evaluate in the closed secret hearings that take place. They can't take notes [at the secret hearings], they can't take their staff [to the secret hearings], and they can't take experts [to the secret hearings]. It's like putting Kindergartners in a college setting and expecting them to figure it out. We've got the wrong people making very important decisions that affect all of us on this planet."[9]

Despite an absence of evidence definitively linking HAARP to any natural disasters there has been no shortage of speculations over the years. At 4:53 pm ET on January 12, 2010, a 7.0 Mw earthquake decimated Haiti and the Dominican Republic resulting in 200,000 deaths and causing approximately $8.5 billion in damage. Venezuelan President Hugo Chavez blamed the US government for "playing God by testing devices capable of creating eco-type catastrophes."[10] It has been reported that the state-run Venezuelan media proposed that the Haitian earthquake "may be associated with the project called HAARP, a system that can generate violent and unexpected changes in climate."[11]

In an October 26, 2012, article published on the popular and controversial conspiracy website Infowars.com, Kurt Nimmo reported that the convenient timing of Hurricane Sandy had raised suspicions that the disaster had been engineered by the "ruling elite."[12] Following a presidential debate between Barack Obama and Mitt Romney, Hurricane Sandy had served as a distraction from the sitting president's perceived lackluster performance, while encouraging the American public to see him as a heroic savior. To support his assertions, Nimmo cited information from Haarpstatus.

com that claimed that HAARP frequency levels were elevated in the ionosphere over the East Coast in the week leading up to the storm. Nimmo referenced Operation Popeye to show that there was historical precedent for secret weather modification programs.

HAARP is also suspected of causing the phenomenon known as the "Windsor Hum." Since 2010, residents of Windsor, Canada— an industrial city across the river from Detroit in southwestern Ontario—have reported hearing a pulsing, *vump vump* bass sound that comes and goes with no discernible cause, or point of origin. The Hum has resulted in insomnia, headaches, irritability, and mood disorders among Windsorites, and also among the citizens of McGregor and Cleveland, Ontario, 20 miles (32 km) to the south and 90 miles (145 km) to the east, respectively. It has reportedly caused windows to rattle, floors to vibrate, and pets to cower in fear. However, although the sound has been determined to exist, only some people can actually hear it.

Inventor Woody Norris, who has worked on projects for DARPA, believes that the Hum is the result of so-called sky quakes, which he describes as "the equivalent of a spectral sound that seems to come from nowhere except above your head."[13] Norris proposes these sky quakes could only be produced by HAARP because there are no other known sources that are capable of generating the amount of energy necessary to create this sound. For instance, where the US's most powerful radio stations put out a comparatively meager 50,000 watts, HAARP is capable of radiating 3 million! Rather than intentionally targeting Windsor with noise pollution, Norris proposes the city's notorious hum is a biproduct of HAARP manipulating the ionosphere and forcing air molecules to collide, creating sound— similar to how lightning gives birth to thunder. But this assumes that the Windsor hum is definitely a sky quake.

Reflecting on the earliest responses to the Windsor hum, local activist Gary Grosse recalled, "The first thing we needed to do is ask the question 'is it coming from the ground?' or 'is it coming from the sky?' Natural Resources Canada came in [to Windsor].

They set up three seismometers and through triangulation, what they found was that it was coming from the vicinity of Zug Island."[14] This spot has similarly been identified as the likeliest origin by researchers from the University of Windsor.

Zug Island falls on the American side of the border, and is technically part of River Rouge, Michigan. A major manufacturing center, this "highly guarded, smoke- and steam-belching, fire-spewing wasteland"[15] is home to a historic steel mill with three blast furnaces and several other industrial facilities owned by US Steel. These blast furnaces are considered the most plausible cause of the Windsor Hum, even by the city of River Rouge itself.

Another school of conspiratorial thought holds that the sky needs to be filled with electrical conductive materials in order for HAARP to function. This aerial seeding is done through another alleged practice linked to weather modification known as "chemtrails."

—

One of the most prevalent conspiracy theories of the 21st century, chemtrails—nefarious chemicals, metals, or biological agents supposedly sprayed across the skies by airplanes on orders from the government—first entered the culture in 1996 when the USAF Issued a report on weather modification operations.[16]

The word "chemtrail" is a portmanteau word combining "chemical" and "trail." Similarly, "contrails"—"condensation" plus "trails"—are the white lines left in the sky behind airplanes owing to moisture in the air. Many of us see them on a daily basis and are so accustomed to the phenomenon that we usually don't take note of them. From a scientific perspective, contrails form when an airplane is flying at an altitude of 25,000 to 30,000 ft (7620 to 9144 m), where the temperature hovers around -40°F (-4.4°C)—well below freezing. The plane's jet engine sucks in moist air, heats it, and spews it back out. When this warmed, moist air collides with freezing temperatures, it forms small ice crystals that linger in the sky before eventually dissipating. Hence, the more moisture there is in the air, the longer the contrail and the greater its duration.

Though contrails had been a fixture of life for over half a century, since the late '90s, numerous individuals began to view them as "chemtrails," including celebrities such as actress and comedian Roseanne Barr, former Smashing Pumpkins frontman Billy Corgan, the late music virtuoso Prince, and reality TV star Kylie Jenner.[17] Leading this conspiratorial charge was investigative journalist William Thomas, a regular guest on the late Art Bell's hugely popular *Coast to Coast* radio program, which focused on paranormal incidents and conspiracy theories. In 2004, Thomas published his findings in *Chemtrails Confirmed*—the canonical text on this particular conspiracy theory—which exacerbated the chemtrail hysteria.

Another influential proponent is filmmaker Michael Murphy, whose 2012 documentary *Why In the World Are They Spraying?* (*WITWATS*) features a variety of former USDA scientists and other talking heads who claim that testing has revealed aerosol and metal particulates, notably aluminum, in rainwater. Among them are former television weatherman Scott Stevens. They propose these substances are causing widespread ecological catastrophe, as well as increasing the prevalence of allergies, asthma, attention-deficit disorder, Alzheimer's disease, and autism. These effects are the unintended consequences of geo-engineers' attempts to control the weather for a variety of nefarious purposes: to wage covert warfare; profit from weather derivatives; enable corporate land-grabs; and increase the market value of genetically modified crops. Conspiracy theorists claim that these weather ops work in tandem with HAARP.

To the layman, *Why In the World Are They Spraying?* can be fairly convincing as it points the finger at controversial private enterprises such as the Monsanto corporation, famous for producing genetically modified seeds, along with well-meaning scientists, who, by trying to solve the world's climatic problems, have naively exacerbated them. The film shows footage of planes with multiple con/chemtrails streaming from their wings, and points out that the plane's engine is located elsewhere. This would seem to rebut the argument that these are simply contrails generated by moist air entering the engine.

Writing for eSKEPTIC.com, geologist Dr. Donald Prothero explains that "in the subfreezing conditions of the upper troposphere or stratosphere . . . sometimes just the disruption of the high atmospheric gases by the tips of wings will cause contrails, even without the benefit of engine fumes . . . often they remain stable for minutes in quiet air."[18] Regarding the notion that specific areas could be targeted, Prothero counters that spraying *anything* at an altitude of 30,000 ft (9,144 m) would cause it to disperse in an unpredictable manner hundreds of miles from where it was actually released, owing to high winds. For this reason, aircraft fly at no more than 30 ft (9 m) when crop-dusting: an altitude where contrails cannot form.

Skeptic Mick West was a particularly painful thorn in *WITWATS*'s side. He noted that the cost of controlling weather globally far exceeded any profit that could be made from the weather-derivatives market. After crunching the numbers, West concluded that an organization would have to spend tens of billion dollars annually for 20 years to even reach a place where there was an above-average probability of profiting.[19] Even more damningly, West noted that the tests *WITWATS* performed to obtain their findings of aluminum in rainwater actually tested sludge—a mixture of dirt and water—and that soil *naturally* consists of 7 percent aluminum.[20]

—

As well as weather manipulation, HAARP and chemtrails have both been accused of being mind-control technologies. A number of conspiracy theorists—including the aforementioned Nick Begich—propose that HAARP also possesses the capacity to disrupt communications systems on a mass scale.

While it is tempting to dismiss these conspiracy theories as mostly harmless, a sincere belief that a malevolent "they" are using HAARP or chemtrails to endanger individuals or the planet as a whole can lead to fears that, in turn, give way to violence. For years, HAARP employees regularly received threatening phone calls from outraged citizens. On Thursday, October 27, 2016, Michael Mancil, 32, and James Dryden, Jr., 22, were arrested by Coffee County Sheriff's officials following a tip-off that the men were purchasing an alarming number of semi-automatic firearms and ammunition. Questioned in custody, Mancil, a known methamphetamine user, divulged the duo's plan to forcibly take over the HAARP facility. He declared that the facility was imprisoning people's souls and preventing them from ascending to heaven, which he intended to stop by blowing up the relevant machine and releasing the confined spirits.[21] Ironically, by the time of Mancil and Dryden's scheduled invasion, HAARP had been shut down for three years, with control of the facility transferred from the US government to the University of Alaska Fairbanks.

Less than two months later, another conspiracy-theory-addled gunman would embark on a mission to save the innocent from a very different manifestation of "them," bursting into a pizzeria in Washington, D.C., armed with an AR-15. It all started with some leaked emails . . .

WikiLeaks and the Murder
of Seth Rich

The 2016 **US** federal election was unlike any other in American history. As Democratic president Barack Obama prepared to exit the White House with a 57 percent approval rating[1] after two terms, the name of his successor was ostensibly a done deal—or was it?

Hillary Rodham Clinton—a former corporate lawyer, FLOTUS, and New York Senator—had run an aggressive campaign for the Democratic presidential nomination in 2008, serving as Secretary of State from 2009 to 2013. Not only did she have name recognition and diverse experience, there was also a sense of historical momentum behind her campaign. Obama had broken through one glass ceiling by becoming the first African American president; now there was a feeling that Clinton would do the same for women. Yet, her detractors often pointed to a perceived sense of entitlement or that she felt she was "owed" the presidency. Some even posited that behind her facade of compassion lay a ruthless careerist who would stop at nothing to serve her own needs and that of globalist corporatism. Moreover, while Clinton gave lip service to progressive values, there was at least one formidable, deceptively charismatic individual with a far richer history of progressive activism to challenge her for the Democratic nomination: Senator Bernie Sanders. And she was overlooking him.

Enter Donald Trump. Like Clinton, he was born the child of a successful businessman and was thoroughly urban, though his wealth and privilege far exceeded her own. From the 1980s to the 1990s, Trump was New York City's most renowned (and arguably powerful) real-estate mogul, one with a conspicuous habit of becoming embroiled in lawsuits and filing for bankruptcy. By the 21st century, Trump had shifted his entrepreneurial focus to branding and the entertainment industry, hosting the successful reality television shows *The Apprentice* and *The Celebrity Apprentice*. After nearly 30 years of publicly musing whether or not to make a serious presidential run, he surprised the world in 2016 by finally throwing his hat into the race for the Republican nomination. From the outset, his campaign was largely disregarded as not being "serious"; however he received overwhelming media attention, and played well to the cameras, thumbing his nose at political correctness and conventional etiquette. Despite widespread accusations of racism, misogyny, xenophobia, and sexual assault Trump shocked the Republican establishment on May 3, 2016, by becoming the presumptive nominee. Unlike Clinton, his rise was anything but predictable.

When Clinton finally defeated Sanders in early June, the stage was set. Two of the most polarizing figures in American political history were now competing for the highest office. And for large swaths of the population, the thought of the "other" candidate winning was absolutely unacceptable. In fact, it meant the end of America as they knew it. Few gave Trump much of a chance.

—

By early summer, the election was already turning out to be the most divisive, dishonest, and vitriolic in recent memory. Then the first of many information bombs exploded. On June 14, Crowd-Strike, a cyber security company, made a shocking public announcement on behalf of the Democratic National Committee: the DNC's computer network had been hacked by two separate computer espionage groups—Fancy Bear and Cozy Bear—both known to work for Russian intelligence. The DNC first became aware of the hacking in April when IT employees noticed unusual activity. Their discovery came shortly after the breach by Fancy Bear, which seemed solely interested in obtaining the DNC's research files on political adversary, Donald Trump. Cozy Bear, which favored a more conventional, long-term espionage approach, had infiltrated the DNC system a year earlier. While Fancy Bear was known to work with Russia's Main Intelligence Directorate (GU), there was less certainty about Cozy Bear's clientele, though American intelligence strongly suspected it was the Federal Security Service of the Russian Federation (FSB).

Having infiltrated the DNC network, the hackers were able to gather every email and other electronic communication that had passed through it: a sizable chunk of what DNC members had written online to one another. Fancy Bear had also made numerous attempts to hack Trump's and Clinton's personal networks, albeit unsuccessfully. Their MO was "spear-phishing": a cyberattack directed at a specific individual or group to collect personal information about them. By doing so, the hacker strengthens their chances of successful hacking endeavors against the target or their social network in the future. Spear-phishing cyberattacks usually arrive in the form of emails which seem to be from a friend, colleague, or trusted business, but actually carry malware or trick the target into revealing passwords or other compromising information.

Naturally, this allegation of Russian meddling was immediately denied by Kremlin Press Secretary Dmitry Peskov. However, all subsequent investigations by the CIA and private American cybersecurity companies confirmed it. It was also no secret that Vladimir Putin loathed Clinton, and vastly preferred the prospect of a Trump presidency. A supposed hacker using the handle Guccifer 2.0 boasted that he had been solely responsible for infiltrating the DNC network and disseminating its emails. Guccifer 2.0 stated that he was not Russian, but Romanian. Subsequent investigations would reveal that Guccifer was most likely a persona used by 12 GU hackers.

According to coworkers at the DNC, one young man who was vocally upset about the hacking and leaked emails, was 27-year-old Seth Conrad Rich.

—

Before dawn swept over the spires of Washington, D.C., on Sunday, July 10, 2016, shots rang out in the residential neighborhood of Bloomingdale. Police raced to the southwest corner of Flager Place and W Street Northwest to find DNC staffer Seth Rich lying in the street, clinging to life. Shot twice in the back within a block of his townhouse, Rich died an hour-and-a-half later. At the time of the attack, he was walking home from Lou's City Bar, where he was a regular patron, while chatting on his cell phone with his girlfriend. Rich had last been seen when Lou's was closing between 1:30 and 1:45 am. Though the establishment was located just under 2 miles (2.9 km) from his address—a 33-minute walk or 8-minute drive—the gunshots were fired at 4:20 am. Information explaining this time discrepancy is absent from public record. According to Seth's mother, "There had been a struggle. His hands were bruised, his knees are bruised, his face is bruised, and yet he had two shots to his back . . . they never took anything . . . they just took his life."[2] Indeed, if it was a robbery, it was an incompetent one: Rich's wallet, cell phone, and watch all remained on his person. Nevertheless, this was the position taken by D.C. police investigators, who were facing and increase in armed robberies in the area, albeit with a different MO.

The next day, DNC chair Debbie Wasserman Schultz released a statement praising Rich's work "to protect the most sacred right we share as Americans—the right to vote."[3] Speaking to a crowd in Portsmouth, New Hampshire, on Tuesday, Democratic Presidential Candidate Hillary Clinton even slipped his name into a soliloquy on gun control, proclaiming "from Sandy Hook to Orlando to Dallas, and so many other places, these tragedies tear at our soul . . . And so do the incidents that don't even dominate the headlines. Just this past Sunday, a young man, Seth Rich, who worked for the Democratic National Committee to expand voting rights, was shot and killed in his neighborhood in Washington. He was just 27 years old."[4] Little did Clinton know that the name "Seth Rich" would not linger in obscurity for long.

—

Founded by the enigmatic Australian hacker Julian Assange in 2006, Wikileaks is a controversial, nonprofit organization that provides a platform to publish classified media from anonymous whistleblowers. Undoubtedly, one of the most influential organizations of the early 21st century, Wikileaks has made waves over the past years, along with powerful enemies, both in the US and abroad.

On Friday, July 22, 2016, Wikileaks began releasing tens of thousands of DNC emails and files. In keeping with the organization's policy, it refused to reveal the source of the leaks, but denied the DNC emails had been provided by the Russian government.[5] Assange made no bones about his preference for a Trump presidency over Clinton, having previously stated in an interview with ITV that "Trump is a completely unpredictable phenomenon . . . The emails we've published show that Hillary Clinton is receiving constant updates about my personal situation. She has pushed for the prosecution of Wikileaks . . . so we do see her as a bit of a problem for freedom of the press more generally. In relation to wars, the emails we revealed about her involvement in Libya and statements by Pentagon generals show that Hillary was overriding the Pentagon's reluctance to overthrow Muammar Qaddafi because they predicted that the post-war outcome would be something like what it is, which is ISIS taking over the country . . . She has a long history of being a liberal war hawk, and we presume that she's going to proceed."[6]

Following the leaks, Assange accused the Clinton campaign of playing the Russia card to distract from the content of their emails. Communications between members of the DNC showed a concerted and anti-democratic conspiracy to undermine the Bernie Sanders campaign prior to Clinton's victory, even encouraging journalists to ask Sanders whether or not he was an atheist. One of these emails read: "It will make no difference but for KY [Kentucky] and WA [Washington, but] can we get someone to ask his belief . . . He had skated on having a Jewish heritage. I read he is an atheist . . . My Southern Baptist peeps would draw a big difference between a Jew and an atheist."[7] Debbie Wasserman Schultz was forced to resign one day before the Democratic National Convention as a result. Ultimately, the toll inflicted on Clinton's campaign was severe, as many fence-sitting voters began to see Trump as the lesser of two evils, while embittered Sanders supporters refused to get behind the party that had thrown their preferred candidate under the bus.

On August 9, the name "Seth Rich" came back from the dead. Julian Assange was being interviewed for the Dutch public broadcast service *Nieuwsuur*, when the newscaster asked about presidential candidate Donald J. Trump's low poll numbers and if Wikileaks was "sitting" on information for an "October surprise."

"Wikileaks never sits on material," Assange replied. "Whistleblowers go to significant efforts to get us material at often very significant risks. There's a 27-year-old that works for the DNC who was shot in the back—murdered—just a few weeks ago for unknown reasons as he was walking down a street in Washington, so--"[8]

"That was just a robbery I believe," the interviewer interrupted, "wasn't it?"[9]

"No," Assange shook his head. "There's no finding, so--"[10]

"What are you suggesting?"[11]

Pausing, Assange continued, "I'm suggesting that our sources take risks and they become concerned to see things occurring like that."[12]

"But was he one of your sources, then?"[13]

"We don't comment who our sources are--"[14]

"But why make the suggestion," interjected the newscaster, "about a young guy being shot in the streets of Washington?"[15]

"Because we have to understand how high the stakes are in the United States . . ." Assange explained. "Our sources face serious risks. That's why they come to us, so we can protect their anonymity--"[16]

"But it's quite something to suggest a murder. That's basically what you're doing."[17]

"Well, others have suggested that," Assange replied composedly. "We are investigating to understand what happened in that situation with Seth Rich. I think it is a concerning situation . . . We wouldn't be willing to state a conclusion, but we are concerned about it. Moreover, a variety of Wikileaks sources are concerned when that kind of thing happens."[18]

While Assange's public statements added fuel to the conspiracist fire, he had a point. Rich's murder had occurred in the early morning hours of July 10, and by July 11, @relombardo3, a vocally pro-Sanders Twitter account had tweeted a photo of Rich along with the words, "1 Week After DNC Lawsuit, DNC Staffer Was Shot Down 4x In The Back In His Own Neighborhood"[19] along with a link to a blog on thehill.com. Replying to Tweets, which now appear to be missing, @relombardo3 wrote: "He was the voter-expansion director. He would be a key witness for sure."[20] There followed a long series of conspiracist replies.

According to journalist Olivia Nuzzi of the *New York Intelligencer*, the conversation then pinged to the now defunct conspiracy site whatdoesitmean.com before making its way to the since-banned r/The_Donald subreddit, to Louise Mensch's "Heat Street" (which now redirects to marketwatch.com), and then onto the Twitter feed of Trump campaign adviser Roger Stone. As Stone's account has been similarly banned by Twitter, the exact contents of his electronic discourse are largely inaccessible. Likewise, an influential Rich-assassination-conspiracy tweet by right-wing political commentator

Mike Cernovich, which Nuzzi cites, is now listed as "unavailable." The conspiracy theory went mainstream when Fox News host Sean Hannity began to discuss it on his radio show, *The Sean Hannity Show*, before the program made its television debut.

By 2017, Dallas businessman Ed Butowsky, a friend and colleague of the Trump campaign's Chief Executive Officer Steve Bannon, recommended and paid the bills of former D.C. homicide detective-turned-private-eye Rod Wheeler. Wheeler was a contributor to Fox News. As the Rich family had seen him on television, they were keen for Wheeler to help investigate their son's death. They were completely unaware of Butowsky's connection to Bannon. Though Wheeler had signed an agreement prohibiting him from talking to the media about his work on the case without their permission, on May 15, 2017, an article written by *Fox News* journalist Malia Zimmerman reported that she had spoken to Wheeler. When asked if his sources had told him about any information linking Seth Rich to WikiLeaks, Wheeler had replied "Absolutely. Yeah. That's confirmed."[21] The article also quoted Wheeler as saying, "I have a source inside the police department that has looked at me straight in the eye and said, 'Rod, we were told to stand down on this case and I can't share information with you.' . . . I don't think it comes from the chief's office, but I do believe there is a correlation between the mayor's office and the DNC . . . "[22]

The next morning, Zimmerman elaborated further in a follow-up article, writing that an anonymous federal investigator had read an FBI forensic report regarding the content of Seth Rich's computer and learned that Rich had contacted WikiLeaks through their now-deceased director, Gavin MacFadyen. Between January 2015 and late May 2016, 44,053 DNC emails with 17,761 attachments had supposedly been passed to MacFadyen through Rich. The article also quoted Wheeler as saying, "My investigation up to this point shows some degree of exchange between Seth Rich and Wikileaks . . . I do believe that the answers to who murdered Seth

Rich sit on his computer on a shelf at the D.C. police or FBI head-quarters … My investigation shows someone within the D.C. government, Democratic National Committee, or Clinton team is blocking the investigation from going forward … That is unfortunate. Seth Rich's murder is unsolved as a result of that."[23]

The Rich family read Zimmerman's articles and immediately issued a public statement decrying the politicization of their son's death and distancing themselves from Wheeler.

Later that day, Wheeler did something entirely unexpected. He told CNN that he had seen no evidence of communication between Seth Rich and Wikileaks, whatsoever, and had only been told of its existence "from the reporter at Fox News."[24]

As Rod Wheeler's statements to CNN directly contradicted those attributed to him in Malia Zimmerman's article, on May 17th, Fox News took down her story from their website. On May 23, they issued a brief explanation, stating "The article was not initially subjected to the high degree of editorial scrutiny we require for all our reporting. Upon appropriate review, the article was found not to meet those standards and has since been removed."[25]

On August 1, 2017, the NYC-based law firm Widger LLP, filed a lawsuit on behalf of their client, Rod Wheeler, against 21st Century-Fox, Fox News, Malia Zimmerman, and Ed Butowsky for defamation and discrimination. They claimed that on May 10, Butowsky and Zimmerman had informed Wheeler that an FBI insider had confirmed that Rich had transferred the hacked DNC emails to WikiLeaks. This was the same anonymous federal investigator who was later mentioned in Zimmerman's May 16 article. On May 11, Zimmerman had sent Wheeler a draft of her article to review, without including his quotes. The reason for their omission, according to the lawsuit, was that several were totally fabricated. Thus, Wheeler had remained completely unaware that Zimmerman was actually crafting fake news.

According to the lawsuit, three days later, Wheeler had received a text message from Butowsky at 9:10 p.m. that read "not to add any more pressure but the president just read the article. He wants the article out immediately. It's now all up to you. But don't feel any pressure."[26] If true, this meant that President Donald Trump was privy to an incendiary article before it was published on Fox News, and was actually providing the news agency with direction.

When Zimmerman's article had finally been printed on May 16, Wheeler had called Zimmerman to confront her about fabricating the quotes she had ascribed to him. She had allegedly explained that it was because Trump wanted this "information" included, and advised Wheeler to simply repeat the story on air. The lawsuit also claimed that President Trump and others wanted to push the Seth Rich angle to shift blame for the email leaks away from Russia and onto Rich. Trump was tired of being accused of colluding with the Russians, and this provided an alternative narrative.

Left with little option but to correct Fox News by turning to their competitor, CNN, Wheeler claimed he had suffered damage to his reputation and career due to a loss of credibility. Furthermore, the statement issued by Fox News on May 23 had made no effort whatsoever to clear his name.

On August 3, 2018, Judge George B. Daniels dismissed the lawsuit on the grounds that there were tape recordings of Wheeler confirming to a Fox 5 reporter that a source had indeed informed him of Rich's ties to the leaked emails. Though Judge Daniels agreed Butowsky and Zimmerman had worked together to fabricate and sensationalize a news article, Wheeler could not "now seek to avoid the consequences of his own complicity and coordinated assistance in perpetuating a politically motivated story not having any basis in fact."[27]

Despite the ruling, the information revealed during the court proceedings provides strong evidence of a conspiracy to manufacture fake news between Butowsky, Zimmerman, Wheeler, and potentially, the President of the United States. It does not, in itself, support or dispel the possibility that Seth Rich had been the source of the leak. Nor does it indicate collusion between President

Trump and elements of the Russian government. At the time of the writing, these claims are still hotly contested. However, it does seem to answer a sad question articulated by one of Seth Rich's friends about the public treatment of his murder: "Is it Seth [the propagandists and conspiracists] care about, or the mythology of Seth they've invented?"[28]

The Mysterious Life and Death of Jeffrey Epstein

In the summer of 2019, the exposure of billionaire Jeffrey Epstein as a sexual predator caused a media storm all over the world. Victim after victim came forward. Epstein's extraordinary list of celebrity connections was revealed. Then, with the furore at its height, the focus suddenly swung back to Epstein himself, mysteriously found dead in his prison cell.

On July 6, 2019, "Lolita Express" financier Jeffrey Epstein was arrested on charges of sex trafficking at New Jersey's Teterboro Airport and held at the Metropolitan Correctional Center in New York City. That same day, FBI agents raided his home on Manhattan's Upper East Side and discovered a trove of print and digital photographs of nude teenagers, many under the legal age of consent. As news of his arrest spread, the world speculated which rich and powerful people the billionaire would name as clients in furtherance of a plea bargain. By now he had not only been linked to excursions with Bill Clinton, but also Donald Trump, Prince Andrew and his then-wife Sarah Ferguson, actor Kevin Spacey, and comedian Chris Tucker.

But who was Jeffrey Epstein? He was obviously incredibly rich and hobnobbed with some of the most powerful and influential people on the planet. Yet, nobody seemed to know from whence he came or how he got there.

To some conspiracists it was obvious—he was a spy.

—

Jeffrey Edward Epstein was born into a lower-middle-class Jewish family on Coney Island, New York, on January 20, 1953. Intellectually gifted, particularly in mathematics, he skipped two grades at Lafayette High School in Brooklyn, graduating in 1969. At the age of 16, Epstein began taking classes in advanced mathematics at prestigious Cooper Union college in the East Village. In 1971, he left Cooper Union, without graduating, to attend New York University's Courant Institute of Mathematical Sciences. Despite Epstein's undeniable genius with numbers, he did not bother to graduate from NYU either. Instead, he obtained a teaching position at Dalton School—an upscale private institution on Manhattan's Upper East Side—where he charmed and educated the privileged sons and daughters of New York's elite. It was here that, in 1976, Professor Epstein came into contact with Alan 'Ace' Greenberg, the father of one of his students and the CEO of Bear Stearns, a global investment bank and securities trading and brokerage firm. Epstein, who was also dating Greenberg's daughter—one of his students—endeared himself to the rags-to-riches CEO who was always scouting for "PSDs"— potential employees who were poor, smart, and determined. Through Ace, Epstein obtained an interview with executive Michael Tennenbaum to work at Bear Stearns. He easily charmed his way into a position as a trader's assistant on the American Stock Exchange, rapidly rising to become a junior partner. Still in his twenties, Epstein entered the special-products division, handling complicated tax issues for the company's wealthiest clients.

In 1981, Epstein resigned from Bear Stearns. This loosely coincided with an investigation into the company by the Security and Exchange Commission (SEC) for insider trading. Epstein continued to collect his $100,000 annual bonus from Bear Stearns; some believe this was a payoff for his refusal to divulge compromising information to the SEC.

From 1982 to 1985, Epstein worked for Ana Obregón, daughter

of a Spanish millionaire, to recover money her father had invested in Drysdale Securities Company. This stock-and-bond-trading firm had gone out of business when its subsidiary, Drysdale Government Securities (DGS), defaulted on $160 million it had borrowed to pay interest on Treasury securities. After three years, Epstein recovered the money from a bank in the Cayman Islands. Though the amount he earned was never disclosed, it would almost certainly have been millions of dollars. During this period, he also earned flat fees of $50 million finding creative solutions for the super-rich to avoid paying taxes.

In 1986, Epstein was introduced to Les Wexner, the CEO of Limited Brands. The following year he became the multibillionaire's financial manager, impressing him with his monetary acumen. Little by little, Wexner became dependent on Epstein to manage most aspects of his life, from his romantic relations and art collection, to the contents of his bank account.

While he was busy tightening his grip on Wexner's life and finances, Epstein became partners in crime with Steven Hoffenberg, Chief Executive Officer of Towers Financial Corporation. According to Hoffenberg, "The CEO of a very large company who had employed Jeffrey Epstein in Europe called me and said, 'This is a brilliant man . . . he has credentials on Wall Street, and he's loaded with energy, but his moral compass is upside down.' Jeffrey Epstein had cheated and stolen money on his expense account. He definitely appealed to us, because we were running a Ponzi scheme. And he understood Wall Street, and he could deliver substantial results in this criminal enterprise."[1]

In 1990, Epstein purchased a gated mansion for $2.5 million in West Palm Beach, Florida.

On July 30, 1991, Wexner signed a power of attorney that granted Epstein "full power and authority to do and perform every act necessary"[2] on his behalf.

—

In November that year, British socialite Ghislaine Maxwell, moved to New York City where she met Jeffrey Epstein at a party. The two became lovers.

Ghislaine had decided to start afresh after her family had been embroiled in a high-profile scandal in the UK. She was distraught at the recent death of her father, the wealthy media mogul Robert Maxwell, who had disappeared on November 5 from his yacht *The Lady Ghislaine* near the Canary Islands. The following day the 68-year-old's naked body had been winched from the ocean by a Spanish helicopter 20 miles (32 km) southwest of Gran Canaria, and identified by his widow, Elizabeth, and son, Philip, at Gando Airforce base. At the height of his success, Robert Maxwell may have been worth up to $1.9 billion—approximately $4.5 billion today—and was considered one of the richest people in the world.

Though the cause of Robert Maxwell's death was officially ruled an accident—he had suffered a heart attack sometime after 4:25 am, probably while urinating off the stern, had fallen into the Atlantic and drowned—the timing was suspicious. Like Ghislaine's new lover, Epstein, her father had been a white-collar crook. On the day of his demise, Robert Maxwell was scheduled to meet with The Bank of England concerning £50 million in loans he had defaulted on from Goldman Sachs which was about to become front-page news. After his death, came the revelation that Maxwell had pilfered £530 million from the pension funds of his 16,000 employees to prevent his flagging media empire from going bankrupt.

Naturally, this led to rumors that Maxwell had committed suicide. Others claimed he had been pushed overboard. But what motive could any of his crew members have had to murder him? Several possibilities presented themselves given the likelihood that Robert Maxwell was a spy.

Born Ján Ludvík Hyman Binyamin Hoch, Maxwell was an Orthodox Jew who had fled occupied east Czechoslovakia in 1939 to fight the Axis Powers, first with the French Foreign Legion and then in the British Army. In 1945, he had earned the rank of captain and was awarded the Military Cross for capturing a German machine-gun nest. He became a naturalized British citizen in 1946, and on June 30, 1948, Ján Hoch officially changed his name to "Robert Maxwell."

The British Foreign Office had investigated Maxwell using its covert Information Research Department, and concluded he was "a thoroughly bad character and almost certainly financed by Russia."[3] Besides being a Soviet agent, he also was linked to MI6 and Mossad.

Robert Maxwell's funeral was held in Jerusalem and attended by Israeli Prime Minister Yitzhak Shamir, President Chaim Herzog, and "no less than six serving and former heads of Israeli intelligence."[4] Maxwell was buried on the Mount of Olives. While eulogizing the late billionaire tycoon, Prime Minister Shamir cryptically remarked that he had "done more for Israel than can be said today."[5]

Former Military Intelligence Directorate agent Ari-Ben Menashe has repeatedly and publicly asserted that Robert Maxwell was a spy for Mossad. When, in 1986, Israeli nuclear technician Mordechai Vanunu had unknowingly approached Maxwell's *Sunday Mirror* to blow the whistle on his nation's nuclear capabilities, Maxwell informed the Israeli embassy. As a result, Vanunu was abducted by agents of Mossad in Rome, whisked back to Israel, and jailed.

With this in mind, Menashe speculates that Maxwell may have been murdered aboard the *Lady Ghislaine* and dumped into the Atlantic because "The British police were about to arrest him over pension funds fraud. And the Israelis were terrified that once he's [sic] arrested he'd start telling stories."[6]

—

Robert Maxwell was not only the only upstart billionaire with potential ties to Israeli intelligence. Steven Hoffenberg alleges Epstein also met Prince Andrew in 1991—the royal's old friend Ghislaine had introduced them. Epstein had called the compromised prince his "Super Bowl Trophy," and bragged about his plan to sell secrets to Mossad. "He told me that Ghislaine Maxwell was going to be the breakthrough to bring him into that orbit."[7] Hoffenberg added.

By this time, Epstein had access to the Herbert N. Straus House, a seven-story manor at 9 East 71st Street on Manhattan's Upper East side. Les Wexner had purchased the residence for $13.2 million in 1989, spending as much again on decoration and furnishings, but had never actually lived in it. According to Hoffenberg, Epstein and Ghislaine "created the plan of installing the honeypot cameras and had taken over the [Herbert N. Straus] house in Manhattan to blackmail the politicians. [Epstein] then took over the house in Florida and put in cameras. The cameras were to record rapes, it wasn't just about gathering intelligence, but compromising the politicians . . . I remember Andrew was at many of his events when he took over the house in Manhattan, that was in the early years . . . Andrew didn't understand he was being used . . . Andrew had a weakness for the girls and fast life, Epstein provided that fantasy."[8]

Ari-Ben Menashe has offered a more nuanced and staggering account of what supposedly happened: "[Robert] Maxwell was working for Israel. Epstein was working for [Robert] Maxwell at the time, and he was introduced to Maxwell's daughter . . . probably sometime in the Eighties . . . Mr. Maxwell also thought he . . . should be introducing a fellow to date his daughter. He tried to do a favor to his daughter to find her a *shidduch* as they say in Hebrew, a match . . . And they were introduced to Israeli intelligence . . . [Epstein's sex trafficking] became, basically, an intelligence operation to entrap different politicians around him . . ."[9]

Both accounts are consistent with statements made by Epstein survivor Virginia Roberts Giuffre who confirmed "I was lent out to all of their friends. They were politicians, they were businessmen, they were powerful people."[10]

—

By the time the law caught wind of Hoffenberg's Ponzi scheme in 1993, Jeffrey Epstein had already left the company. Two years later, Steven Hoffenberg pled guilty to five counts of security fraud, tax evasion, and obstruction of an SEC inquiry. He was sentenced to 20 years in a federal prison. Hoffenberg chose not to finger Epstein, because he was convinced his billionaire accomplice was both well connected and protected. He was probably right. Alexander Acosta, who would later prosecute Epstein at his 2008 Florida trial, would eventually claim he was told to offer the financier a cushy plea deal because Epstein "was connected to intelligence" and that such matters were above Acosta's "pay grade."[11]

As Steven Hoffenberg sat in a cell, Jeffrey Epstein carefully siphoned a small fortune from Leslie Wexner's finances into his own possession. He purchased a 7,500-acre (3,035-hectare) ranch in Stanley, New Mexico; a 72-acre (29-hectare) island near St. Thomas in the US Virgin Islands which he dubbed "Little St. Jeff" (but known locally as "pedophile island"); a second 165-acre (67-hectare) island close by; and an apartment in Paris.

—

At 1:30 a.m. on July 23, 2019, Jeffrey Epstein was found lying semiconscious on the floor of his cell at the Metropolitan Correctional Center with strangulation marks about his neck. His cellmate, former NYPD cop and body-building mass-murderer Nicholas Tartaglione, claimed he had saved Epstein from committing suicide by hanging. According to some sources, Epstein confided in his lawyers that Tartaglione had attacked him.

On July 29, lawyer Spencer Kuvin who represented three of Epstein's victims, told *The Sun* newspaper: "I question whether or not it was a true suicide attempt that Mr. Epstein was involved in in jail or whether or not there may be some powerful people who just don't want him to talk . . . If he goes to trial, everyone he's been in contact with will ultimately be fair game . . . There's no doubt in my mind that no jail will protect you when there's powerful people that want to reach you . . . "[12]

Epstein was transferred to an observation cell, where he was placed on suicide watch. His lights were left on around the clock, all potential suicide implements were supposedly removed, and there were copious windows through which he could be monitored.

Despite these substantial measures, at approximately 6:30 a.m. on August 10, while the guards were serving breakfast, they discovered Epstein's corpse in a kneeling position hanging by a strip of bedsheet from his top bunk. He was officially pronounced dead at New York Downtown Hospital at 6:39 a.m. The next day an autopsy performed on Epstein's body by NYC Chief Medical Examiner, Barbara Sampson, determined he had committed suicide by hanging.

When this finding was announced on August 16, the eyes of the world suddenly fixed on Jeffrey Epstein. How could he have committed suicide while under such strict prison conditions? The official answers to these questions only served to fuel public skepticism. Apparently, night guards Tova Noel and Michael Thomas, had last checked Epstein's cell at 10:30 pm then fallen asleep for approximately three hours and browsed the Internet, instead of performing their duties. Noel and Thomas had later falsified the log books to cover this up. Moreover, it was widely reported that two surveillance cameras in front of Epstein's cells had not worked, while the FBI deemed footage from a third camera in the hallway "unusable." Epstein's cellmate had also been transferred just one day before Epstein's death, leaving him completely alone.

The belief that Jeffrey Epstein had been "suicided"—that is, murdered with the crime scene staged to look like he had taken his own life—bloomed on both sides of the political spectrum. For the left, the culprit was clearly Donald Trump, while right-wingers pointed to the Clintons, viewing Epstein as simply another entry next to Seth Rich on their alleged "kill list."

Mark Epstein, the deceased's younger brother, agreed, challenging the findings of both Dr. Sampson and the Department of Justice. Within 24 hours of Jeffrey's death, Mark Epstein hired forensic pathologist Dr. Michael Baden to witness the autopsy. Baden found the injuries to be more consistent with manual strangulation than hanging. Celebrity pathologist Dr. Cyril Wecht looked at Baden's findings and came to the same conclusion. For the record, Wecht also proclaimed ex-Nirvana frontman Kurt Cobain was murdered, based on a flawed understanding of toxicology, and was the only one of a panel of nine forensic pathologists in the 1978 House Select Committee on Assassinations who rejected the findings of the Warren Commission. "There was no evidence at all to indicate that [Jeffrey Epstein] had jumped or leaped from the bunk," Wecht explained. "I came to learn that there were fractures of the hyoid bone, located high in the neck, directly beneath the mandible, the lower jaw . . . Three factures were found: the horn of the hyoid bone on the left side, and then . . . there were fractures of the thyroid cartilage and then on the right side of the thyroid cartilage. You do not get those three fractures with a suicidal hanging of someone leaning forward. So where, again, is the force that would have been required to produce those fractures from kneeling forward? I can say I've never seen it myself in all of my autopsies. I would say, to have these three fractures in that kind of a suicidal hanging would be extremely rare."[13]

Note: "extremely rare" does not mean "impossible."

To this day, the meme "Epstein didn't kill himself" continues to feature both in mainstream and social media, on signs and t-shirts, and even in the beer industry with the Rusted Spoke Brewing Co.'s New England IPA "Epstein Didn't Kill Himself."[14] The same message has also featured on the bottom of cans of Tactical Ops Brewing's Basher Oatmeal Stout.[15]

Even though more than half of Americans believe Jeffrey Epstein was murdered[16], there is a glaring problem with this theory: A surveillance camera outside his cell *was* working on the night of his demise. In actuality, it was the footage from the night of his *attempted* suicide that had been accidentally deleted. Attorney General William Barr initially suspected that Epstein had been the victim of homicide. However, upon reviewing security footage revealing that no one had entered or approached Epstein's cell on the night of his death[17], Barr declared the events "a perfect storm of screw-ups"[18] that enabled Epstein's suicide. One can argue about the minutiae of broken neckbones and the logistics of hanging endlessly, but given the existence of the camera footage, this is merely an exercise in confirmation bias.

A less thrilling, but more likely, possibility is that Epstein or one of his confederates on the outside bribed the guards to look the other way while he took his own life. Tellingly, the disgraced financier had changed his will on August 8—less than 48 hours before his death—placing more than $577 million in assets into a trust fund entitled 1953 Trust. These actions are completely consistent with a man who is putting his affairs in order before committing suicide.

Multiple formal and informal psychological profiles of Jeffrey Epstein have determined that he was a narcissist: "He tries at all times to be the master of his domain and in control of his world. As soon as he feels he's out of control it's unsettling to him."[19] Epstein possessed both the calculating intellect and criminal cunning to realize that he was almost completely powerless. The life of lust and luxury he had enjoyed for nearly 40 years had been replaced with prison bars, bare necessities, and the constant threat of violence. In the same way that his 1953 Trust had been prepared as an obstacle to victims accessing his fortune, Epstein's suicide was a final exercise of power—a demonstration that he had escaped the punishment and judgment that was to be meted out to him. Given his rise from humble beginnings on Coney Island to one of the wealthiest men in the world, it is foolish to say he lacked the will to hang himself. To give the devil his due: Jeffrey Epstein got things done.

While the perverted life and controversial death of Jeffrey Epstein continued to fascinate the world well into 2020, the question of the whereabouts of his alleged accomplice and former girlfriend, Ghislaine Maxwell, loomed over the case. She was finally located in New Hampshire and charged with grooming underage girls on July 2. But by now, there was something stalking the world that was far more nebulous and terrifying than Epstein's activities—a 21st-century plague dubbed COVID-19 . . .

COVID-19

In the early days of 2020, the first whisperings of a new, virulent, flu-like virus began to emerge. Its causes were unknown, inviting all sorts of wild theories. Soon it was sweeping the globe. There had been pandemics before, but never anything like Covid-19.

In November 2016, Donald Trump declared in his presidential victory speech: "It is time for America to bind the wounds of division . . . I pledge to every citizen of our land that I will be President for all of Americans . . ."[1] However, the next four years saw ever-worsening political and cultural polarization. The deluge of misinformation proliferating online and in legacy media throughout the 21st century mushroomed during the 2016 election, and continued to do so across the political spectrum. Nor was it confined to the United States. With "countless news media organizations [constantly] broadcasting vastly conflicting reports."[2]

When the world was blindsided by the Covid-19 pandemic in 2020, it became apparent that the sheer volume of information and speculation pouring from news outlets of every description had severely compromised the collective intellectual and cultural immune system of the West. Citizens of the same country were now viewing events and reality from such vastly different perspectives (supported by wildly divergent "facts") that they could no longer reach a functional consensus even during a major crisis. Many months after the virus' onset, an official narrative regarding the origins, nature, implications, and appropriate handling of COVID-19 had yet to be established. Therefore, unlike the more historical conspiracies in this book—whether, confirmed, suspected, disputed, or debunked—the event had no official anchoring point.

—

One of the few things that has been established about COVID-19, a novel coronavirus, is that it originated in Wuhan, China. Initially, the virus was said to have been spawned in the city's "wet markets," a cluster of open-air stalls selling meat, seafood, fruit, and vegetables. Often, live and wild animals are kept in tanks and cages to be slaughtered on site in less than hygienic conditions.

In the spring of 2020, the creature considered most likely to have transferred the virus to humans was a horseshoe bat (considered a delicacy in parts of southeast Asia), with pangolins (perhaps the world's most trafficked wild animal) acting as an intermediary. However, another possible origin of the coronavirus was the Wuhan Institute of Virology—a local laboratory where bats were routinely used as test subjects. This hypothesis, first put forth by Senator Tom Cotton on February 16, 2020, and frequently reaffirmed by President Trump as of April, was met with ridicule by the media and prominent medical experts alike. Subsequently, many original detractors began to take this suggestion far more seriously.

The Communist Party of China (CPC) unsuccessfully attempted to shift the blame onto the US, claiming that "it might be [300 athletes from the] US army who brought the epidemic"[3] to China in October 2019, when they attended the 7th Military World Games in Wuhan. This claim is undermined by the historical over-representation of coronaviruses that have originated in China, as well as scientific evidence of COVID-19's etiology. As the Chinese government has a veritable state monopoly over the media, many of the country's citizens have blithely accepted the CPC's narrative.

Opinions regarding the pandemic in the West have ranged from it being a tragic accident, to one that the Chinese government capitalized on, and even a calculated biowarfare attack by China on the West itself. The latter two explanations fall into the category of "conspiracy theory," though evidence has continued to mount that the Chinese government *at least* knew about the virus in late 2019. "This is worse than Pearl Harbor. This is worse than the World Trade Center. There's never been an attack like this," President Trump opined to reporters in the Oval Office on May 6. "And it should never have happened . . . It could have been stopped in China . . . and it wasn't."[4]

Indeed, in early January, Chinese ophthalmologist Dr. Li Wenliang had notified medical students of the deadly outbreak in an online chat room. For his efforts, Chinese authorities knocked on his door in the middle of the night, and compelled him to sign a statement retracting his warning, and affirming that he had repeated an illegal and baseless rumor. Li soon contracted the virus and died on February 7.

Even the chronology of COVID-19 is disputed. The most commonly cited date of when it was first identified is late December 2019 in Wuhan, though there were reports of suspected cases dating back to October 2019.[5] The first reported case outside China was on January 13 in Thailand. By January 21, the virus had reached the US. On January 30, 2020, the World Health Organization (WHO) declared COVID-19 a Public Health Emergency of International Concern, upgrading it to a pandemic on March 11. There were 21.5 million documented cases of COVID-19 infection in nearly 200 countries and territories as of August 17, 2020, with 13.5 million recoveries, and deaths in excess of 773,000. By October 23, the number of deaths worldwide had reached 1,738,780, according to the European Centre for Disease Prevention and Control.

In March 2020, President Donald Trump touted hydroxychloroquine, a highly affordable anti-malaria drug, as a "game-changer"[6] in the fight against COVID-19 which showed "very, very encouraging results"[7]. He immediately faced pushback from the media and influential members of the medical community, including Dr. Anthony Fauci, director of the National Institute of Allergy and Infectious Disease (NIAID). However, not all medical practitioners and researchers concur with this criticism, though it seems many are afraid to speak out. Such is the level of polarization in the US that influential comedian and podcaster Joe Rogan recently disclosed: "My friend got tested [for COVID-19], turned out positive, and the doctor asked him what his political leanings are. And he said 'why?' And [the doctor] said, 'Well, I really believe in hydroxychloroquine but a lot of people who are Democrats who don't like the president don't want to use it . . .' And he goes, 'hydroxychloroquine, especially when used in the early stages of the virus seem to be very effective.'"[8]

—

On May 4, 2020, a 26-minute video entitled *Plandemic* was posted on Facebook, Twitter, YouTube, and Vimeo. Within three days it had been removed and banned from these big-tech platforms in a seemingly coordinated effort.

Purporting to be a trailer for a feature-length documentary to be released in the summer of 2020, *Plandemic* consisted primarily of an interview between producer and director Mikki Willis and medical researcher Dr. Judy Mikovits, whom Willis introduces as "one of the most accomplished scientists of her generation."[9] A 2009 *New York Times* article calls Mikovits a "virus expert,"[10] while another published in the *Ventura County Star* in 2014 states that she is a "world-known Oxnard researcher."[11] Willis claims her doctoral thesis, published in 1991, "revolutionized the treatment of HIV/AIDS."[12] The respected academic journal *Science* has disputed each of these claims.

In the interview, Mikovits accused Fauci of being a self-serving propagandist whose steady torrent of medical disinformation had caused the deaths of millions since he became NIAID director in 1984. As a 25-year-old, Mikovits had been part of a team working on a confirmatory study that isolated Human Immuno-Deficiency

Virus (HIV) from saliva and blood, supposedly producing an important research paper. She claimed to have been approached by Fauci, who demanded to see the article before it was published. Despite his threats to fire her for insubordination if she failed to comply, Mikovits stood her ground. She explained that he could talk to her superior, Dr. Frank Ruscetti, when he returned to town. When Ruscetti arrived, Fauci allegedly browbeat him into relinquishing the paper. This delayed the paper's publication for months—which Mikovits claims resulted in mass deaths—allowing Fauci's colleague, Dr. Robert Gallo, to pen his own article. In doing so, Gallo became known as the ingenious savior who had identified HIV as the retrovirus that caused Acquired Immune Deficiency Syndrome (AIDS). According to Mikovits, Dr. Robert Redfield, director of the Centers for Disease Control and Prevention, was also a member of this alleged medical cabal.

As Fauci and his cohorts had allegedly done with HIV/AIDS, Mikovits proposed their goal was to secretly enable COVID-19 and capitalize on the virus by developing and administering an unnecessary vaccine. These inoculations would be conducted on a mass scale, earning Fauci and his colleagues billions of dollars in profit from the patent. Mikovits believed such a vaccine would not only be ineffective, but would result in additional deaths as, "There is no vaccine currently on the schedule for any RNA virus that works."[13]

Mikovits concurred with Trump's appraisal of hydroxychloroquine's effectiveness in combating the coronavirus, but explained that big pharma's propaganda machine would discredit this view as there was no money to be made by endorsing it: "It's not the scientists who are in any way dishonest. They're listening to people who, for more than 40 years, have controlled who gets funded, what gets published. And I'm sorry to say many, many people will simply just take the money and the fame and support things that absolutely aren't true."[14]

While *Plandemic* has been censored and dismissed as a dangerous conspiracy-theory video, some of its assertions merit further exploration. Firstly, it drew attention to an alarming practice that has almost certainly led to a statistical over-inflation of recorded COVID-19 deaths in the United States. Both Mikovits and Minnesota Senator Scott Jensen, a practicing physician, revealed that Medicare was offering hospitals $13,000 for every patient recorded as having COVID-19. Jensen added that if such a patient was treated with a ventilator this amount went up to $39,000. Theoretically, this financially incentivized these institutions to classify patients as suffering from the virus, even if they did not have it. However, according to the Kaiser Family Foundation, this monetary amount applied to all "respiratory infections and inflammations with major comorbidities."[15] Nor did it necessarily prove any American hospitals were actually making false claims about their patients' medical conditions. *Plandemic* provided testimony from medical doctors to support these assertions. For instance, according to Dr. Dan Erickson of Bakersfield, California, "When I'm writing up my death report, I'm being pressured to add COVID [to the report]. Why is that? . . . To maybe increase the numbers and make it look a little bit worse than it is? I think so."[16] According to this line of thought, while hospitals might have been fudging the numbers to increase the amount of funding they received from government, overinflating COVID-19's prevalence served the Fauci cabal's secret, profit-driven agenda.

Another claim made in *Plandemic* that has since gained traction, was Mikovits' assertion that, "Somebody didn't go to a market [and] get a bat [to eat]. The virus didn't jump directly to humans. That's not how it works. That's accelerated viral evolution. If it was a natural occurrence, it would take up to 800 years to occur . . . This family of viruses was manipulated and studied in a laboratory, where the animals were taken into the laboratory. And this [manipulated virus] is what was released, whether deliberate or not. That cannot be naturally occurring."[17] This notion that the virus must have been manipulated was also supported by the biologist and evolutionary theorist Dr. Bret Weinstein and Dr. Peter Chumakov, head of the Englehardt Institute of Molecular Biology. However, the wider scientific community scoffed at it.

Mikovits believed that COVID-19 originated "between the North Carolina laboratories, Fort Detrick US Army Research Institute of Infectious Disease (USAMRIID), and the Wuhan laboratory."[18] She says that while working at the USAMRIID at Fort Detrick in 1999, she was tasked with manipulating Ebola to infect human cells without causing their death, something it could not do "until we took it in the laboratories and taught them."[19]

In this regard, her statements are largely in line with Dr. Chumakov's. The Russian microbiologist disclosed that the Wuhan lab had done "absolutely crazy things"[20] during more than ten years of developing coronavirus variants, adding, "the Chinese and Americans who worked with them published all their works in the open (scientific) press. I think that an investigation will nevertheless be initiated, as a result of which new rules will be developed that regulate the work with the genomes of such dangerous viruses."[21]

But who is Dr. Mikovits, and can she be trusted?

—

Judy Mikovits received a PhD in biochemistry from George Washington University in 1991. Mikovits stated she then went on to conduct postdoctoral research from 1993-94 under one David Ders, before accepting a position at Ruscetti's Laboratory of Leukocyte Biology at the National Cancer Institute in 1996. After nearly five years at the NCI, in May of 2001, Dr. Mikovits began working for EpiGenx Biosciences—a pharmaceutical research company in Santa Barbara, California.

Interestingly, her Wikipedia page states: "By late 2005, Mikovits was working as a bartender at the Pierpont Yacht Club in Ventura, California,"[22] implying a significant downturn in her personal fortunes. However, one of the two accompanying citations for this information links to a *Ventura County Star* article which provides context that is both relevant and absent from the Wikipedia entry: "She served on a race committee at the Pierpont Bay Yacht Club, *volunteering her services as a club bartender* [emphasis added]."[23] Nor is there any mention of when Mikovits began tending bar at the yacht club in this citation or the second: a *New York Times* article.

Mikovits became a research director for the Whittemore Peterson Institute for Neuro-Immune Disease (WPI) in the fall of 2006, a facility which both the *New York Times* and *Ventura County Star* accurately state is located in Reno. Yet, the Wikipedia entry citing them says it was "located in Las Vegas"[24]—fairly ironic, given the entry asserts that Mikovits "is known for her discredited medical claims"[25].

The primary purpose of the WPI was to research and find a cure for Chronic Fatigue Syndrome, a task which Mikovits appeared to accomplish quickly. Drawing upon the findings of Dr. Daniel L. Peterson and Dr. Robert Silverman, Mikovits hypothesized that CFS was caused or abetted by a virus known as xenotropic murine leukemia virus–related virus (XMRV). According to an article in the science journal *Nature*, "She and her postdoc, Vincent Lombardi, known as Vinny, asked a graduate student to test for XMRV DNA in white blood cells from some of the most seriously ill people being studied at the WPI. The first try turned up just two positives out of 20. But by tweaking the conditions of the test, Mikovits says her team found XMRV in all 20 . . . They spent the next few weeks convincing themselves that they were onto something, and soon conscripted Silverman and Mikovits' former mentor at the NCI, Frank Ruscetti, to help prove that XMRV infection was behind chronic fatigue.."[26]

In 2009, *Science* published their research article on XMRV and CFS, however, by early 2010, multiple attempts to replicate these findings by scientists in a number of countries proved negative. On December 23, 2011, *Science* retracted the article, explaining that it had "lost confidence in the Report and the validity of its conclusions. We note that the majority of the authors have agreed in principle to retract the Report but they have been unable to agree on the wording of their statement."[27]

A year later, Mikovits contributed to a scientific research article which concluded that the team's latest analysis "reveals no evidence of either XMRV or pMLV infection"[28]—a fairly important omission from *Plandemic*. A later article in *Science* also claimed that Mikovits eventually conceded that "there is no evidence that XMRV is a human pathogen"[29], although it provides no supporting citation.

In November 11, the WPI filed a lawsuit against Mikovits for supposedly stealing lab notebooks and storing proprietary information on her laptop, flash drives, and email account. Seven days later, acting on a warrant from the Washoe County Sheriff's Office, Ventura County sheriffs arrested Mikovits, and charged her with being a fugitive from justice. According to Mikovits, "I was held in jail with no charges. I was called a fugitive from justice. No warrant. Literally drug me out of the house. Our neighbors are looking at what's going on here. They search my house without a warrant, literally terrorize my husband for five days. They said, 'If you don't find the notebooks, if you don't find the material,' which was not in my possession, but planted in my house . . . Heads of our entire HHS colluded and destroyed my reputation. And the Department of Justice and the FBI sat on it and kept that case under seal, which means you can't say there's a case, or your lawyers are held in contempt of court. So, you can't even get a lawyer to defend you. So, every single due process right was taken away from me, and to this day, remains the same. I have no constitutional freedoms or rights . . . [I was put under a gag order] for five years. If I went on social media, if I said anything at all, they would find new evidence and put me back in jail. And it was one of the few times I cried. It was because I knew there was no evidence the first time. And when you can unleash that kind of force . . . to force someone into bankruptcy with a perfect credit score so that I couldn't bring

COVID-19

my 97 witnesses, which included the heads—Tony Fauci, Ian Lipkin—the heads of the public health in HHS, who would've had to testify that we did absolutely nothing wrong . . . "[30]

Four days after the release of *Plandemic*, Martin Enserink and Jon Cohen authored a fact-checking article for *Science* that methodically addressed and countered Mikovits' claims. Whether her reputation was destroyed, or she destroyed it herself, she is clearly not in good standing with the scientific community.

—

Within a month-and-a-half of the release of the *Plandemic* preview, Dr. Fauci confessed that he had told a potentially crucial untruth. Having stated in March that there was no reason for healthy citizens to wear protective facial masks because they had unintended consequences and did not offer the level of protection people believed they did, in mid-June, Fauci reversed his position and admitted that he had deceived the American people: "The public health community . . . were concerned that it was at a time when personal protective equipment including the N95 mask and the surgical masks were in very short supply, and . . . the healthcare workers who were brave enough to put themselves in harm's way to take care of people who you *know* were infected with the coronavirus . . . we did not want them to be without the equipment that they needed. So, there was non-enthusiasm about . . . everyone buying a mask or getting a mask. We were afraid that they would deter away from the people who really needed it. Now we have masks . . . so right now, unequivocally, the recommendation is when you're out there, particularly if you're in a situation where there's active infection, keep the distance physically and wear a mask. So, though there might appear to be some contradiction of 'you were saying this then, and why are you saying this now', actually the circumstances have changed. That's the reason why."[31]

Even if Fauci's explanation can be justified as a necessary

practical measure to serve the greater good, it unfortunately undermined trust in a vital institution: healthcare. Was it any wonder
conspiracies sprang up like weeds under such conditions?

—

Naturally, there are the "COVID deniers," ranging from those
who view the pandemic as no worse than the common flu to the
lunatic fringe that believe the virus is a total fabrication concocted
by an alliance of "thems" to destroy civil liberties. Then there are
conspiracists who attribute the emergence of the virus to the Deep
State or Shadow Government—a loosely defined conglomerate of
intelligence agencies, which, depending on the source, also
includes the military industrial complex; rich, influential businessmen; and bureaus. The existence of a Deep State that has far
greater influence on the US than its elected officials, is actually not
an unreasonable assertion, and its existence has been confirmed by
the controversial NSA whistleblower Edward Snowden, former
Democratic congressman Dennis Kucinich, retired Libertarian
presidential candidate Ron Paul, and his son Republican senator
Rand Paul of Kentucky, along with many others across the political spectrum. What is far less believable is that Bill Gates, who has
donated billions of dollars to Gavi, The Vaccine Alliance, to
develop a coronavirus inoculation, is conspiring to hide microchips in forthcoming mandatory COVID-19 vaccines in order to
track and control the global population.

One particularly pernicious coronavirus conspiracy theory is
linked to 5G cell phone technologies. This idea seems to be most
popular in the United Kingdom, where its proponents have set
over one hundred 5G towers ablaze. The most prominent theory
holds that these emit waves which either cause or enable COVID-
19. A second, less popular variant, is that the coronavirus does not
exist at all, rather, citizens are experiencing illnesses related to
mankind's biological incompatibility with 5G. The danger of this

conspiracy theory is that, once debunked, people may ignore credible threats associated with 5G, specifically, Chinese spy capabilities
inherent in the Huawei company's 5G phones.

—

According to conspiracists, the timing of the COVID-19 outbreak
was suspiciously fortuitous for the government in Beijing. President Trump, who had advocated imposing tariffs on Chinese
goods since the 1980s, made renegotiating trade agreements with
Beijing one of the central tenets of his 2016 presidential run. By
July 2018, the Trump administration had placed $550 billion in
tariffs on Chinese products, prompting economic retaliation from
the Chinese government. With the coming of 2020, the incum-
bent president had a 56 percent approval rating regarding the
economy and his standing in the country at large had been largely
unaffected by the so-called "Russia Probe" which sought evidence
of his alleged collusion with the Putin administration during the
2016 presidential election. It was now election year once again, and
for many Americans, his opponents in the Democratic Party had
emerged from the investigation with egg on their faces. Trump,
the brash, anti-China president, stood a reasonable chance of being
reelected: a possibility that was contrary to Beijing's interests.

Furthermore, in March 2019, anti-Chinese government protests
had broken out in Hong Kong in response to draconian measures
imposed on this special administrative region by Beijing. As the
year went on, the Chinese government resorted to force to quash
the civil unrest, spurring a violent reaction from some protesters.
As a response to these human rights violations, on November 27,
the US congress passed the Hong Kong Human Rights and
Democracy Act, creating a federal law that compelled the American government to place sanctions on mainland China and Hong
Kong. With the eyes of the world on China, a diversion was highly
convenient.

With this in mind, the Chinese government certainly had the motive and means to deliver a crushing blow, in viral form, to Trump's America. The only question is, "Would they go to such extremes?" Though the deaths of tens of millions of Chinese during Chairman Mao Zedong's rule may not accurately reflect 21st-century China's treatment of its own citizens, one might look to the torture, "re-education," organ harvesting, and cultural genocide of practitioners of the Falun Gong religious movement and Uyghur ethnic minority as possible indicators of the value President Xi Jinping's government places on human life.

From a logistical standpoint, a biological attack against the US, or the West in general, would be an ingenious destabilizing tactic because it creates plausible deniability. Unlike ballistic, chemical, or even cyberwarfare, which all require a human hand, viruses can arise naturally and spontaneously as "acts of God." With Western hospitals overcrowded, economies nearing collapse, and socially isolated citizens becoming increasingly psychologically unhinged, their governments' attention and resources would be diverted from global issues to focus on handling domestic crises. Western governments would be far less likely, for instance, to concern themselves with the "national security law" imposed on Hong Kong, which allowed Chinese authorities to crack down on the media, and arrest prominent newsmen. Another non-priority would be the June 10 advancement of the People's Liberation Army 3 to 5 miles (4.8 to 8 km) into disputed territory with India. Better still, if blatantly accused of releasing COVID-19 as an act of biological warfare, China could simply point to the deaths of its own citizens as a response. Furthermore, the process can be repeated as often as necessary, until the CPC has achieved its objectives, whatever they may be.

As of August 18, 2020, China reported a total of 4,634 deaths from COVID-19, an astoundingly low number, given the virus' point of origin. This meant that China had had fewer known COVID deaths than the USA, Brazil, Mexico, India, the United

Kingdom, Italy, France, and virtually every other major country in the world. Although 21 million cell phone subscriptions in China were cancelled between January and February 2020—prompting speculation that Beijing had covered up tens of millions of coronavirus deaths—the state-owned China Mobile Ltd explained to the Associated Press (AP) that this was due to "reduced business and social activities."[32] Was China obfuscating its real death toll? As of this writing, this is simply speculation.

In the fall of 2020, events connected to the pandemic continued to be fast-moving and unpredictable. In early October, President Trump himself was diagnosed with the virus, yet seemingly made a swift recovery. He promised to make the drugs he had been given available to all, but many commentators doubted this would be possible. Those looking for a potential conspiracy even questioned whether he had really caught the virus at all, but was using his seeming ability to shrug off the disease to boost his standing in the polls for the upcoming presidential election.

As soon as COVID-19's pernicious effects were discovered in early 2020, it had rapidly become clear that the only lasting solution to the pandemic would be an effective vaccine. Ever since, the search for this has preoccupied governments around the world, leading to accusations that some nations—the US in particular—are secretly stockpiling supplies for their own people. On October 9, China pulled off something of a public-relations coup when a government spokesman announced that it would support a World Health Organization program to vaccinate two billion people around the world.

Picture Credits

The publisher would like to thank the following for their kind permission to reproduce their photographs:

(Key: a–above; b–below/bottom; c–centre; f–far; l–left; r–right; t–top)

Insert 1 Alamy Stock Photo: Chronicle (tl); Classic Image (tr); Carol and Mike Werner (bl). **Getty Images:** Hulton Archive / Stringer (c); Stefano Bianchetti / Corbis (crb). **Insert 2 Alamy Stock Photo:** Heritage Image Partnership Ltd (clb); Keystone Press (tc); Peter Horree (tr); World History Archive (cr); Sueddeutsche Zeitung Photo (br). **Getty Images:** ullstein bild Dtl. / Contributor (cla). **Insert 3 Alamy Stock Photo:** Everett Collection Inc (cl); Sueddeutsche Zeitung Photo (cr). **Getty Images:** HO / AFP (tr); Handout (tl); Robert Nickelsberg / The LIFE Images Collection (cb); Bettmann (clb, bc). **Insert 4 Alamy Stock Photo:** Keystone Press (tc). **Getty Images:** AFP / Stringer (tr); Universal History Archive / Universal Images Group (tl); Bettmann (cl); Mondadori Portfolio / Contributor (cr); Keystone / Stringer (bl); Bettmann / Contributor (br). **Insert 5 Alamy Stock Photo:** hpbfotos (t); Oreolife (crb). **Getty Images:** Jerod Harris / Contributor (bc); DigitalGlobe / ScapeWare3d / Contributor (c). **Insert 6 Alamy Stock Photo:** Chronicle (cr); Niday Picture Library (t); Everett Collection Inc (clb); ClassicStock (crb); Granger Historical Picture Archive (bl). **Getty Images:** Bettmann / Contributor (c). **Insert 7 Alamy Stock Photo:** American Photo Archive (cb); Chronicle (tl); Shawshots (tr); Columbia Pictures / AA Film Archive (c); Granger Historical Picture Archive (br). **Insert 8 Getty Images:** National Archives - JFK / Corbis (tr); Bettmann / Contributor (tl, cl); Terry Ashe / The LIFE Images

Collection (cra); New York Daily News / Contributor (crb, bl). **Insert 9 Alamy Stock Photo:** Everett Collection Historical (tl); Keystone Press (bl); GL Archive (br). **Getty Images:** Bettmann / Contributor (cr); Virginia / Ullstein Bild (tr); John Dominis / The LIFE Picture Collection (clb) **Insert 10 Getty Images:** Bettmann / Contributor (c, cr); Bill Eppridge / The LIFE Picture Collection (cla); Abbie Rowe / PhotoQuest (bl); Patrick T. Fallon for The Washington Post (br). **Rex by Shutterstock:** Warren Winterbottom / AP (tr). **Insert 11 Alamy Stock Photo:** Heritage Image Partnership Ltd (tr). **Getty Images:** NASA / AFP (b); NASA / Gamma-Rapho (cl). **NASA:** (tl). **Insert 12 Alamy Stock Photo:** Historic Images (br). **Getty Images:** Imagno / Contributor (cra); Joel Forrest / Barcroft Media (t); Kent Photo News (K.P.N.) / Express / Hulton Archive (cl). **Insert 13 Alamy Stock Photo:** imageBROKER / Hartmut Schmidt (cra); Tommy E Trenchard (tl); Paul Andrew Lawrence (b/1). **Insert 14 Alamy Stock Photo:** Paul Hennessy (br); Fred Mack (bl); MPI10 / MediaPunch Inc (cr). **Insert 15 Alamy Stock Photo:** © Netflix / Courtesy Everett Collection / Ron Harvey (tr); Pictorial Press Ltd (tl); Richard Levine (bl). **Getty Images:** Emily Michot / Miami Herald / Tribune News Service (cr); Mirrorpix (cl); Scott Winters / Icon Sportswire (br). **Insert 16 Alamy Stock Photo:** amnat (tr); Jeremy Pembrey (cla); ZUMA Press, Inc. (cra); Mr Pics (clb/1). **Getty Images:** Yuri Cortez / AFP (crb); Chris Kleponis / Polaris / Bloomberg (bc)

Cover images: *Front:* **NASA**

All other images © Dorling Kindersley
For further information see: www.dkimages.com

Endnotes

"Them"

1 https://www.oed.com/oed2/00048049;jsessionid=0389830C
953F30EA35E2A97FD896F289
2 *Conspiracy Theories & Secret Societies for Dummies* by Christopher Hodapp & Alicia Von Kannon.
3 *Conspiracy Theories & Secret Societies for Dummies* by Christopher Hodapp & Alicia Von Kannon.
4 *Secret Rulers of the World - David Icke, The Lizards and the Jews* directed by Jon Ronson.

Operation Grey Wolf

1 *The Last Days of Hitler: The Classic Account of Hitler's Fall From Power* by Hugh Trevor Roper.
2 *Grey Wolf: The Escape of Adolf Hitler* by Simon Dunstan and Gerrard Williams.
3 *Grey Wolf: The Escape of Adolf Hitler* by Simon Dunstan and Gerrard Williams.
4 *Grey Wolf: The Escape of Adolf Hitler* by Simon Dunstan and Gerrard Williams.
5 *Humanitarians at War: The Red Cross in the Shadow of the Holocaust* by Gerald Steinacher.
6 "Identification of the Skeletal Remains of Martin Bormann by mtDNA Analysis" in *International Journal of Legal Medicine* by K. Anslinger, G. Weichhold, W. Keil, B. Bayer, & W. Eisenmenger.

Nazi Ratlines

1 *Unholy Trinity: The Vatican, the Nazis, and the Swiss Banks* by Mark Aarons and John Loftus.

2 *The Nazi Doctors: Medical Killing and the Psychology of Genocide* by Robert Jay Lifton.

3 *Unholy Trinity: The Vatican's Nazis, Soviet Intelligence and the Swiss Banks* by Mark Aarons and John Loftus.

4 *Unholy Trinity: The Vatican's Nazis, Soviet Intelligence and the Swiss Banks* by Mark Aarons and John Loftus.

5 *Unholy Trinity: The Vatican's Nazis, Soviet Intelligence and the Swiss Banks* by Mark Aarons and John Loftus.

6 *Hitler's Pope: The Secret History of Pius XII* by John Cornwell.

7 *Hitler's Pope: The Secret History of Pius XII* by John Cornwell.

8 https://www.c-span.org/video/?174865-1/depth-martin-gilbert

9 *Washington Post*, March 3, 2020—"Pope Pius XII was silent during the Holocaust. Now Vatican records may reveal whether he collaborated with the Nazis."

10 *Unholy Trinity: The Vatican's Nazis, Soviet Intelligence and the Swiss Banks* by Mark Aarons and John Loftus.

11 *Unholy Trinity: The Vatican's Nazis, Soviet Intelligence and the Swiss Banks* by Mark Aarons and John Loftus.

12 *Washington Post*, March 3, 2020—"Pope Pius XII was silent during the Holocaust. Now Vatican records may reveal whether he collaborated with the Nazis."

13 *The Guardian*, March 1, 2020—"Unsealing of Vatican archives will finally reveal truth about 'Hitler's pope.'"

14 *Operation Paperclip* by Annie Jacobsen.

15 *Operation Paperclip* by Annie Jacobsen.

16 *BBC Future*, September 7, 2014—"V2: The Nazi rocket that launched the space age."

17 *Operation Paperclip* by Annie Jacobsen.

18 *Cross Currents: Cultures, Communities, Technologies* by Kristine L. Blair, Jen Almjeld, & Robin M. Murphy.
19 *Operation Paperclip* by Annie Jacobsen.

Area 51

 1 *Bob Lazar: Area 51 & Flying Saucers* directed by Jeremy Corbell.
 2 *Bob Lazar: Area 51 & Flying Saucers* directed by Jeremy Corbell.
 3 *Area 51* by Annie Jacobsen.
 4 *Bob Lazar: Area 51 & Flying Saucers* directed by Jeremy Corbell.
 5 *Alamogordo Daily News*, 26 July 1982—"This is a real hot rod."
 6 *Bob Lazar: Area 51 & Flying Saucers* directed by Jeremy Corbell.
 7 https://www.youtube.com/watch?v=COCRjd4YH-k
    UFO Top Secret
 8 https://www.youtube.com/watch?v=COCRjd4YH-k
    UFO Top Secret
 9 https://www.youtube.com/watch?v=COCRjd4YH-k
    UFO Top Secret
10 The Joe Rogan Experience #1315—Bob Lazar & Jeremy Corbell.
11 *Bob Lazar: Area 51 & Flying Saucers* directed by Jeremy Corbell.
12 The Joe Rogan Experience #1315—Bob Lazar & Jeremy Corbell.
13 *Bob Lazar: Area 51 & Flying Saucers* directed by Jeremy Corbell.
14 *Area 51* by Annie Jacobsen.
15 http://www.stantonfriedman.com/index.php?ptp=articles&fdt=2011.01.07
16 http://www.stantonfriedman.com/index.php?ptp=articles&fdt=2011.01.07

The Men in Black

 1 *Men In Black: A Preliminary Report* by Robert Bull.
 2 *Men In Black: The Secret Terror Among Us* by Gray Barker.
 3 *Men In Black: A Preliminary Report* by Robert Bull.

4 *Starstruck: Cosmic Visions in Science, Religion, and Folklore* by Albert Harrison.

5 *Men In Black: A Preliminary Report* by Robert Bull.

6 *Men In Black: The Secret Terror Among Us* by Gray Barker.

7 *Men In Black: The Secret Terror Among Us* by Gray Barker.

8 *Men In Black: The Secret Terror Among Us* by Gray Barker.

9 *Men In Black: The Secret Terror Among Us* by Gray Barker.

10 *Starstruck: Cosmic Visions in Science, Religion, and Folklore* by Albert Harrison.

11 *The Mothman Prophecies: A True Story* by John A. Keel.

12 *The Mothman Prophecies: A True Story* by John A. Keel.

13 *The Mothman Prophecies: A True Story* by John A. Keel.

14 *The Mothman Prophecies: A True Story* by John A. Keel.

15 *The Mothman Prophecies: A True Story* by John A. Keel.

16 *The Mothman Prophecies: A True Story* by John A. Keel.

17 *The Mothman Prophecies: A True Story* by John A. Keel.

18 *Operation Trojan Horse: The Classic Breakthrough Study of UFOS* by John Keel.

19 *Men In Black: The Secret Terror Among Us* by Gray Barker.

20 *Men In Black: The Secret Terror Among Us* by Gray Barker.

21 *Area 51: An Uncensored History of America's Top Secret Military Base* by Annie Jacobsen.

22 *Men In Black: The Secret Terror Among Us* by Gray Barker.

23 *Men In Black: The Secret Terror Among Us* by Gray Barker.

24 *Men In Black: The Secret Terror Among Us* by Gray Barker.

The Assassination of John F. Kennedy

1 *The Warren Report: The Official Report on the Assassination of President John F. Kennedy* by The Warren Commission.

2 *The Warren Report: The Official Report on the Assassination of President John F. Kennedy* by The Warren Commission.

3 https://web.archive.org/web/20081202011802/http://www.jfk.org/go/collections/about/abraham-zapruder-interview-transcript

4 *Who Was Lee Harvey Oswald?* directed by William Cran & Ben Loeterman.

5 *The Warren Report: The Official Report on the Assassination of President John F. Kennedy* by The Warren Commission.

6 *The New York Times*, December 24, 1963—"Johnson Feared a Plot in Dallas"

7 *Who Was Lee Harvey Oswald?* directed by William Cran & Ben Loeterman.

8 *Global News*, August 29, 2019—"Jim Leavelle, Dallas cop cuffed to Lee Harvey Oswald at his shooting, dies at age 99"

9 *Global News*, August 29, 2019—"Jim Leavelle, Dallas cop cuffed to Lee Harvey Oswald at his shooting, dies at age 99"

10 https://web.archive.org/web/20081202011802/http://www.jfk.org/go/collections/about/abraham-zapruder-interview-transcript

11 *Who Was Lee Harvey Oswald?* directed by William Cran & Ben Loeterman.

12 *The Warren Report: The Official Report on the Assassination of President John F. Kennedy* by The Warren Commission.

13 *Family of Secrets: The Bush Dynasty, America's Invisible Government, and the Hidden History of the Last Fifty Years* by Russ Baker.

14 *The Warren Report: The Official Report on the Assassination of President John F. Kennedy* by The Warren Commission.

15 *Edwin A. Walker and the Right Wing in Dallas* by Chris Cravens.

16 *Who Was Lee Harvey Oswald?* directed by William Cran & Ben Loeterman.

17 *Who Was Lee Harvey Oswald?* directed by William Cran & Ben Loeterman.

18 *HCSA Final Assassinations Report* by House Select Committee on Assassinations.

19 https://texashistory.unt.edu/ark:/67531/metapth346593/m1/1/

20 *Men In Black: The Secret Terror Among Us* by Gray Barker.

21 *Men In Black: The Secret Terror Among Us* by Gray Barker.

22 *Who Was Lee Harvey Oswald?* directed by William Cran & Ben Loeterman.

23 *Who Was Lee Harvey Oswald?* directed by William Cran & Ben Loeterman.

24 https://www.nbcchicago.com/news/local/journalist-stripper-refute-jack-ruby-mob-conspiracy/2047811/

25 https://www.nbcchicago.com/news/local/journalist-stripper-refute-jack-ruby-mob-conspiracy/2047811/

26 https://www.nbcchicago.com/news/local/journalist-stripper-refute-jack-ruby-mob-conspiracy/2047811/

27 *Chaos: Charles Manson, the CIA, and the Secret History of the Sixties* by Tom O'Neill.

28 *Chaos: Charles Manson, the CIA, and the Secret History of the Sixties* by Tom O'Neill.

29 *Chaos: Charles Manson, the CIA, and the Secret History of the Sixties* by Tom O'Neill.

30 *Chaos: Charles Manson, the CIA, and the Secret History of the Sixties* by Tom O'Neill.

MK-ULTRA

1 *LSD—My Problem Child* by Albert Hofmann.

2 *I Swear By Apollo: Dr. Ewen Cameron and the CIA-Brainwashing Experiments* by Don Gillmor.

3 *Poisoner in Chief: Sidney Gottlieb and the CIA Search for Mind Control* by Stephen Kinzer.

4 *Poisoner in Chief: Sidney Gottlieb and the CIA Search for Mind Control* by Stephen Kinzer.

5 *Poisoner in Chief: Sidney Gottlieb and the CIA Search for Mind Control* by Stephen Kinzer.

6 *Poisoner in Chief: Sidney Gottlieb and the CIA Search for Mind Control* by Stephen Kinzer.

7 *Poisoner in Chief: Sidney Gottlieb and the CIA Search for Mind Control* by Stephen Kinzer.

8 *Poisoner in Chief: Sidney Gottlieb and the CIA Search for Mind Control* by Stephen Kinzer.

9 *Poisoner in Chief: Sidney Gottlieb and the CIA Search for Mind Control* by Stephen Kinzer.

10 https://www.theguardian.com/film/2011/aug/06/lsd-ken-kesey-pranksters-film

11 https://www.theguardian.com/film/2011/aug/06/lsd-ken-kesey-pranksters-film

12 https://www.telegraph.co.uk/films/0/charles-manson-murders-cia-conspiracy-theory-lsd-labs-truth/

13 *Chaos: Charles Manson, the CIA, and the Secret History of the Sixties* by Tom O'Neill.

14 *Chaos: Charles Manson, the CIA, and the Secret History of the Sixties* by Tom O'Neill.

15 *The Search for the Manchurian Candidate* by John D. Marks.

16 https://www.theatlantic.com/magazine/archive/2000/06/harvard-and-the-making-of-the-unabomber/378239/

The Assassination of Robert F. Kennedy

1 https://voicesofdemocracy.umd.edu/lyndon-baines-johnson-withdrawal-speech-31-march-1968/

2 *A Lie Too Big to Fail: The Real History of the Assassination of Robert F. Kennedy* by Lisa Pease.

3 https://www.democracynow.org/2008/6/5/democracy_now_special_robert_f_kennedy

4 *The Assassinations: Probe Magazine on JFK, MLK, RFK and Malcolm X* by James DiEugenio, Lisa Pease, & Judge Joe Brown.

5 "The Assassination of Robert F. Kennedy: an analysis of the senator's injuries and neurosurgical care" in *Journal of Neurosurgery* by Jordan M. Komisarow, Theodore Pappas, Megan Llewellyn, and Shivanand P. Lad.

6 http://rfktapes.com/ep4-transcript/

7 https://www.youtube.com/watch?v=Ma_RpEcm7NY&list=
   PLtP10qqTzKD_cE1IezrkojuN92a DDWM8k

8 *The Assassinations: Probe Magazine on JFK, MLK, RFK and Malcolm
   X* by James DiEugenio, Lisa Pease, & Judge Joe Brown.

9 *The Assassinations: Probe Magazine on JFK, MLK, RFK and Malcolm
   X* by James DiEugenio, Lisa Pease, & Judge Joe Brown.

10 *Who Killed Bobby?: The Unsolved Murder of Robert F. Kennedy* by
    Shane O'Sullivan.

11 *Who Killed Bobby?: The Unsolved Murder of Robert F. Kennedy* by
    Shane O'Sullivan.

12 *Who Killed Bobby?: The Unsolved Murder of Robert F. Kennedy* by
    Shane O'Sullivan.

13 *Who Killed Bobby?: The Unsolved Murder of Robert F. Kennedy* by
    Shane O'Sullivan.

14 *Who Killed Bobby?: The Unsolved Murder of Robert F. Kennedy* by
    Shane O'Sullivan.

15 *Who Killed Bobby?: The Unsolved Murder of Robert F. Kennedy* by
    Shane O'Sullivan.

16 *Who Killed Bobby?: The Unsolved Murder of Robert F. Kennedy* by
    Shane O'Sullivan.

17 *Who Killed Bobby?: The Unsolved Murder of Robert F. Kennedy* by
    Shane O'Sullivan.

18 *Who Killed Bobby?: The Unsolved Murder of Robert F. Kennedy* by
    Shane O'Sullivan.

19 *Who Killed Bobby?: The Unsolved Murder of Robert F. Kennedy* by
    Shane O'Sullivan.

20 *Who Killed Bobby?: The Unsolved Murder of Robert F. Kennedy* by
    Shane O'Sullivan.

21 *Who Killed Bobby?: The Unsolved Murder of Robert F. Kennedy* by
    Shane O'Sullivan.

22 *Who Killed Bobby?: The Unsolved Murder of Robert F. Kennedy* by
    Shane O'Sullivan.

23 *Who Killed Bobby?: The Unsolved Murder of Robert F. Kennedy* by
    Shane O'Sullivan.

24 *The Assassinations: Probe Magazine on JFK, MLK, RFK and Malcolm X* by James DiEugenio, Lisa Pease, & Judge Joe Brown.

25 *The Assassinations: Probe Magazine on JFK, MLK, RFK and Malcolm X* by James DiEugenio, Lisa Pease, & Judge Joe Brown.

26 *The Assassinations: Probe Magazine on JFK, MLK, RFK and Malcolm X* by James DiEugenio, Lisa Pease, & Judge Joe Brown.

27 *The Assassinations: Probe Magazine on JFK, MLK, RFK and Malcolm X* by James DiEugenio, Lisa Pease, & Judge Joe Brown.

28 *The Assassinations: Probe Magazine on JFK, MLK, RFK and Malcolm X* by James DiEugenio, Lisa Pease, & Judge Joe Brown.

29 *The Assassinations: Probe Magazine on JFK, MLK, RFK and Malcolm X* by James DiEugenio, Lisa Pease, & Judge Joe Brown.

30 *The Assassinations: Probe Magazine on JFK, MLK, RFK and Malcolm X* by James DiEugenio, Lisa Pease, & Judge Joe Brown.

31 *The Assassinations: Probe Magazine on JFK, MLK, RFK and Malcolm X* by James DiEugenio, Lisa Pease, & Judge Joe Brown.

32 *The Assassinations: Probe Magazine on JFK, MLK, RFK and Malcolm X* by James DiEugenio, Lisa Pease, & Judge Joe Brown.

33 *The Assassinations: Probe Magazine on JFK, MLK, RFK and Malcolm X* by James DiEugenio, Lisa Pease, & Judge Joe Brown.

34 *The Assassinations: Probe Magazine on JFK, MLK, RFK and Malcolm X* by James DiEugenio, Lisa Pease, & Judge Joe Brown.

35 *The Assassinations: Probe Magazine on JFK, MLK, RFK and Malcolm X* by James DiEugenio, Lisa Pease, & Judge Joe Brown.

36 *The Assassinations: Probe Magazine on JFK, MLK, RFK and Malcolm X* by James DiEugenio, Lisa Pease, & Judge Joe Brown.

37 *The Assassinations: Probe Magazine on JFK, MLK, RFK and Malcolm X* by James DiEugenio, Lisa Pease, & Judge Joe Brown.

38 *Bobby Kennedy for President* directed by Dawn Porter.

39 *Bobby Kennedy for President* directed by Dawn Porter.

40 https://www.dailymail.co.uk/news/article-7456521/Robert-F-Kennedy-assassinated-Thane-Eugene-Cesar-Sirhan-Sirhan-says-RFK-Jr.html

41 *The Killing of Robert F. Kennedy: An Investigation of Motive, Means, and Opportunity* by Dan E. Moldea.

42 https://historynewsnetwork.org/article/50532

43 https://historynewsnetwork.org/article/50532

44 http://hnn.us/articles/38496.html

45 *The Assassinations: Probe Magazine on JFK, MLK, RFK and Malcolm X* by James DiEugenio, Lisa Pease, & Judge Joe Brown.

46 https://www.youtube.com/watch?v=Ma_RpEcm7NY&list= PLtP10qqTzKD_cE1IezrkojuN92a DDWM8k

The Moon-Landing "Hoax"

1 https://youtu.be/lw9azZmLxtw

2 *Area 51: An Uncensored History of America's Top Secret Military Base* by Annie Jacobsen.

3 *Apollo* by Charles Murray and Catherine Bly Cox.

4 https://www.history.com/news/moon-landing-fake-conspiracy-theories

5 Conspiracies. Faking the Moon Landing.

6 *Room 237* directed by Rodney Ascher.

7 *The Shining* directed by Stanley Kubrick.

8 *Room 237* directed by Rodney Ascher.

9 https://youtu.be/nEPA22ja0MU

10 *Room 237* directed by Rodney Ascher.

11 https://www.youtube.com/watch?v=ThE3UTWHwMk

12 https://www.youtube.com/watch?v=ThE3UTWHwMk

13 https://www.youtube.com/watch?v=ThE3UTWHwMk

14 https://www.youtube.com/watch?v=ThE3UTWHwMk

15 https://www.youtube.com/watch?v=-5yh2HcIlkU&t= 7617s

16 https://www.youtube.com/watch?v=-5yh2HcIlkU&t= 7617s

17 https://youtu.be/lw9azZmLxtw

Endnotes

Is the Earth Really Flat?

1 *Dinosaur in a Haystack: Reflections in Natural History* by Stephen J. Gould.
2 *Earth Not a Globe (Illustrated Edition)* by Samuel Birley Rowbotham (Parallax).
3 https://www.oxfordreference.com/view/10.1093/oi/authority.20110810104644335
4 https://www.youtube.com/watch?v=0KRVNzLzg3I
5 *Behind the Curve* directed by Daniel J. Clark.
6 *Behind the Curve* directed by Daniel J. Clark.
7 *Behind the Curve* directed by Daniel J. Clark.
8 *Behind the Curve* directed by Daniel J. Clark.
9 *Behind the Curve* directed by Daniel J. Clark.
10 *Behind the Curve* directed by Daniel J. Clark.
11 *Behind the Curve* directed by Daniel J. Clark.
12 *Behind the Curve* directed by Daniel J. Clark.

Environmental Modification Weapons

1 *Joe Rogan Questions Everything* (TV series, episode 2).
2 *Angels Don't Play This HAARP: Advances in Tesla Technology* by Nick Begich and Jeane Manning.
3 *Angels Don't Play This HAARP: Advances in Tesla Technology* by Nick Begich and Jeane Manning.
4 https://www.wired.com/2010/01/irans-nuclear-molemen/
5 https://www.gi.alaska.edu/facilities/haarp
6 *The Imagineers of War: The Untold Story of DARPA, the Pentagon Agency That Changed the World* by Sharon Weinberger.
7 *Area 51: An Uncensored History of America's Top Secret Military Base* by Annie Jacobsen.
8 *The Sun*, November 13 , 2018—"No Darping Matter"
9 *Joe Rogan Questions Everything* (TV series, episode 2).

10 https://www.livescience.com/8071-chavez-tectonic-weapon-caused-haiti-quake.html

11 https://www.livescience.com/8071-chavez-tectonic-weapon-caused-haiti-quake.html

12 https://www.infowars.com/hurricane-sandy-divine-wind-for-obama/

13 *Joe Rogan Questions Everything* (TV series, episode 2).

14 *Joe Rogan Questions Everything* (TV series, episode 2).

15 https://science.howstuffworks.com/science-vs-myth/unexplained-phenomena/zug-island-mysterious-spot-likely-behind-windsor-hum.htm

16 *The Times*, September 27 , 2013—"Weather Eye: contrail conspiracy"

17 *New York Intelligencer*, May 26 , 2015—"Kylie Jenner Isn't the Only Celebrity Who Believes in Chemtrails"

18 https://www.skeptic.com/eskeptic/14-10-15/#feature

19 https://www.metabunk.org/threads/debunked-why-in-the-world-are-they-spraying.300/

20 *Joe Rogan Questions Everything* (TV series, episode 2).

21 *Douglas Now*, October 28 , 2016—"Sheriff's Office Uncovers Potential Domestic Terrorism Plot, Two Arrested"

WikiLeaks and the Murder of Seth Rich

1 http://www.gallup.com/poll/116479/barack-obama-presidential-job-approval.aspx

2 https://www.nbcwashington.com/news/local/man-shot-killed-in-northwest-dc/2074048/

3 https://www.washingtonpost.com/local/public-safety/police-identify-man-fatally-shot-in-bloomingdale/2016/07/11/4236fd1a-4754-11e6-90a8-fb84201e0645_story.html

4 https://www.washingtonpost.com/news/true-crime/wp/2016/07/12/hillary-clinton-invokes-name-of-slain-dnc-aide-seth-rich-in-calling-for-gun-control

5 https://www.belfasttelegraph.co.uk/news/world-news/julian-assange-russian-government-not-source-of-leaked-dnc-and-podesta-emails-wikileaks-editor-contradicts-cia-claims-in-new-interview-35300175.html

6 https://www.itv.com/news/update/2016-06-12/assange-on-peston-on-sunday-more-clinton-leaks-to-come/

7 https://wikileaks.org/dnc-emails/emailid/7643

8 https://www.youtube.com/watch?v=Kp7FkLBRpKg

9 https://www.youtube.com/watch?v=Kp7FkLBRpKg

10 https://www.youtube.com/watch?v=Kp7FkLBRpKg

11 https://www.youtube.com/watch?v=Kp7FkLBRpKg

12 https://www.youtube.com/watch?v=Kp7FkLBRpKg

13 https://www.youtube.com/watch?v=Kp7FkLBRpKg

14 https://www.youtube.com/watch?v=Kp7FkLBRpKg

15 https://www.youtube.com/watch?v=Kp7FkLBRpKg

16 https://www.youtube.com/watch?v=Kp7FkLBRpKg

17 https://www.youtube.com/watch?v=Kp7FkLBRpKg

18 https://www.youtube.com/watch?v=Kp7FkLBRpKg

19 https://twitter.com/relombardo3/status/752697104003264514

20 https://twitter.com/relombardo3/status/752697104003264514

21 https://web.archive.org/web/20170516061720/http://www.fox5dc.com/news/local-news/254852337-story

22 https://web.archive.org/web/20170516061720/http://www.fox5dc.com/news/local-news/254852337-story

23 https://web.archive.org/web/20170516112429/www.foxnews.com/politics/2017/05/16/slain-dnc-staffer-had-contact-with-wikileaks-investigator-says.html

24 https://money.cnn.com/2017/05/16/media/seth-rich-family-response-claims-of-wikileaks-contact/index.html

25 https://www.foxnews.com/politics/statement-on-coverage-of-seth-rich-murder-investigation

26 https://assets.documentcloud.org/documents/3906804/Seth-Rich-Fox-News.pdf

27 https://www.npr.org/2018/08/03/635272922/judge-dismisses-suits-against-fox-news-over-seth-rich-story

28 https://nymag.com/intelligencer/2017/05/is-this-even-about-seth-rich-at-all.html

The Mysterious Life and Death of Jeffrey Epstein

1 *Jeffrey Epstein: Filthy Rich* directed by Lisa Bryant.

2 https://www.nytimes.com/2019/07/25/business/jeffrey-epstein-wexner-victorias-secret.html.

3 https://www.telegraph.co.uk/news/uknews/1445707/FO-suspected-Maxwell-was-a-Russian-agent-papers-reveal.html

4 *Gideon's Spies: The Secret History of the Mossad* by Gordon Thomas.

5 https://www.timesofisrael.com/the-maxwells-scandal-conspiracy-and-more-than-a-few-days-in-court/

6 https://youtu.be/TO_z7Fu_6D0

7 https://www.nzherald.co.nz/lifestyle/news/article.cfm?c_id=6&objectid=12303369

8 https://www.nzherald.co.nz/lifestyle/news/article.cfm?c_id=6&objectid=12303369

9 https://youtu.be/TO_z7Fu_6D0

10 *Jeffrey Epstein: Filthy Rich* directed by Lisa Bryant.

11 https://www.newsweek.com/alex-acosta-epstein-sex-trafficking-department-labor-1448568

12 https://www.thesun.co.uk/news/9605078/jeffrey-epsteins-life-in-jeopardy-pals-dont-want-secrets-out/

13 *Jeffrey Epstein: Filthy Rich* directed by Lisa Bryant.

14 https://www.metrotimes.com/table-and-bar/archives/2019/11/11/michigan-brewery-reminds-us-that-jeffrey-epstein-probably-didnt-kill-himself

15 https://kutv.com/news/nation-world/fresno-brewery-prints-epstein-didnt-kill-himself-on-the-bottom-of-cans

16 https://www.washingtonexaminer.com/news/majority-believe-epstein-murdered-because-he-knew-too-much-poll

17 https://www.businessinsider.com/jeffrey-epstein-jail-cell-footage-night-suicide-justice-department-2019-11

18 https://www.businessinsider.com/ag-barr-epsteins-death-was-a-perfect-storm-of-screw-ups-2019-11

19 *Jeffrey Epstein: Filthy Rich* directed by Lisa Bryant.

COVID-19

1 https://www.cnn.com/2016/11/09/politics/donald-trump-victory-speech/index.html

2 *I Kill, Therefore I Am: The Expressive/Transformative Process of Violence* [dissertation] by Lee Mellor.

3 https://twitter.com/zlj517/status/1238111898828066823

4 https://www.cbc.ca/news/world/coronavirus-covid-china-united-states-political-campaign-1.5555245

5 https://allianceforscience.cornell.edu/blog/2020/05/covid-pandemic-might-have-begun-as-early-as-october-experts-say/

6 https://www.cnbc.com/2020/03/26/trumps-claim-that-malaria-drug-can-treat-coronavirus-gives-hope-but-little-evidence-it-will-work.html

7 https://www.cnbc.com/2020/03/26/trumps-claim-that-malaria-drug-can-treat-coronavirus-gives-hope-but-little-evidence-it-will-work.html

8 https://www.youtube.com/watch?v=WMXTiCJSl_0

9 *Plandemic* directed by Mikki Willis.

10 https://www.nytimes.com/2009/11/12/giving/12SICK.html?pagewanted=1&_r=1

11 https://archive.vcstar.com/news/local/oxnard/world-known-oxnard-researcher-claims-she-was-smeared-pushed-out-ep-792662230-350412251.html

12 *Plandemic* directed by Mikki Willis.

13 *Plandemic* directed by Mikki Willis.

14 *Plandemic* directed by Mikki Willis.

15 https://www.kff.org/uninsured/issue-brief/estimated-cost-of-treating-the-uninsured-hospitalized-with-covid-19/

16 *Plandemic* directed by Mikki Willis.

17 *Plandemic* directed by Mikki Willis.

18 *Plandemic* directed by Mikki Willis.

19 *Plandemic* directed by Mikki Willis.

20 https://torontosun.com/news/world/wuhan-lab-did-crazy-things-in-covid-19-research

21 https://torontosun.com/news/world/wuhan-lab-did-crazy-things-in-covid-19-research

22 https://en.wikipedia.org/wiki/Judy_Mikovits

23 https://archive.vcstar.com/news/local/oxnard/world-known-oxnard-researcher-claims-she-was-smeared-pushed-out-ep-792662230-350412251.html

24 https://en.wikipedia.org/wiki/Judy_Mikovits

25 https://en.wikipedia.org/wiki/Judy_Mikovits

26 https://www.nature.com/news/2011/110314/full/471282a.html

27 https://science.sciencemag.org/content/334/6063/1636.1

28 *A Multicenter Blinded Analysis Indicates No Association between Chronic Fatigue Syndrome/Myalgic Encephalomyelitis and either Xenotropic Murine Leukemia Virus-Related Virus or Polytropic Murine Leukemia Virus* by Harvey J. Alter et al.

29 https://www.sciencemag.org/news/2020/05/fact-checking-judy-mikovits-controversial-virologist-attacking-anthony-fauci-viral

30 *Plandemic* directed by Mikki Willis.

31 https://www.youtube.com/watch?v=0XHC5Kxxv_w

32 https://www.ctvnews.ca/health/coronavirus/drop-in-cellphone-users-in-china-wrongly-attributed-to-coronavirus-deaths-1.4878923